CW01302402

FIGHTER PILOT TACTICS

FIGHTER PILOT TACTICS

The techniques of daylight air combat

Mike Spick

PSL Patrick Stephens, Cambridge

© Mike Spick 1983

All rights reserved. No part of this publication may be reproduced, stored in a retrieval system or transmitted, in any form or by any means, electronic, mechanical, photocopying, recording or otherwise, without prior permission in writing from Patrick Stephens Limited.

First published in 1983

British Library Cataloguing in Publication Data

Spick, Mike
   Fighter pilot tactics.
   1. Air warfare   2. Tactics
   I. Title
   358.4'3   UG630

ISBN 0-85059-617-3

Photoset in 10 on 11pt Times by Rowland Phototypesetting Limited, Bury St Edmunds, Suffolk. Printed in Great Britain on Antique Wove Vol 18 80 gsm, and bound, by The Garden City Press, Letchworth, Herts, for the publishers, Patrick Stephens Limited, Bar Hill, Cambridge, CB3 8EL, England.

Contents

	Introduction	7
Chapter 1	Finding the way	10
Chapter 2	The day of the dogfight	22
Chapter 3	Which way now?	36
Chapter 4	The great leap forward	41
Chapter 5	The storm breaks	52
Chapter 6	The conflict widens	73
Chapter 7	Crescendo over Europe	92
Chapter 8	The setting of the Rising Sun	115
Chapter 9	The road to Mig Alley	120
Chapter 10	The nuclear threat: Some answers	132
Chapter 11	Limited wars	140
Chapter 12	Summary	160
	Appendix	171
	Bibliography	173
	Index	174

Introduction

The massive F-14 Tomcat of Fighting Squadron 41 quivered as all five stages of its afterburners lit up. The steam catapult fired and the huge fighter leaped forward. In less than three seconds it was climbing away from its carrier, *USS Nimitz*. It was shortly after 6 am on August 19 1981. Commander Henry Kleeman was off on another routine patrol in company with a second Tomcat flown by Lieutenant Lawrence Muczynski.

The previous day had been eventful. Fifteen ships of the United States 6th Fleet, including the aircraft carriers *Nimitz* and *Forrestal*, were conducting a missile firing exercise in the southern Mediterranean. Despite the standard international warning issued several days earlier, no less than 35 patrols of Libyan aircraft had approached the exercise area and six Libyan aircraft had actually entered it. In every case they had been intercepted by American fighters and turned away without incident.

Kleeman and Muczynski flew towards their designated operating area where they would orbit at 20,000 ft ready to intercept intruders and escort them away from the hazardous missile firing zone. Other pairs of Tomcats were doing the same, taking up positions on the perimeter of the exercise area.

At about 7.15 am Commander Kleeman's radar intercept officer sitting about 6 ft behind him, reported a radar contact to the south and heading in their direction. The fighter controller on board *Nimitz* directed them to investigate and the pair of Tomcats set course towards the contact, flying a formation known as defensive combat spread, between 1 and 2 miles apart, with Muczynski slightly behind Kleeman and higher. Commander Kleeman now takes up the story: 'At approximately 8 miles I saw the section of two SU22 Fitters on the nose. They were flying a formation we refer to as welded-wing, within about 500 ft of each other. The pass (was) nose to nose with No 102 (Kleeman's Tomcat) very nearly on the flight path with the two SU22 Fitters. . . . I rolled my wings and began a turn to keep the Fitters in sight and turn around and rendezvous on them. About 500 ft above them and 1,000 ft out in front, I observed a missile being fired from the right station of the Fitter. As I saw the missile come off, I communicated to my wingman that we had been fired at. I then continued a very hard turn across their tails to come back and find them. I kept both of them in sight through this area. The lead Fitter did a climbing left-hand turn in the general direction of my wingman. I was initially turned around to go after the man who had fired, as I saw my wingman come in. He came into view in front of me, starting to come into a position behind the

Fig 1A Gulf of Sidra incident, August 19 1981.

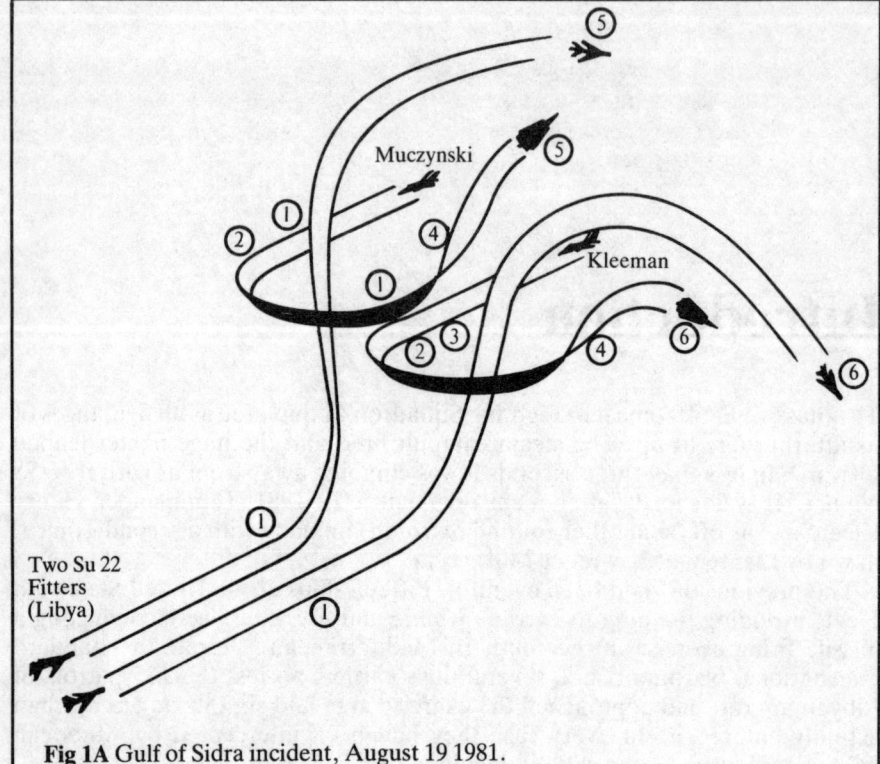

1) Leading Fitter launches missile at Kleeman.
2) Both Tomcats break hard left.
3) Fitters execute a defensive split.
4) As Kleeman pulls round against his attacker, Muczynski cuts in front of him. Kleeman then switches to the second Libyan fighter.
5) Muczynski reaches a firing position and launches a Sidewinder.
6) Kleeman launches a Sidewinder. Both Fitters are destroyed.

lead Fitter as he continued off in that direction. Since I saw that he had him under control, I switched my attention to the wing Fitter who had done a climbing right hand turn. My Fitter was approaching the sun; as I intended to use a Sidewinder heat-seeking missile, I realised that that was not a good position to shoot. I waited about ten seconds until he cleared the sun, fired my missile. The missile guided, struck him in his tailpipe area causing him to lose control of the airplane and he ejected within about five seconds.'

Meanwhile Muczynski had dropped in behind the lead Fitter and launched a Sidewinder. It guided straight into the tail pipe of the Libyan aircraft and exploded.

At the time of writing the incident just described was the most comprehensively documented recent fight between aircraft. It was two versus two with the Libyans having the advantage of the first shot. However, there the similarities end. The Tomcat is arguably the world's most sophisticated weapon system and, with a two man crew and twin-engines, it is best suited to fleet defence.

The SU22 is a single-seat single-engined attack aeroplane; not a machine with which to tackle an advanced fighter on even terms.

The missile fired by the Libyan pilot was probably a Russian-made Atoll, similar to the Sidewinders fired by the Tomcats. It was fired from an unfavourable angle and range. By contrast, the two American pilots manoeuvred into a favourable position before launching their Sidewinders.

The formation flown by the Americans was tactically better than that of the Libyans. The wide spacing between the Tomcats enabled Muczynski to swing in on the tail of the leading Fitter, thus allowing Kleeman to pursue the wingman. The close 'welded wing' formation of the Libyans permitted no real alternative to the defensive split which they attempted as soon as it became apparent that their missile had missed.

The combat was over within 60 seconds. The American flyers demonstrated a high degree of professionalism in disposing of their opponents rapidly and with the minimum possible expenditure of missiles. Sixty-seven years had passed since the first shots were exchanged between aeroplanes. This is the story of those years. I have tried to keep technicalities to a minimum, but some aerodynamics have perforce crept in. In common with many thousands of aviation fans, I have eagerly devoured accounts of war in the air. Frequently one encounters a passage which goes something like: 'He was sitting on my tail. I hauled into a climbing turn, booted the rudder bar hard over and rolled out behind him!' The reaction is all too often, 'How the hell did he manage that?' However, by the end of the book I hope the reader will know how it was done. To this end some previously published combat accounts have been used and reconstructed in diagrammatic form.

Air combat appears at first sight to be a open-ended, manoeuvre-countermanoeuvre process with limitless possibilities but this is not the case. In any given situation, the fighter pilot has a limited number of options open to him. These are dependent on relative positions and speeds at the start of the encounter and the flying qualities of the opposing aircraft, as we shall see later.

For the sake of simplicity all speeds are given in statute miles per hour, despite the fact that the nautical mile per hour, or knot, has been in widespread use for many years. The knot was brought into use for ease of navigation, and varies from statute mph by about 15 per cent. Thus 600 knots is approximately 690 mph.

Tactics is generally defined as the art or science of manoeuvring forces in battle according to established principles. A better definition would be the art of achieving maximum results with minimum risk and effort. I have made little attempt to include up to date tactical theory, although it has been touched upon briefly in the summary chapter. Modern tactical theory is based on twin foundations; the technical means available and the type of war that aircraft will be called upon to fight. Much technical information is classified and many technical devices may not be used. Typical is the controversy about communications jamming. Does one attempt to make life difficult for the enemy by jamming his communications, or are greater advantages to be derived from monitoring? Much also depends on the type of war that aircraft are called upon to fight. The lesson of history is that all too often air forces have trained for one type of war and found themselves fighting a totally different one.

Chapter 1

Finding the way

October 5 1914 was a memorable day in the annals of air warfare. A Voisin Type 3 of the French Air Service, flown by two young Sergeants, Joseph Frantz and Louis Quenault, slowly approached a German Aviatik which was reconnoitring the lines. The Germans either did not see the Voisin, or ignored it. At this time no aeroplane had ever shot down another and they may well have thought that they had little to fear from the lumbering French biplane. A stream of bullets from Quenault's machine-gun made them aware of their peril, but too late. The mortally stricken Aviatik fell from the sky, the first victim of a new dimension in warfare.

The need to command the skies had been foreseen long before the outbreak of World War 1. The Royal Flying Corps Manual of June 1914 clearly stated: 'It is not to be expected that aircraft will be able to carry out their duties undisturbed. In war, advantages must be fought for and the importance of aerial reconnaissance is so great that each side will strive to prevent the other making use of it.'

The means were to hand. The Vickers FB (Fighting Biplane) 5, usually known as the Gunbus, had been designed the previous year and was armed with a machine-gun. Both France and Germany had experimented with machine-gun armed aeroplanes before war broke out, but the lack of practical experience meant that no one really knew for certain what the requirements of air fighting would be, although the theorists were active. Perhaps the most remarkable piece of prophecy came from the pen of F. W. Lanchester, in an article for the magazine *Engineering* dated October 23 1914: '. . . the taking of the upper position at the start, or perhaps we may say, before the start, gives the power to outmanoeuvre an enemy, in spite even of inferior speed capacity in the ordinary acception of the term. The initial difference in altitude represents a store of potential energy which may be drawn upon when the opportunity occurs. . . . It will probably prove to be, and will remain, the key or pivot on which every scheme of aeronautical tactics will, in some way or another, be found to hang.'

Shortened to 'He who has height controls the battle', this was to become holy writ for the next few decades. To have a height advantage meant added speed in a diving attack, a better chance of surprising the opponent and speed to escape if the attack failed.

Meanwhile pilots on both sides were trying to develop methods of fighting each other, with varying degrees of success. The difficulty of catching an opponent tended at the time to obscure what was later to become obvious; the use of the machine-gun as the primary weapon. The loss of performance owing to the weight of these weapons and their ammunition was widely held to be unacceptable and alternatives were sought. The rifle, carbine and pistol were used, together with steel darts or *flechettes* and small bombs, but with little success. Some idea of the problem is given by the anonymous author of a Royal Flying Corps report which is undated but almost certainly from very early 1915. He starts by very reasonably pointing out that flying his machine with one hand, while aiming a pistol with the other is not conducive to good marksmanship, and aiming a single bullet by aiming the whole aeroplane is a difficult operation. We may assume from this that he was a single-seater pilot and was referring to the use of a cavalry carbine carried in a fixed rest, pointing forwards and outwards at an angle to miss the propeller. The report continues: 'There are two methods by which good results are likely to be obtained. (i) *Blunderbusses*: A heavy and scattering charge of grape and chain shot fired from a smooth bore weapon something like a large blunderbuss, affords a pilot a better chance of bringing down a hostile aeroplane by aiming his own than when aiming a single bullet in this manner . . . the pattern should be not less than 20 ft wide at 50 yds range; this means a cone of dispersion of about 8 degrees from the moment of leaving the muzzle. . . .'

His next idea was even better, a small bomb fixed to a grapnel, trailed below a fast scout on a 100 ft of wire and detonated electrically from the cockpit. The intrepid fast scout pilot then flew above this opponent and hooked the grapnel on to the trailing edge of his wings. Accelerating, he tore the grapnel through the structure until it reached the rear spar, then with a deft flick of a switch, he detonated the bomb. His unfortunate adversary, who no doubt watched this feat of aerial virtuosity in open-mouthed admiration, then went down to destruction.

With the advantage of 65 years of hindsight it is easy to be critical of this report. However, the writer was right about one thing; it was very difficult to get results with the means available to him.

During the early months of the war none of the combatant nations possessed specialist air fighting units. The aeroplanes were sent out on a specific task, usually singly, and if they met the enemy they fought him, if they had the means to do so. The Royal Flying Corps were no exception. Each squadron had one or two fast scouts to which those pilots who showed a flair for fighting naturally gravitated. Lieutenant Duncan Grinnell-Milne of No 16 Squadron later wrote: 'By a fortunate succession of accidents, my own role in the squadron became gradually more that of a fighting pilot than of an artillery spotter or photographer'.

Another Royal Flying Corps report of the period bore the exciting title *Method of Attack of Hostile Aeroplanes*. However, it contained little of value to the aspiring fighter pilot. Lieutenant Penn-Gaskell listed lots of suitable firing positions for use against different opponents, but neglected to advise on how to achieve them. Major Raleigh stated that one should always endeavour to face an adversary from about an equal height. Captain Todd remarked that the machine-gun was a splendid weapon but went on to say: '. . . but in a "Tractor" the small number of occasions on which it could be used firing backwards, and the ease with which the attacked aeroplane can avoid being fired at, do not justify the extra weight'. The report was concluded by Lieutenant-Colonel

Trenchard, commanding the 1st Wing, who recommended the development of a three-seater pusher aeroplane armed with two Lewis guns. Little about methods of attack was evident in the report. It is of interest mainly because it illustrated so clearly the difficulties of the early days. Perhaps we should give Grinnell-Milne the last word: 'In those unsophisticated days, each man had to learn and progress from his own experience'.

Some were doing better than others. Roland Garros, a noted French pilot, remembered pre-war trials with an interrupter gear fitted to a machine-gun. This device enabled the gun to be fired through the propeller arc by preventing the gun from firing when the propeller blade was in line with the gun muzzle. Faulty ammunition had caused this project to be abandoned (the Germans had conducted similar trials with similar results), but not before Raymond Saulnier, in charge of the trials, had come up with the idea of fitting wedge-shaped steel deflectors to the part of the propeller at risk. These deflectors would have dealt with the occasional misfire for the loss of some propeller efficiency, and at the added risk of straining the engine. The risk was felt to be unacceptable in peacetime, but with a war in progress, Garros went to Saulnier and asked for the interrupter gear to be fitted.

After some discussion, the deflectors only were fitted and on April 1 1915, Garros' Morane-Saulnier Type L attacked a German Albatros two-seater and sent it down. Success followed success and during the next two and a half weeks Garros shot down another four Germans, thus becoming the first fighter ace. But on April 18 he was himself hit and crash-landed behind the German lines, becoming a prisoner of war.

Garros had received much publicity during his short but successful phase, and the Germans were quick to examine his machine. Aware of the potential of the fixed forward-firing machine-gun, they asked the Dutch designer Anthony Fokker to copy it. Fokker's engineers examined the deflectors and promptly went one better; they designed a workable synchronisation gear and fitted it to their newest aeroplane, the Eindecker.

Few aeroplanes made such an impact on air combat as the new Fokker monoplane. By mid-1915, combats were becoming more frequent but were more often than not inconclusive. There were of course exceptions, such as the action on July 25 for which Captain Lanoe Hawker won the Victoria Cross. Flying a Bristol Scout armed with a Lewis gun fixed to fire outwards and downwards past the propeller, he drove down two German two-seaters and shot down a third in flames. Much more typical were the engagements described in a letter home by a young German officer, Oswald Boelke: 'When the others take off on artillery flights, etc, I go up with them, fly about in their neighbourhood and protect them from enemy attacks. So if a Frenchman comes along, I pounce on him like a hawk, while our other machine goes on calmly flying and observing. Meanwhile I whack the Frenchman by flying up to him and giving him a good hammering with our machine-gun. Those chaps bolt so quickly that it is really glorious. I have whacked about a dozen Frenchmen in this way. It is great fun for me.'

Shortly after this letter was written, Boelke shot down his first victim, a French Morane, after a long chase. He then took over the first of the new Fokkers to be delivered to his section and started his meteoric rise to fame.

The Eindecker was not particularly fast for its time but it climbed well and could be dived at a steep angle without shedding its wings. In the hands of its

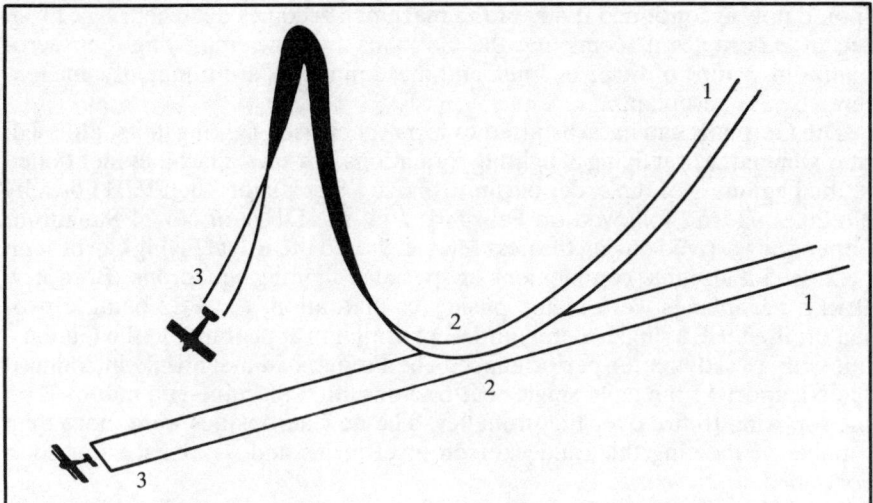

Fig 1 The Immelmann turn.

1) Immelmann swoops down on his victim.
2) He fires, then pulls sharply up.
3) He stall-turns at the top of his climb, ready to attack again. Regardless of what evasive action his quarry takes, Immelmann can vary the angle of roll-out following the stall-turn to give himself a good attacking position. Immelmann was the first recorded pilot to use vertical manoeuvre.

two greatest exponents, Boelke and Max Immelmann, it was a deadly weapon. The usual methods of attack, depending on the relative position of the quarry when first sighted, were the careful stalk from the blind spot beneath the tail or the steep dive, preferably from out of the sun, continued past and down after the attack. This last was developed by Immelmann into his famous turn. There has been a certain amount of controversy as to what this actually was, but contemporary accounts described a diving attack, after which the nose was pulled up vertically. The aeroplane was then ruddered over sideways, leaving it well placed for a further attack.

Before he became a Fokker pilot, Boelke had flown the two-seater LVG. In the single-seat Eindecker he discovered that he was unable to concentrate on an attack and still keep a good lookout. His answer to this problem was for aircraft to fly in pairs, one to guard the other's tail.

The Germans gradually gained tactical experience and confidence in their machines. With this came increased aggression, and a moral as well as a material ascendancy. The Allied situation finally became so serious that on January 14 1916, the Royal Flying Corps issued the following order: 'Until the Royal Flying Corps are in possession of a machine as good as or better than the German Fokker, it seems that a change in the tactics employed becomes necessary. It is hoped very shortly to obtain a machine which will be able to successfully engage the Fokkers at present in use by the Germans. In the meantime, it must be laid down as a hard and fast rule that a machine proceeding on reconnaissance must be escorted by at least three other fighting machines. These machines must fly in close formation, and a reconnaissance should not be continued if any of the machines becomes detached.... From recent experience it seems that the Germans are now employing their aeroplanes in groups of three or four, and these numbers are frequently encountered by our aeroplanes.'

The Germans had in fact started to form specialised fighting units, although they were not as yet flying in fighting formations. The new machines mentioned at the beginning of the order began to arrive a week later, the FE2B flown by No 20 Squadron followed on February 7 by the DH2s of No 24 Squadron. Other units arrived during the next few weeks and the Royal Flying Corps soon possessed a sizeable complement of specialist fighting squadrons. Both new British aeroplanes were of the pusher configuration, the FE2 being a two-seater, the DH2 a single-seater, and were similar in appearance to the Gunbus, but with a vastly better performance. The French had meanwhile introduced the Nieuport 11, an agile single-seat tractor with a machine-gun mounted on the top wing to fire over the propeller. The new aeroplanes were more than capable of meeting the Eindecker on level terms and its menace was soon contained.

Until 1916 aeroplanes had generally flown singly, and fights involving more than three or four machines had been rare. But now came the first formations, of between three and six aircraft. It was no longer a question of outfighting an adversary in single combat so much as outfighting an enemy unit.

The greatest aerial tactician of the time was Oswald Boelke, often referred to as the father of aerial combat. During the summer of 1916 he set down eight principles of air fighting which have changed remarkably little since then. These principles are listed below with relevant comments.

1 *Try to secure advantages before attacking. If possible keep the sun behind you*: The greatest advantage in any form of warfare is the element of surprise. Four out of five aeroplanes shot down never see their assailant until it is too late. Boelke showed his awareness of this critical point by recommending attacks out of the sun, which render the attacker almost invisible. Surprise could also be gained by the use of cloud cover where possible, or by approaching an opponent from the blind spot under his tail. As Lanchester had already predicted, superior height was also an advantage. The additional speed gained in a diving attack enabled the attacker rapidly to close on his quarry, thus giving him less time to spot his assailant and take evasive action. Decoys also came under this heading. The usual decoy was a solitary aeroplane wandering about at medium altitude looking vulnerable, with a whole gaggle of his friends a mile higher and up-sun ready to spring the trap. Fighting over your own lines was also an advantage in those days of mechanical unreliability. A forced landing on the wrong side of the lines, for whatever reason, was likely to be a serious inconvenience. On at least one occasion, Boelke feigned damage and lured an unwary British machine 15 miles over the German lines before setting about it. This particular advantage was more easily obtained by the Germans as the prevailing south-westerly winds blew aircraft toward their lines.

2 *Always carry through an attack when you have started it*: Determination was (and still is) the fighter pilot's most important attribute and morale is the most important factor in war. An attack broken off too early would have achieved nothing and almost certainly have encouraged the enemy to fight back harder.

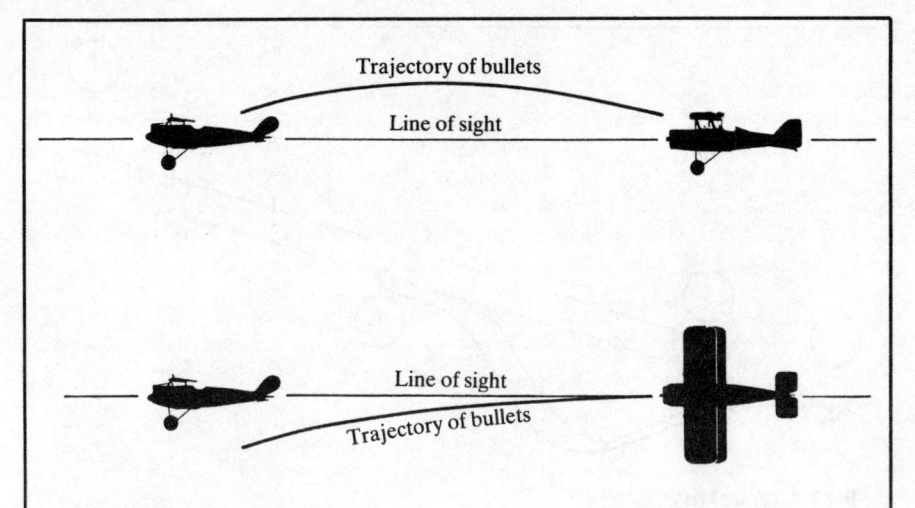

Fig 2 Gunnery problems.

Guns are aligned above the line of sight. The bullets fired drop under the influence of gravity until, at optimum range, their trajectory coincides with the line of sight. At shorter ranges the difference would not matter; at longer ranges the attacker needs to aim above the target to compensate for gravity drop.
In the lower illustration, gravity is acting at right angles to the line of sight and the attacking pilot must allow for this.

3 *Fire only at close range and only when your opponent is properly in your sights:* This was not quite as obvious as it looks. Many successful attacks in World War 1 were made from 25 yds or less. On a firing range, a marksman could achieve respectable scores at several hundred yards. Hitting a manoeuvring target with a machine-gun attached to a vibrating aeroplane, which was probably not flying straight and level, was a very different matter. If the attacking aeroplane was turning or sideslipping, a sideways motion was imparted to the bullets which would therefore not go where they were aimed. The sights on the gun were set to compensate for the force of gravity acting on the bullets if fired in level flight. If the fighter was banking at 90 degrees, the compensating allowance would need to be sideways to the pilot. And finally there was the difficulty of accurate deflection shooting, where the bullets had to be fired ahead of a turning target so that both target and bullets arrived in the same place at the same time. This required such skill that only a few naturally gifted pilots ever mastered it. As Boelke suggested, all these problems could be overcome by firing from so close that they did not matter.

4 *Always keep your eye on your opponent, and never let yourself be deceived by ruses:* This can be summed up in two points. Do not be lured into a false position by any of the tricks described earlier for instance by decoys. Also be sure that your opponent really is dead and not shamming. The other ruse which caught out a lot of pilots of all nationalities, came when they tried to break off an action and had gained a 300–400 yd lead. The devilishly clever pursuer would open fire, although he was well out of effective range. The fleeing pilot often became nervous and instinctively took evasive action, thus allowing the

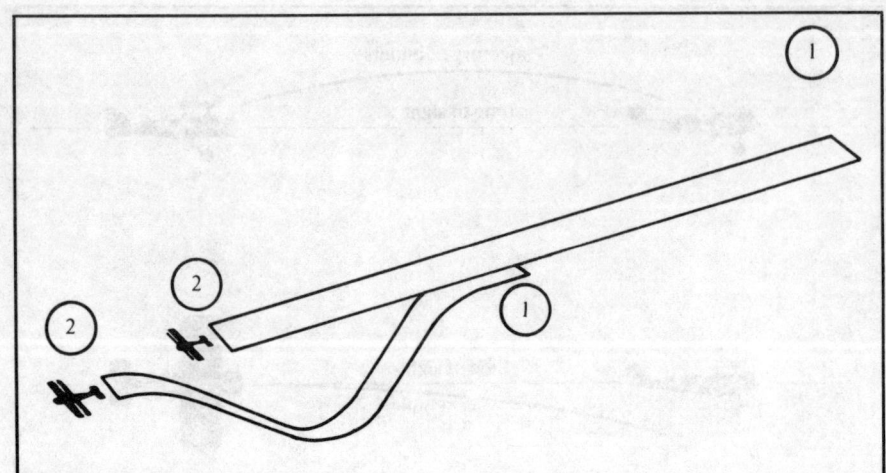

Fig 3 A typical ruse
1) The attacking aeroplane opens fire out of effective range. His opponent takes evasive action.
2) This allows the pursuer to close the distance.

pursuer to cut the corner and close the range. The correct course of action would have been to fly straight on at full speed since there was little chance of being hit.

5 *In any form of attack it is essential to assail your opponent from behind:* There were four reasons for this rule. Firstly it was likely to give an easy no-deflection shot. Secondly the time available to aim and fire was longer during a stern attack and thus such an attack was more likely to be effective. Thirdly, if the target was a single-seater it would have been unable to return fire. Fourthly, the attacker was less likely to be seen from astern and, even if spotted, was well placed to retain the initiative. In this connection it should be remembered that the attacker was usually going to have to change course before starting his attack. To do this he had to bank his aeroplane and one of the surest signs to the enemy was sunlight reflecting from the wings as the aeroplane banked. This tended to catch the eye even if the victim was not looking in the right direction.

6 *If your opponent dives on you, do not try to evade his onslaught but fly to meet it:* This was based on the assumption that an opponent diving to attack would have been overtaking too fast to be evaded. This being so, the only possible countermove was to turn and face him. Both aeroplanes would thus have obtained a fleeting head-on shot at each other, which, other things being equal, gave a slight advantage to the heavier armed aircraft. If the time was insufficient for the victim to have been able to turn completely into the attack, at least the attacker would be forced to attempt the more difficult shot. Either way the victim would have shown that he was undaunted by the attack and was prepared to fight.

7 *When over the enemy's lines, never forget your own line of retreat:* This applied at two levels. At the most basic level an inexperienced pilot could easily have got lost, run out of fuel and been compelled to make a forced landing

behind the enemy lines. At a more advanced level, pilots involved in a pursuit or a fight would need to have kept a sharp look-out for a superior enemy force getting across their line of retreat.

8 *Attack on principle in groups of four or six. When the fight breaks up into a series of single combats, take care that several do not go for one opponent:* The group attack was recommended to inflict maximum damage during the first pass, which might easily have taken the enemy unawares. The cautionary second sentence was both a warning of the risk of collision and an injunction to keep as many of the enemy as possible occupied in saving their own necks.

Shortly after formulating his eight principles, Boelke formed the first real German fighting unit, Jagdstaffel (usually abbreviated to Jasta 2. His pilots were hand-picked and carefully trained in his methods. They studied the flying capabilities of their own machines, also those of their opponents, using captured aeroplanes. Jasta 2 were based just outside Cambrai, and started operations in September 1916.

Directly across the lines from Cambrai was Bertangles airfield, the home of No 24 Squadron, Royal Flying Corps, who flew the DH2. Commanded by Major Lanoe Hawker, No 24 Squadron had earlier played a leading role in countering the Fokker menace.

Hawker seems to have been more of a technician than a tactician, although a more aggressive man would have been hard to find. During June 1916 his tactical orders were pinned on the squadron notice board. Brief and to the point, they read: Attack Everything! Hawker wanted his pilots to be able to do tight turns without losing height and an upward spiral was his preferred evasive manoeuvre. He wanted them to engage the enemy at every opportunity and he flew constantly, at a time when this was not considered a squadron commander's job and was positively discouraged by higher authority.

One of his preoccupations was effective gunnery; he was always seeking ways of hitting the enemy, and one of his bright ideas was the upward firing gunsight. A bullet pursues a parabolic path when fired, the curve becoming more pronounced as its momentum is lost and gravity takes over. A bullet fired at an angle to the line of flight has the force of the slip-stream imposed upon it, giving another parabolic trajectory. Hawker's calculations showed the speed and angle at which the curved trajectory of an upward fired bullet was cancelled out by the slip-stream caused by the forward motion of the firing aircraft, and the bullet then followed an absolutely straight path for a considerable distance. While useless in a dogfight, it proved effective against reconnaissance machines which would be approached from 1,000 ft below and behind.

Jasta 2 were equipped with the new Albatros single-seater, with a much better top speed and climb performance than the DH2. No 24 Squadron, their opponents in many encounters, covered up the inadequacies of their machines with a spirited show of aggression. But the battles were nearly all of the Germans' choosing; the aging British pusher had not the performance to force the enemy to fight. It was, however, still accorded a healthy respect by its opponents, as an action fought on October 28 proved.

That day, two DH2s of No 24 Squadron encountered Boelke at the head of six Albatroses, soon to be reinforced by a further six from another unit. Facing odds of six to one, flying slower aeroplanes, the British machines had no option but to fight. And fight they did. The squadron combat report reads: 'It was after about five minutes of strenuous fighting that two hostile aircraft collided. One dived at Lieutenant Knight, who turned left-handed. The hostile aircraft zoomed right-handed and its left wing collided with the right wing of another hostile aircraft which had started to dive on Lieutenant Knight.'

After a further 15 minutes' fighting, the Germans broke off the action and the British machines returned safely to Bertangles. The sole victim of this engagement was Boelke, who crashed to his death as a result of a collision with one of his own men.

Just over three weeks later there was an engagement which showed the way the earlier fight should by rights have gone. Three DH2s of No 24 Squadron led by Captain Andrews and accompanied by Major Hawker and Lieutenant Saundby, were patrolling near Bapaume. Sighting two enemy aircraft below, they dived to the attack. The Germans saw them coming and dived away eastwards and the experienced Andrews, suspecting a trap, scanned the sky above. Sure enough there were two German patrols above them and Andrews immediately broke off his pursuit and turned right, accompanied by Saundby. Hawker, however, continued the pursuit, only to be attacked from astern by the German high cover. Andrews had turned back and succeeded in warding off Hawker's assailant, but was hit in the engine almost at once and forced to break away. Saundby evaded the initial attack with an upward spiral, then closed with Andrews' opponent, driving him down. While doing this he lost sight of Hawker and the remaining Germans. He escorted the crippled Andrews back to the lines, then resumed the patrol alone.

Meanwhile Hawker had found trouble. Only one Albatros was with him, but it was flown by Baron Manfred von Richthofen, looking for his eleventh victory. Starting at about 10,000 ft they desperately tried to out-turn each other. Von Richthofen takes up the story: 'So it went, both of us flying like madmen in a circle, with engines running full out at 3,000-m altitude. First left, then right, each intent on getting above and behind the other. I was soon acutely aware that I was not dealing with a beginner, for he did not dream of breaking off the fight. He had a very manoeuvrable crate, but mine climbed better, and I finally succeeded in coming in above and behind him. . . . The circles that we made about each other were so narrow that I estimated them to be not further than 80 to 100 m. I had time to view my opponent. I peered perpendicularly at him in his cockpit and could observe every movement of his head . . . he finally had to decide whether to land on our side or fly back to his own lines. Naturally he attempted the latter, after trying in vain to evade me through looping and such tricks. As he did so my first bullets flew by his ears, for prior to that I had not fired a shot. At about 100 m altitude he tried to escape towards the Front by flying zigzag, making his plane a difficult target to hit. It was now the given moment for me. I followed him from 50 down to 30 m altitude, firing steadily. About 50 m behind our lines he plunged down with a shot through the head.'

This combat was documented in greater detail than most, and several interesting features emerge on close examination. The early phase of the fight was confused, with aircraft taking fleeting pot-shots before being attacked themselves. In the general muddle, Hawker and von Richthofen became separated from the rest and began their private war free from outside interference. This initially took the form of trying to out-turn each other. When turning hard an aeroplane loses speed and at the same time its stalling speed rises considerably. Calculations based on the known performances of both aeroplanes coupled with von Richthofen's estimate of the diameter of the circles would suggest that their speed was 70 to 75 mph which was perilously close to stalling. Consequently, they were both forced continually to trade altitude for speed and this accounted for the tremendous loss of height during the combat. To maintain height, one or the other would have had to slacken the turn and thus have given the advantage to his opponent. If the estimated speed seems low to the reader it should be remembered that both aeroplanes were turning a full circle in under ten seconds. Much faster than this and the wings would have been torn off by the centrifugal force.

The faster Albatros could have broken off the fight at any time and escaped. No such option was open to Hawker. Had he broken away when von Richthofen was exactly across the circle, he would have gained an initial lead of about 600 yds. Three-quarters of a mile further on and about 30 seconds later, the Albatros would have been back on his tail within easy shooting distance. His only chance was to fly as erratically as possible and present a difficult target. Against anyone but von Richthofen, the master marksman, he might have succeeded in escaping.

Basic principles of flight

Lift An aeroplane flies by virtue of the lift created by its wings. As air rushes over the wing a low pressure area forms on the top surface. The air pressure on the undersurface of the wing is either normal or slightly higher than normal. The difference in air pressure between the top and bottom surfaces makes the wing try to rise to fill the low pressure area. This is called lift.

Stall Lift is dependent on the flow of air over the wings being smooth. When this is not so the air flowing over the top of the wing swirls and destroys the low pressure area and with it the lift. When this happens the aeroplane cannot continue to fly and falls. There are two reasons for this happening. Either the aeroplane is not moving fast enough to keep the flow of air smooth, or the wing is meeting the air at too steep an angle owing to violent manoeuvres.

Air The atmosphere becomes thinner the higher one goes. The aeroplane has to fly faster to avoid stalling. If it stalls at 40 mph at ground level, the stalling speeds will increase to 43 mph at 5,000 ft, 47 mph at 10,000 ft and just over 50 mph at 15,000 ft. The pilot, however, works on indicated airspeed, the speed shewn on his indicator. If he is flying at 15,000 ft and his indicator reads 40 mph he is really doing 50! As the air becomes thinner the drag becomes less. The engine needs air to burn with its petrol. As the air becomes thinner the engine loses power.

Ceiling As the engine loses power and the stalling speed increases with altitude, the aeroplane reaches a theoretical maximum height at which its top speed equals its stall speed. In practice this would never be achieved.

Banking When a pilot wishes to turn an aeroplane he must tilt it over sideways, which is called banking. The tightness of the turn is determined by the angle of the bank. In the combat between Hawker and von Richthofen both aeroplanes were banking at about 70 degrees. Tight turns cause a lot of extra drag and also increase the stall speed. This is why aircraft in a fight in World War 1 lost height continually. This subject will be dealt with in more detail later.

Normal pressure area

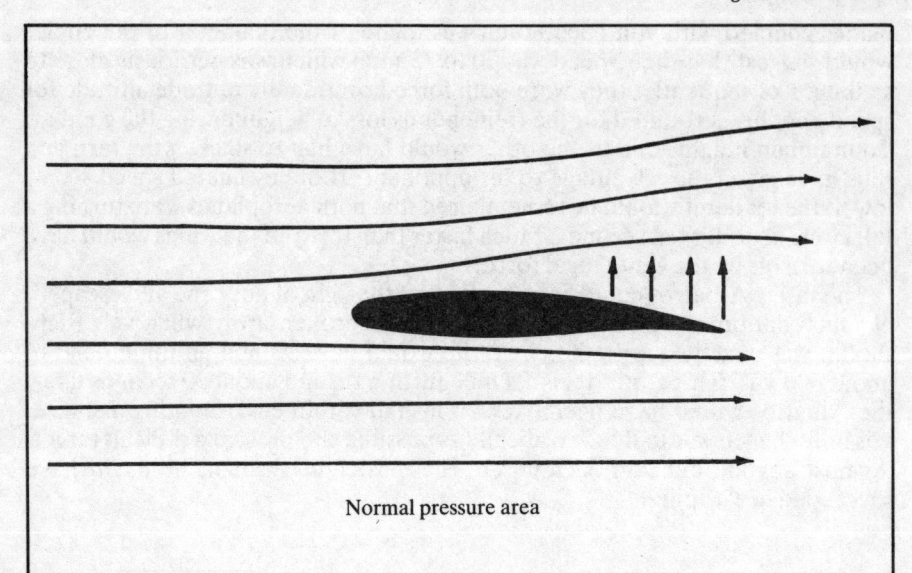

Low pressure area

The airstream swirls into the low pressure area destroying lift.

Figs 4 and 5 Basic principles of flight.

Finding the way

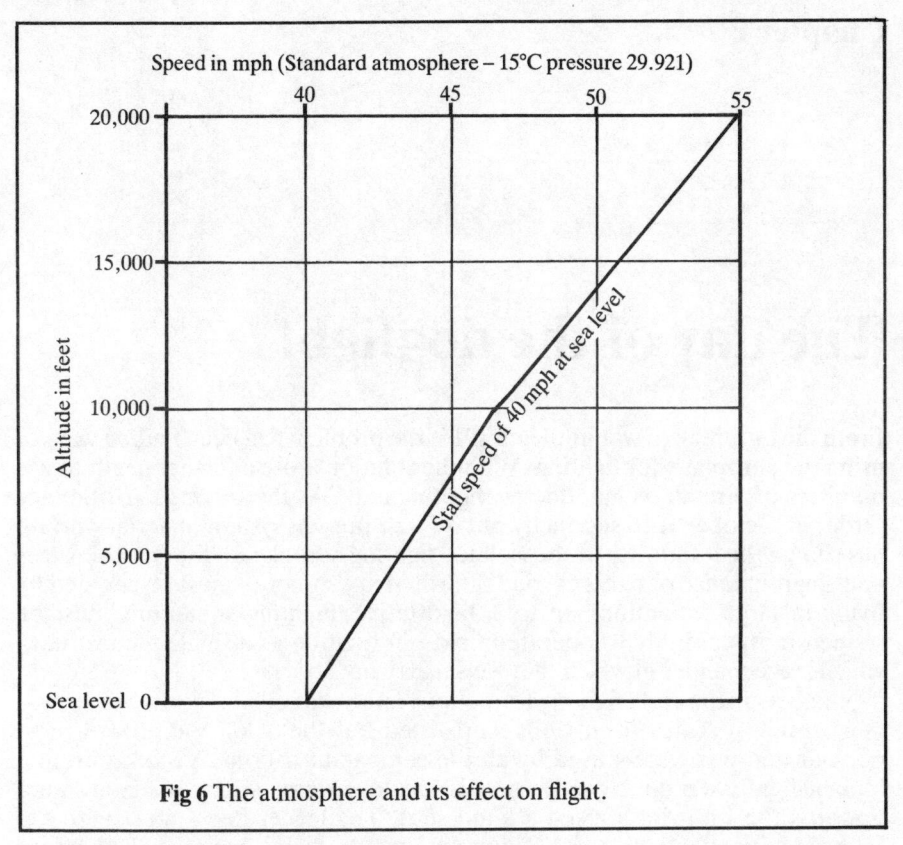

```
Speed in mph (Standard atmosphere – 15°C pressure 29.921)
```

Fig 6 The atmosphere and its effect on flight.

Drag This is the resistance of air around the aeroplane. As the aeroplane flies it pushes the air in front of it out of the way. The air causes friction along the skin of the aeroplane and slows it down. The faster the aeroplane flies, the greater the friction becomes. Drag increases in direct proportion to the square of the speed. The same aeroplane flying at 120 mph has to overcome four times the drag that it has at 60 mph.

Zoom Climbing was a leisurely affair in early aeroplanes. But if an aeroplane had gained speed during a dive, or even by flying level as fast as possible before pulling its nose up. it could then climb very fast for a short distance until its momentum had been used up.

Chapter 2

The day of the dogfight

From the outbreak of war until late 1916, the problem had been finding ways of using the aeroplane for fighting. With the solution arose a further need; to use numbers of aircraft as an effective fighting unit. As the German Air Service Order of October 1916 succinctly put it: 'The present system of aerial warfare has shown the inferiority of the isolated fighting aeroplane; dispersal of forces and a continuance of fights carried out when in a minority must be avoided by flying in large formations up to a Jagdstaffel. Fighting squadrons must be trained most carefully to operate in close formation as a single tactical unit, which is the manner in which they must carry out attacks.'

Numbers in the early fighting formations rarely exceeded nine; five or six was most usual. Various formations were tried but the V or Vic proved most popular and was widely used by all the combatant nations. Visibility from a biplane fighter was quite good forwards and downwards, whereas forwards and upwards the top wing caused a blind spot. The leader flew lowest with the following aircraft stepped upwards and outwards, from where they had a clear view of him. In addition, the following machines had a small reserve of height which could be exchanged for speed should they lag in a turn. If a radical change of course was made this was a distinct possibility.

Other formations used were echelon, in which all the aircraft were stepped upwards and outwards from the leader, and line abreast. In all of these formations, changing course was a difficult business, the inside aeroplane throttled back turning tightly, while those on the outside of the turn had to cut the corner at full throttle to stay in position.

Line astern seems never to have been used. There were several good reasons for this. They would have had to fly stepped down from the leader to enable each pilot to keep the preceding aircraft in view. This meant that no one could have seen the leader's signals clearly. Furthermore, once an aeroplane lost station it was difficult for its pilot to catch up the others and regain position in the formation.

The task of the leader was to search the sky ahead and navigate. The other pilots kept station and searched the sky above and behind. On sighting the enemy, the leader manoeuvred his flight to obtain a good attacking position, preferably high and up-sun. He tried to avoid silhouetting his formation against high cloud, which would have made them easy to see, and equally tried to avoid flying over any undercast which would have exposed him to a higher enemy formation. Until the time came to launch his attack, he tried to avoid turning his back to the sun. Surprise was much more difficult to achieve with a formation, than with a single aeroplane. A formation was more easily seen from a distance, and the jockeying for position took longer, which gave the enemy more time to discover their danger.

Signalling in the air was basic and consisted of hand signals, coloured Very lights, and movements of the entire aeroplane. Hand signals were of little use in combat and could be easily missed by members of the formation. Coloured Very lights were often used, typical meanings being: red (if fired by the leader), 'Attacking, follow me'; or if in a dogfight, 'Break off and reform'. Fired by any other pilot, a red meant 'Help!' A green light could mean 'Engine giving trouble', and a white, 'Let's go home'. Rocking the entire machine gently from side to side indicated that the leader was about to start a turn and rocking fore and aft showed a dive or climb was imminent. The leader was easily recognisable in the air by streamers tied to the interplane struts while the deputy leader had a streamer on his tail. Individual markings, such as red spinners or rudders were tried but these found more favour with the Germans, culminating in the highly individualistic colour schemes almost universally adopted by their scout pilots.

Paradoxically, the period which first saw the advent of the fighting formation was also the heyday of the lone wolf aces. Albert Ball and Georges Guynemer were among the first and most outstanding and in many ways were typical of the breed. Neither hesitated to attack superior numbers and both were badly shot-up on many occasions. Guynemer was probably the more reckless of the two, attacking from any angle, while Ball would carefully stalk his opponents when opportunity offered. Both were masters of the head-on attack, which called for very fine judgement. Two scouts 200 yds apart and approaching each other head-on at a combined speed of 180 mph, would be just over two seconds from a collision. Few pilots were sufficiently determined to push their attack closer. Ball and Guynemer were the exceptions who held on, thus gaining a free shot when their opponent broke away. Ball also used a trick which called for a great deal of nerve. He would fly straight and level below a hostile machine and invite the German to dive on his tail. Choosing his moment precisely, he would break hard upwards and into his assailant and often succeeded in reversing their positions. At first sight this ploy seems suicidal. Closer examination reveals that for an expert pilot it was quite feasible. Until the range closed to less than 150 yds, Ball was fairly safe. His opponent could seldom start his attack from directly astern; he would need to come down in a curving dive. This would be done either gently, throttled back so as not to overshoot, or flat out and hell for leather. As Ball watched his foe curve around in pursuit, he would have been able to gain a fair idea of his speed. This judging of the attacker's speed was critical. As the German came closer his concentration was on flying smoothly and aiming carefully at his unsuspecting quarry. Then suddenly Ball's Nieuport would rear up and around and in a couple of seconds have gained a height and positional advantage. If the German pilot was alert and had kept his speed high, he could break off the fight and escape. If not, he was not a good insurance risk.

Ball and Guynemer both possessed the usual attributes of the great fighter pilots; confidence and determination, flying and shooting ability. They also displayed another quality to a remarkable degree, luck. This is not intended to belittle their achievements in any way, but is purely an observation based on a

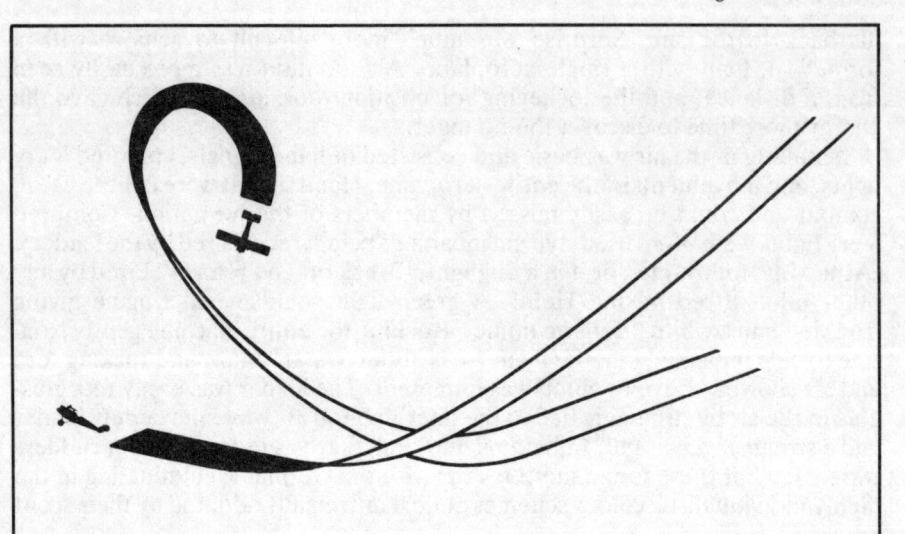

Fig 7 A ruse commonly used by Captain Albert Ball.

This manoeuvre called for a great deal of nerve and fine judgement. It depended on lulling the attacker into a false sense of security. Surprised by the hard upward break, the hunter quickly became the hunted.

comparison of their records with those of some of the more cautious but equally renowned air fighters. The aircraft of Manfred von Richthofen, Rene Fonck, Edward Mannock and James McCudden were rarely hit in combat, in contrast to those of Ball and Guynemer which often staggered home full of holes. In retrospect it seems that both felt obliged to live up to their reputations and were thus forced to ride their luck until it ran out. Ball fell in May 1917, Guynemer in September.

Another top-scoring pilot was Major James McCudden. His methods were completely opposite to the 'let's have a fight' attitude of Ball and Guynemer. His philosophy was to inflict maximum damage on the enemy at minimum risk. While much of his time was spent leading his flight, he also flew alone on many occasions, usually in pursuit of high-flying enemy reconnaissance aircraft. His SE5a was modified to give maximum high altitude performance and his method was to wait until the enemy machine crossed the lines, then climb after it at a distance. He made the best possible use of cloud cover and his solitary pursuits often took nearly an hour.

His final approach was made from the blind area under the enemy's tail and where possible he aligned his SE with the haze on the horizon to make himself less visible, before closing to about 100 yds. This was not easy. The enemy observer stood in a large round cockpit and he could lean over and peer under the tail quite easily. Therefore McCudden waited until the enemy were busy with their primary mission of observation and photography, before closing when their look-out was least efficient.

Like many other pilots, McCudden had a great deal of respect for the observer's machine-gun and took pains to keep out of the line of fire. If the crew of the two-seater saw him, they would turn the machine to bring the gun to bear. McCudden's counter to this was to open the throttle and turn in the opposite direction, thus keeping under the tail of the other aircraft. He then reversed his turn and used the SE's superior speed to hold his position in his opponent's blind spot. Having failed to get a shot by turning in one direction, the reconnaissance machine would often turn the other way. McCudden would then haul his nose around and fire a quick burst. The enemy pilot frequently reacted by diving away. His speed rose sharply and the slipstream would blow the observer flat along the top of the fuselage, preventing him from using his gun. When this happened, McCudden slid in behind for an easy no-deflection shot. But despite his successes, McCudden always maintained that a well handled two-seater could match a single-seater.

The first large-scale air combats, or dogfights, began in 1917. These gave rise to two new problems. The first was tactical; whether to attempt to fight as a formation, or to use the formation to get large numbers to the fight efficiently. The second was technical; whether to use a very fast aeroplane to strike rapidly and break off, or an extremely manoeuvrable machine to stay and outfight the enemy. The technology of the period did not allow both qualities.

The answer to the tactical problem was conditioned by the aircraft flown by the individual unit. Major Sholto Douglas commanded No. 43 Squadron, Royal Flying Corps, between January and May 1917. This squadron flew with Sopwith 1½ Strutter, a two-seater armed with one Vickers fixed machine-gun firing forwards and a free Lewis gun in the rear cockpit. Lacking performance, their tactical options were limited as Major Douglas was at pains to point out. He wrote: 'Offensive patrols were carried out by a flight of five or six machines flying in close formation. Owing to the superior performance of the enemy fighting machines, it was rarely possible in the course of an offensive patrol to attack an enemy formation. It was usually necessary, in order to bring the enemy to battle, to fly underneath his formation, lure it into attacking one, and then trust to the good shooting of one's observers to pick off the enemy machines as they came diving to the attack. This is a poor method of carrying out an offensive patrol; it is difficult to be really offensive. It is also bad for one's morale. But it was the method that was forced on us by the inferior performance at height of our machines. This experience, more than any other, brought home to me the supreme importance of performance in a fighting machine: for performance means the initiative – the most valuable moral and practical asset in any form of war.'

Other British squadrons were even worse equipped than No 43. The obsolete FE2 was still in service and a new tactic evolved at about this time. The originator of it will probably never be known, but Major Douglas first noted its use by No 25 Squadron. A pusher was singularly ill-defended from the rear. It could fire backwards but only if the gunner stood precariously on his seat, with the coaming of the nacelle barely above his ankles. Even then his field of fire was restricted by the arc of the propeller. The answer was for the formation to fly in a circle, each gunner defending the tail of the machine in front. To quote Major Douglas again: 'As long as pilots followed closely in the wake of the machine in front, and the circle was unbroken, it was impossible for the enemy to attack the rear of any individual FE without coming under strong fire from at least one other FE; in fact a formation was formed without a rear or blind side that could be attacked. By making a slightly wider sweep at each revolution of

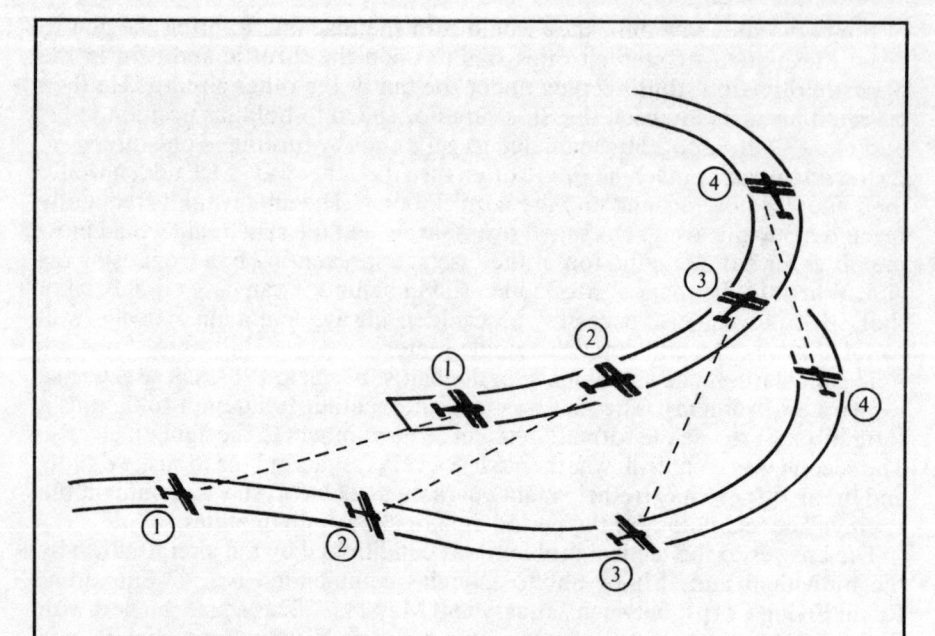

Fig 8 McCudden's method of tackling a two-seater.

1) McCudden closes a two-seater from astern and below.
2) The two-seater turns away to allow its observer to fire. McCudden also turns away, remaining in the two-seater's blind spot below and behind.
3) The two-seater continues to turn. McCudden reverses his turn to stay in the blind spot, using the superior speed of his SE 5A.
4) McCudden reaches a firing position below and astern.

the circle, the leader would gradually work the whole formation back to our lines.'

No 43 Squadron experimented with the circle but found that as the pilot of a tractor aeroplane had a poor forward view, he could not easily keep the preceding machine in sight. However, the French Escadrille Lafayette used it successfully and it became widely known as the Lufbery after one of their pilots.

The German Air Service had no doubts about the value of formation fighting. The first of the so-called 'Flying Circuses' was formed on July 26 1917 under the command of Manfred von Richthofen. Jastas 4, 6, 10 and 11 were combined to form Jagdgeschwader 1. The idea was to have a numerically large self-contained unit which could be rapidly moved from place to place to meet the demands of the moment. The Jastas quickly became used to working as an integrated unit as shown by the account of an action fought against them by six Sopwith 1½ Strutters of No 45 Squadron in late July.

The Sopwiths were on a photographic mission 15 miles into hostile territory when the Germans arrived in four separate formations of eight or nine aircraft. The Jastas took station all around, to left and right ahead, and to left and right astern of the British formation, all with a height advantage. The sequence of attacks was perfectly co-ordinated. The first formation came in from the left rear, diving below then attacking in a shallow climb under the tail of the Sopwiths. This was immediately followed by the second unit from high astern on the right as the defenders' attention was focused low and to the left. As the first two German units broke away, the third unit attacked from high front left, followed by the fourth from level front right. The hapless British pilots could not turn to meet either of these attacks without breaking formation, which in the face of the German technical and numerical superiority, would have been to risk total annihilation. Three out of the six Sopwiths were lost.

Had No 45 Squadron been attacked by a single Jasta they could have manoeuvred to meet it. If a single Jasta had split into sub-formations to carry out a co-ordinated attack, each thrust would have consisted of two or three aeroplanes only, and been much less deadly. But against this perfectly timed sequence of attacks by whole units, the British formation was helpless.

The early months of 1917 were a bad time for the British. Their pilot replacements were arriving at the front with as little as 15 hours flying experience and were incapable of handling their machines in combat. The German Air Service had introduced new and improved aircraft, the Albatros D5, the Pfalz D3 and the Halberstadt. Casualties were high, reaching a peak in 'Bloody April'. With the arrival of the latest British types, the SE5 and the Sopwith Camel, the situation eased and with the introduction of better training methods it finally stabilised.

Combat manoeuvres were fairly standard in all air arms. The stall turn or Immelmann was widely used. It enabled the aeroplane to reverse its direction very quickly in the lateral space of about 30 ft. The barrel roll was used effectively on occasion, as the extra distance flown around a helical path was

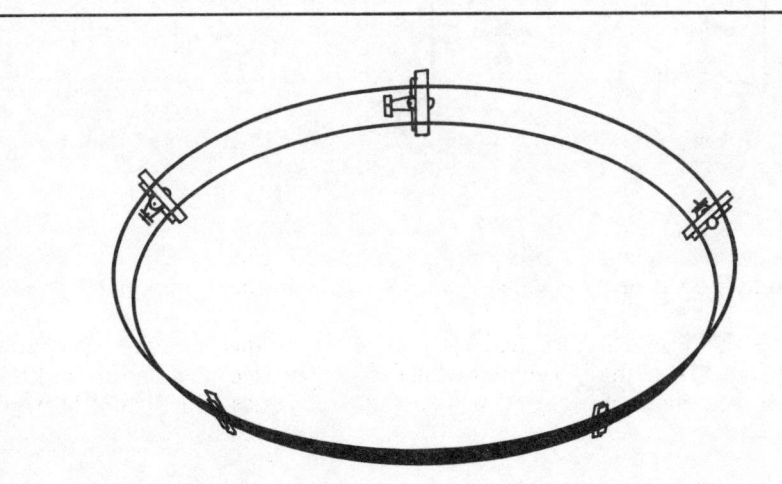

Fig 9 The defensive circle.
Any attacker coming in astern of an aircraft in this formation will come under fire from the one following. The tail of every plane is covered but height is gradually lost and plenty of fuel is needed to hold out against a prolonged attack.

Fig 10

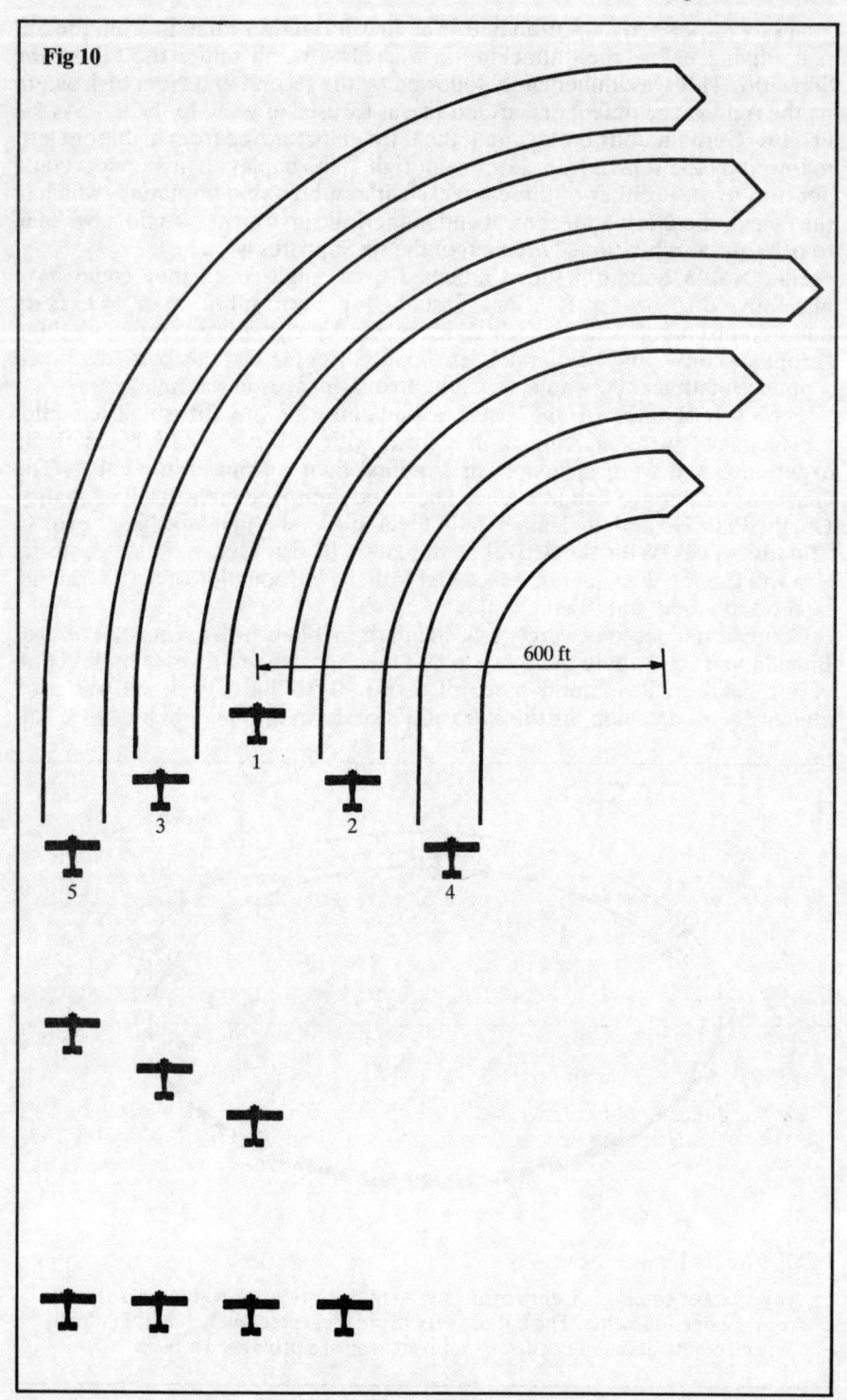

600 ft

worth about 60 yds in a straight line. An aircraft close behind a rolling opponent would have found himself out in front unless he broke off his attack. Looping was not recommended as the aircraft performing it became a slow-moving sitting target as it came over the top. Should a loop have become necessary, the method recommended was to throttle back the engine when nearing the top. On arriving inverted at the end of the climb, the nose was pushed up, causing a stall, from which the machine recovered at a higher level than when it started the manoeuvre. Spinning was taught as a method of evasion, shamming dead. It was frequently used in combat to fool the opposition. Sometimes it failed to work. Major Edward Mannock of No 74 Squadron once spun down after a spinning German, firing short bursts while spinning. He had no chance of scoring, and was later asked why he had fired. His reply was 'to increase his wind up'. The principle was sound; the more worried the German became the more likely he was to make a mistake. He did, and was shot down!

The German Air Service has often been accused of lack of aggression as its fighting units mainly operated on their own side of the lines. The reason for this is not hard to find. The German armies almost invariably occupied high ground from which they overlooked the Allied lines. Consequently the Allies were far more dependent on reconnaissance from the air than were the Germans. Their observation machines had to be protected and this could only be done by offensive patrols over German-held territory. A lesser factor was that the German Air Service was numerically inferior to the combined British and French forces. Fighting over their own lines was more economical in that a pilot shot down but surviving was not lost to them. But with their opponents so willing to carry the fight to them, they could afford to wait for trouble to come, rather than go looking for it.

Major Douglas returned to France in September 1917 leading No 84 Squadron, equipped with the SE5a, a fast and robust aeroplane. It was not the most agile of machines, but Douglas did not think this mattered a great deal. He later wrote: 'In the present development of aerial fighting, it is the flight that fights as one unit. Therefore it is the manoeuvrability of the flight that counts, not the manoeuvrability of the individual machine. If then a machine is sufficiently handy to keep its place in the formation in any flight manoeuvre, it is of minor importance whether that machine is individually of a high degree of manoeuvrability or not. . . . After much debate and in spite of opposition from

---

Opposite
Fig 10 A 90-degree turn in typical World War 1 formations.

Vic The difficulties of keeping station are apparent; with the leader turning on a 600 ft radius, No 4 must turn on a radius of 480 ft and No 5 on a radius of about 720 ft. If the leader is moving at 80 mph the two outside men would need speeds of 65 mph and 95 mph to keep station. In practice, the outside men would cut the corner and the inside men would throttle back and climb slightly during the turn.

Echelon Turning right presents the same problem as does Vic for the inside men. In a left turn the formation would have dropped into line astern, resuming formation when the turn was complete.

Line abreast This manoeuvre involved the ever present risk of collision in the turn and was not popular for this reason. It was rarely used.

the individualists of the squadron, we finally made a strict order that no pilot was on any account to leave the formation, even to take an apparently easy opportunity of shooting down an enemy machine. The initiative in any attack lay wholly with the flight leader: if he dived to the attack, the whole flight dived with him: when he zoomed away after the attack, even if he had failed to shoot down the enemy attacked, all pilots zoomed away with him, still keeping formation. This was found to be the only way of keeping the formation together during a combat; otherwise the flight was split up at the first onset, each pilot breaking off in pursuit of a different enemy machine; and then being defeated in detail. The natural consequence of this order was that it was usually the flight commander who actually shot down the enemy machine. But being the most experienced pilot, he was the most capable of doing this quickly and effectively. In addition, with his flight behind him to act as a buffer against any attack from behind, he could afford to concentrate all his powers on the destruction of the enemy machine; there was no need for him to be peering over his shoulder all the time, anxious lest he himself be attacked. His aiming and shooting were therefore the more careful and deliberate.'

This rigid doctrine was far from universal. Many squadrons recognised the value of the initial attack in formation but once battle was joined, the pilots were free to fight as they pleased until the recall signal was given. Most German units also operated on this principle. The damage was most often done in the first pass, the subsequent dogfight consisting of much shooting but few hits.

As formations increased in size, caution became the order of the day. Major Mannock's dictum 'Always above, seldom on the same level, never underneath,' was widely practised. To return to Major Douglas' report: 'Another lesson that we soon learnt was that there are occasions when it is wrong to accept battle: that one must always strive to take the enemy at a disadvantage: equally that one must not be taken at a disadvantage oneself: and this often entails a deliberate refusal of battle and a retirement, so that the enemy's advantage may be nullified. If for instance that advantage is height, then one should retreat, climb hard, and go back and seek out the enemy at his own height or higher. Of course there are occasions when battle has to be accepted at a disadvantage – if, for instance, one sees another British squadron being overwhelmed by superior numbers, then obviously whatever the odds, one must accept battle. But normally one should force the battle upon the enemy, not have the battle forced upon oneself.'

It is interesting to note that at a time when big dogfights were a common occurrence on the western front, Major Douglas was advocating avoiding them wherever possible. His analysis of squadron combats showed that casualties mainly occurred when the flight broke up and that it was more likely to break up when attacking, than when being attacked. Thus his insistence on rigid flight discipline. His handling of the squadron as a whole was no less positive. 'A' flight was the spearhead, covered by 'B' flight 500 ft higher, about half a mile away to one flank and slightly astern. 'C' flight acted as top cover, 2 to 3 miles astern of 'A' flight and up-sun, only joining the other two flights in battle in dire necessity.

Big dogfights were seldom planned but arose from a chance meeting of two small formations. A handful of SPADs would join in, followed by an Albatros Jasta followed in turn by a flight of Camels until between 50 and 100 aeroplanes were whirling around in an area possibly 5 or 6 miles across. Captain Bill

C flight

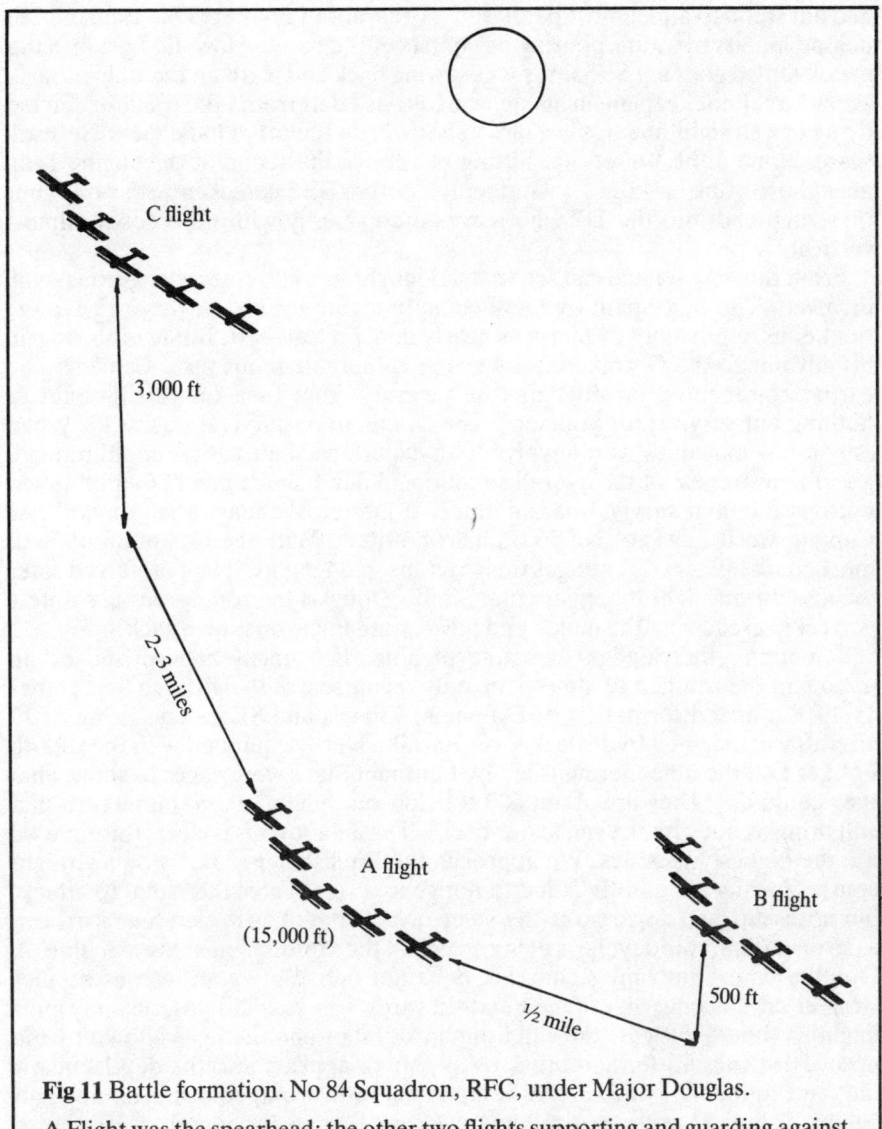

3,000 ft

2–3 miles

A flight
(15,000 ft)

B flight

½ mile

500 ft

Fig 11 Battle formation. No 84 Squadron, RFC, under Major Douglas.
A Flight was the spearhead; the other two flights supporting and guarding against surprise.

Lambert, an American flying with No 24 Squadron, Royal Flying Corps described what it was like: 'At that moment a bright blue aeroplane flashes by me. He is only 10 yds off my right wing-tip and going in the same direction. Down goes my nose; slight right rudder, my eye glued to the Aldis sight. Ease off on the rudder, back on the stick a bit. Just right. How can I miss this? Before I can press the button for both guns I find out. At that instant something crashes around my cockpit; I feel a slight jerk on the right side of my suit collar. What is that? Several ragged holes appear in my dashboard. I look over my shoulder and am stunned and almost paralysed. A red-nosed Fokker D7 is about 50 yds behind me, its two guns pouring out bursts of red flame. How did I get into this mess? Down goes my SE5a, my legs sawing back and forth on the rudder bar. I know he cannot keep me in his sight so long as I dart from side to side and avoid flying in a straight line. Only a lucky shot will do the job. I look back. He's still there. None of his bullets are hitting but above the sound of the engine I can hear those guns barking . . . suddenly another SE5 comes in with both guns throwing lead into the D7 who leaves me instantly with nose down, almost vertical.'

From this account we can see that a dogfight was extremely dangerous to all involved. The time spent by Lambert in lining up his first adversary gave the Fokker its opportunity, which was nearly fatal for Lambert. But in following up his advantage the German pilot became vulnerable in his turn. Lambert had earlier commented on dogfights in general, 'from then on you thought of nothing but survival for yourself'. The comment on survival was valid. When only a few machines were involved, an experienced air fighter could retain a general awareness of the overall situation. When large numbers fought, it was not possible and survival became more a matter of chance than of skill. As Captain Cecil Lewis of No 56 Squadron noted, 'With the exception of Ball, most crack fighters did not get their victims in dogfights. They preferred safer means.' In this light it appears that Sholto Douglas' reasoning was absolutely correct in eschewing the melee and advocating the formation attack.

Sometimes the dogfight was unavoidable. If a unit was surprised by an opponent determined to attack, the only recourse was to fight. On September 15 1918 a mixed formation of Dolphins, Camels and SE5as consisting of 17 aircraft were sighted by Jasta 35 over Baralle. Newly equipped with the superb Fokker D7, the nine Germans led by Leutnant Stark were eager to show what they could do: 'They are about 600 ft below our height; we go into a turn that will bring us out with the sun at our backs. The air above us is clear; this time we are the highest machines. We approach the Englishmen. The fly on a straight course, having apparently failed to notice us as yet. I give the signal to attack; our noses dip, and down we go in a steep dive. Schmidt on my left seems to be in a particular hurry today; he is flying at almost the same height as my machine. A Dolphin comes into my sights. He does not notice my approach as he flies straight on, unconcerned. One hundred yards – 80 yds – 50 yds, now my guns begin to shoot – 30 yds, the Englishman sideslips and then goes down by the nose. His wings flutter and break away. He disappears into the depths below me, and suddenly I find myself in the midst of his companions. The dogfight begins. Schmidt is sitting on a Sopwith (Camel) while Stoer and an SE go into turns. The others are engaged in a tail-chasing bout with the rest of the English.'

From this extract we can see that however desirable it was to avoid a general melee, it was not always possible if the enemy had other ideas. Dogfights were to remain a major feature of air warfare until the Armistice. Two different types of single-seat fighting scout had been developed, each with their own exceptional qualities, and controversy arose as to which type was the best fighter. One type was fast and strong, ideally suited to the surprise attack from above; the other not so fast but incredibly agile, well-suited to the tight turning of the dogfight. It was not possible to combine the two qualities to any great degree as the difference lay primarily in the type of engine. Exceptional

Pfalz DIII

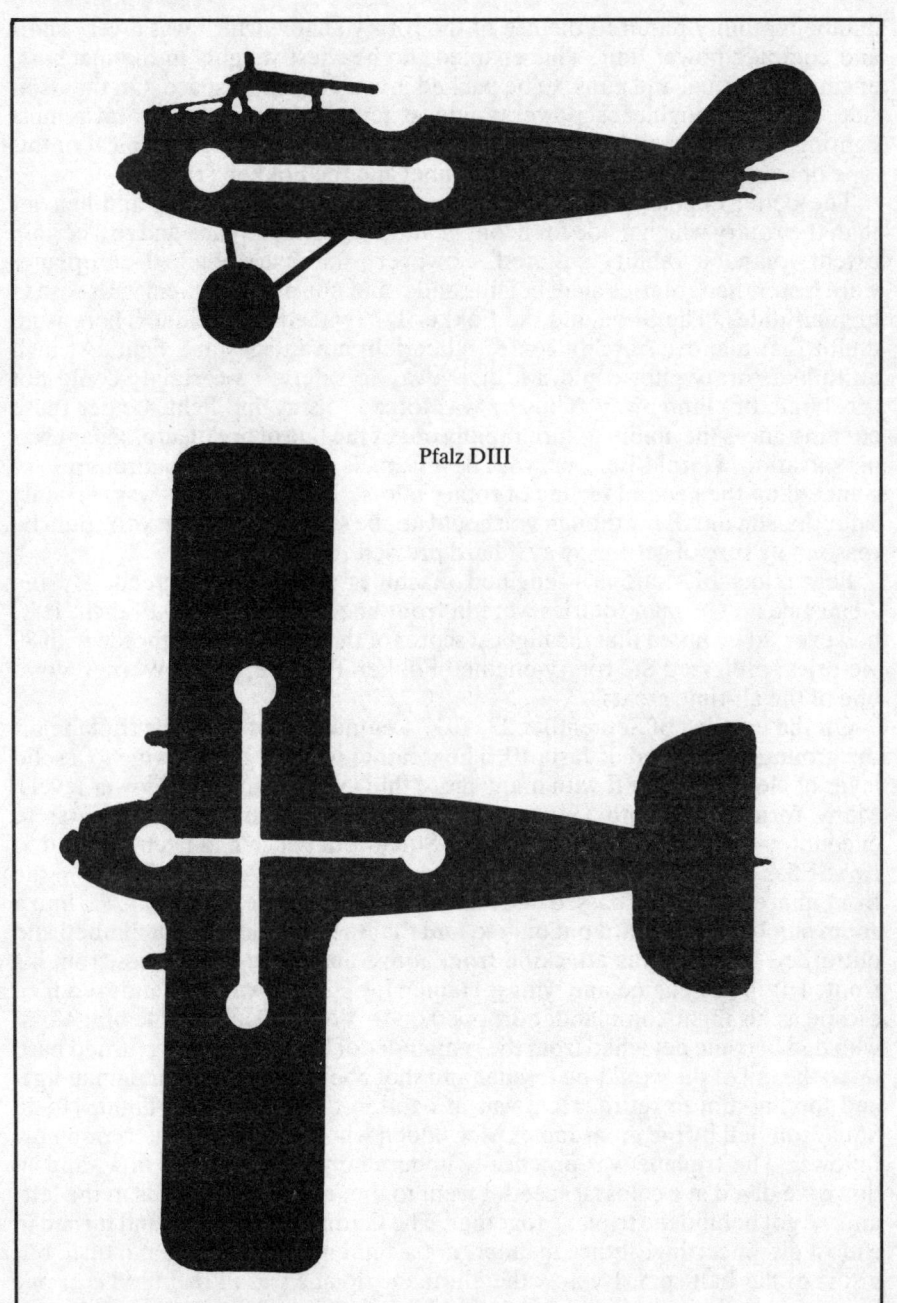

Fig 12 Manoeuvre commencement capability.
The dumb-bells represent the turning moments of the weight of the aeroplane about the centre of gravity. The further from the centre the weights, the slower the response to a change in direction of flight will be.

manoeuvrability required the use of the rotary engine which was a very short and compact power unit. This enabled the heaviest weights in the machine, engine, pilot, fuel and guns, to be packed into a very short space. On the debit side, the rotary engine lost power rapidly at heights above 12,000 ft and as most fighting took place higher than this, they were out-performed. Typical of this type of aeroplane were the Sopwith Camel and the Fokker Triplane.

The better engine was the stationary engine. This was longer and heavier than the rotary which made for a longer and heavier aeroplane and to a certain extent, manoeuvrability suffered, however, stationary-engined aeroplanes were faster than rotaries at all heights and could out-perform them with ease at high altitudes. The SE5a and the Fokker D7 typified this model. There is no doubt that manoeuvrability conferred certain advantages in a fight. At high altitude a rotary pilot could not dive away to safety; he certainly could not accelerate or climb away. Thus he was forced to stay and fight. Under these circumstances the ability to turn rapidly out of the line of fire of an assailant was his salvation. Harold Balfour, who flew Camels with No 43 Squadron in 1917 summed up the general feeling of rotary pilots: 'Life on a Camel was certainly safer than on an SE for though you could not be sure of your man, you could be reasonably sure of getting away if hard pressed'.

Few pilots of stationary engined machines would have agreed. By the Armistice no German rotaries were in front line service and few French. It is, however, to be noted that the highest scorer of the war, von Richthofen with 80 victories, preferred the rotary-engined Fokker Triplane, as did Werner Voss, one of the all-time greats.

On the evening of September 23, 1917 Leutnant Voss lifted his triplane off the ground at the head of Jasta 10. The weather was not good, owing to a solid layer of cloud at 9,000 ft with many more thin layers scattered at lower levels. Many formations, both German and British were up on patrol. First to encounter Voss was 'A' flight of No 60 Squadron, which had been reduced to two SE5as. Lieutenant Hamersley at once attacked in a shallow dive from the front quarter. As Voss passed underneath him, Hamersley pulled his SE into a zoom climb, turning hard but only to find that the triplane had outclimbed and outturned him and was attacking from above and about 30 degrees from his front. Hit in the engine and wings, Hamersley spun down in an endeavour to escape as his flight-commander dropped on to Voss' tail in a rescue bid. Voss, who had become detached from the remainder of his Jasta by now, turned hard on to the tail of the would-be rescuer and shot about his rudder bar damaging it and forcing him to retire. Help was at hand in the shape of 'B' flight, No 56 Squadron, led by the great James McCudden whose account of the action now follows: 'The triplane was practically underneath our formation now, and so down we dived at a colossal speed. I went to the right, Rhys-Davids to the left, and we got behind the triplane together. The German pilot saw us and turned in a most disconcertingly quick manner, not a climbing nor Immelmann turn, but a sort of flat half spin. By now the German triplane was in the middle of our formation and its handling was wonderful to behold. The pilot seemed to be firing at all of us simultaneously, and although I got behind him a second time, I could hardly stay there for a second. His movements were so quick and uncertain that none of us could hold him in sight at all for any decisive time. I now got a good opportunity as he was coming towards me nose on, and slightly underneath, and had apparently not seen me. I dropped my nose, got him well in my sight, and pressed both triggers. As soon as I fired up came his nose at me, and I heard clack-clack-clack-clack, as his bullets passed close to me and through my wings. . . . By this time a red-nosed Albatros Scout had arrived, and was apparently doing its best to guard the triplane's tail, and it was well handled too. . . .'

Three more SEs of No 56 Squadron's 'C' flight now joined in, led by Captain Bowman. The Albatros vanished and no-one noticed its going, they had their hands full with Voss. The fight had drifted down to about 2,000 ft and at this height Voss could have broken off the fight and climbed away at any time. But no, back he came into the fray every time. Such an action could have only one end. As he passed across Bowman's nose, he applied full rudder without bank, hauled his nose up and fired a short burst while skidding sideways, then corrected. This left Rhys-Davids right on his tail at point blank range. His shots struck home. Shortly afterwards, the triplane hit the ground. Thus fell the man who may well have been Germany's greatest air fighter. Virtually single-handed he had fought 11 SE5s for ten minutes. Three were subsequently written off, two seriously damaged and all the rest were holed. This fight was a striking example of the capability of manoeuvre when opposed by faster but less agile machines, but it was the exception rather than the rule.

We can sum up the speed versus manoeuvreability argument quite simply. A cursory glance through any biographical work of the period shows that roughly four out of every five pilots shot down did not see their assailant until it was too late, if at all. An aeroplane could be seen at 2 to 3 miles in average weather conditions; a formation at even greater distances. The fast aeroplane such as the SE5a closed the gap much more quickly than the agile Camel and thus had a much better chance of surprising an unwary opponent and it was by the element of surprise that most victories were obtained. Many victories were gained in dogfights, but as we have seen, the element of surprise was still the dominant factor. Extreme manoeuvreability helped a pilot little if his attackers' first shots were on target. We can thus conclude that speed, coupled with a good rate of climb to obtain a height advantage, was the most important attribute of a fighting aeroplane in World War 1.

Chapter 3

Which way now?

World War 1 ended, the German Air Service was disbanded and the British and French Air Forces were reduced to a fraction of their former strength. The hard-won experience of the fighting pilots was distilled and reduced to textbook stuff. With the pressure of war lifted, ideas could be tried at leisure, the good accepted and the not so good rejected. As Harold Balfour commented nearly 60 years later, while the war was in progress they had been too busy fighting to worry about the business of clever tactics.

During 1918, the Royal Flying Corps had become the Royal Air Force. In 1922 the Royal Air Force Training Manual was first issued and it is of interest to examine the sections dealing with air fighting. The Vic formation had become standard; it gave members a good view of the leader and was by far the best formation for flying through cloud. This was an important consideration in Europe where bad weather is common; it was useless for the leader to emerge from cloud minus the rest of the squadron. One advance on wartime practice was the use of distinct sub-formations which could operate independently if unavoidably split from the main formation.

Communications were standardised as movements of the leader's aeroplane. Hand signals were not encouraged and pyrotechnics thought unsuitable for use by single-seaters. Typical signals were; 'close up', a lateral rocking movement; 'open out', a violent porpoising; 'about turn', a short gentle climb; 'change direction', twice banking in the direction of the turn, etc. The simple turn was still used, pilots on the outside were instructed to accelerate, by losing height if necessary, and cut the corner, afterwards climbing back into position as quickly as possible. The cross-over turn was also taught. This was a much better way of turning through 90 degrees as all aircraft flew at the same speed, reversing their positions in the formation as they did so. Collisions were avoided by the aircraft on the inside of the turn pulling up and over their opposite numbers. It needed much practice to perfect but was far superior to the simple turn.

Turning through 180 degrees was obviously a combat requirement. The simple turn was too slow, the inside aeroplanes would have been nearly stalling, the outside ones lagging. The double cross-over was very complicated; the pilot's attention would have been concentrated on keeping station to the exclusion of keeping a look-out. The method adopted was for the leader to turn hard left, while the others turned outwards using the Immelmann turn, then regained formation as quickly as possible. The defensive circle was adopted as a standard tactic and pilots were trained to form the circle as quickly as possible.

Which way now?

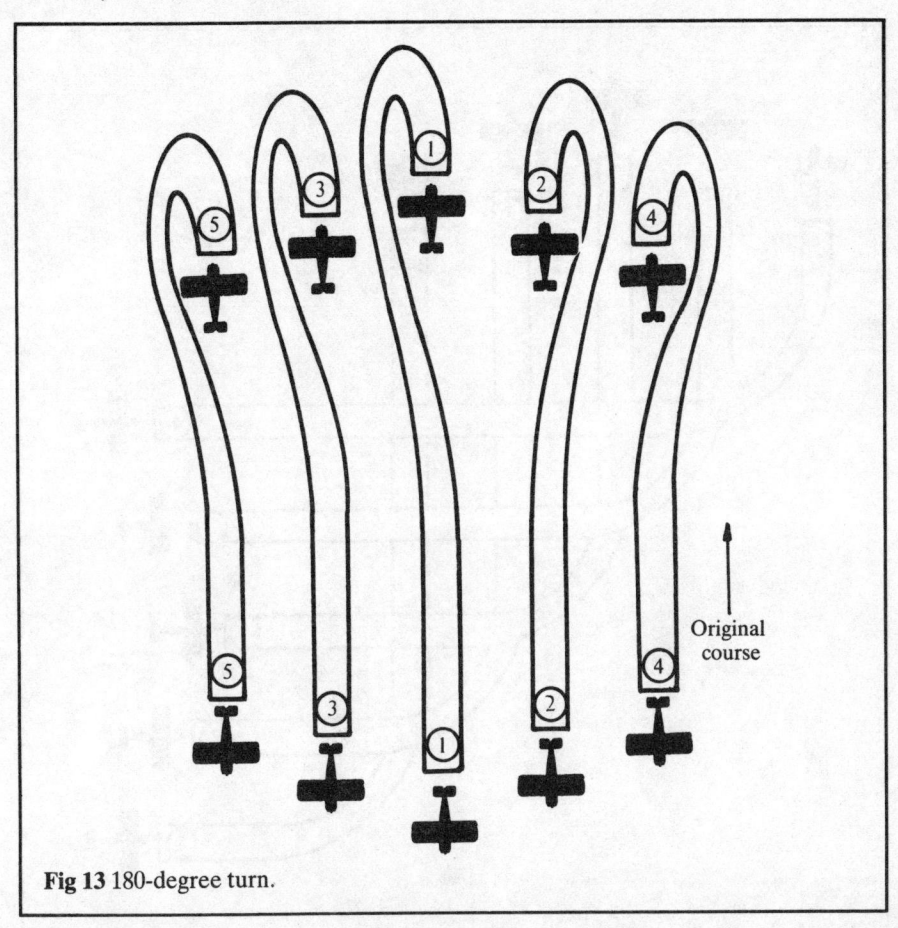

Fig 13 180-degree turn.

It can be seen that there was nothing very original in the manual except the cross-over turn. This was almost certainly evolved during the war, but the difficulties of introducing it to the front line units would have been extreme. Fighting a war left no time to practice complex manoeuvres. The manual stressed three fundamental principles: (1) Victory can only be achieved by a display of the true offensive spirit. (2) Every attack must be driven home with implacable determination to destroy the opponent. (3) Surprise must be employed whenever possible. It was realised that ascendancy in the air could be won by the cumulative effect of a series of material and moral successes. These could be achieved by pursuing a relentless offensive to establish a general superiority. Absolute air superiority could only be attained by the complete destruction of the enemy. This was unlikely and local enemy concentrations were always likely to reverse the general situation temporarily.

The choice of surprise as the third fundamental principle bears out what has already been noted, that most victims never saw their assailant. Von Richthofen and others had often referred to the chivalry of the air. In truth there was precious little. Surprise was the weapon of the assassin, not the chevalier: the means of murderous ambush rather than the fair fight.

Fig 14 The cross-over turn.

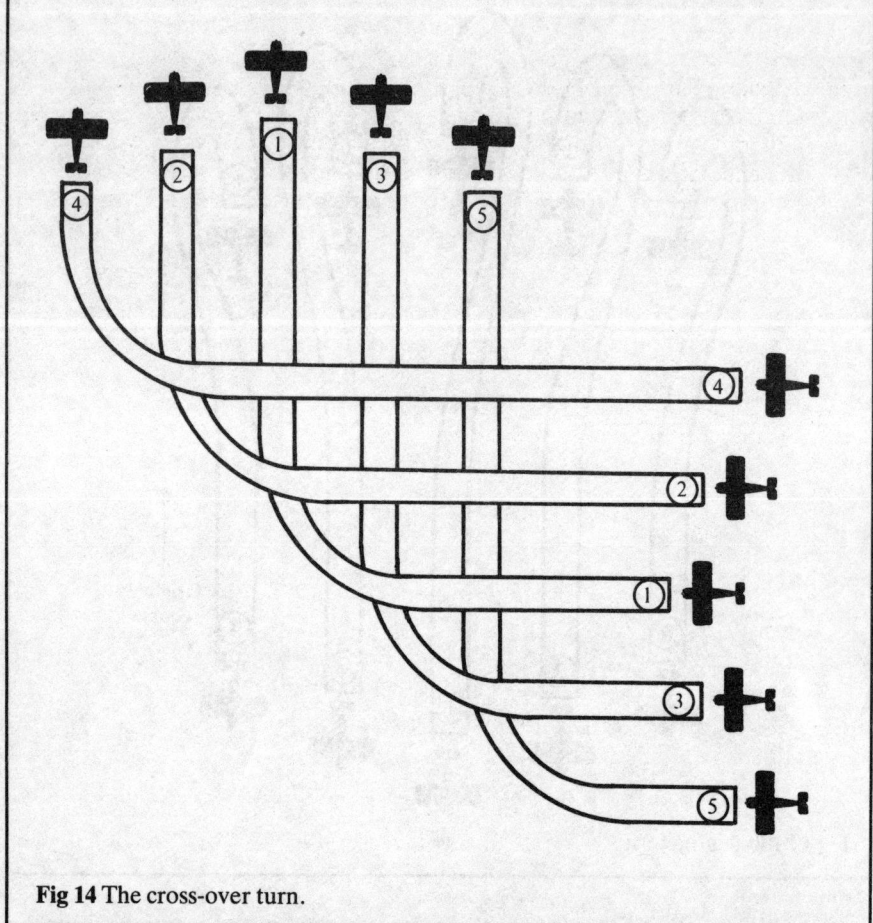

This took a lot of practice admittedly, but the advantages were so great that it seems amazing that it fell into disuse, to be re-invented by the Germans during the Spanish Civil War.

Pilots were taught to take advantage of their background and to use the sun or cloud to approach their victim unobserved. Great stress was laid on using the blind spots of the enemy, which in the biplanes of the time were considerable. Finding the blind spots of a formation was more difficult, but some angles were more favourable than others. The best angles were from below but there was little future in climbing up beneath a formation of hostile fighters. The best shooting range was agreed to be as close as possible without risking collision, and the best shooting position directly astern. A great deal of the air fighting section of the manual was devoted to single aircraft combats. While useful, this was unrealistic in the context of the fighting formations generally advocated.

Keeping an efficient look-out, and expertise in aircraft recognition were stressed. To see and identify the enemy first would give the pilot a few vital seconds to take the initiative.

Which way now?

In 1921, the Italian General Guilio Douhet published a book called *The Command of the Air*, which made him the international evangelist of air power. As there can be no doubt that Douhet did for a time considerably influence military aviation thinking, it is relevant to examine exactly what he said; and why he made such an impact.

Even in translation, Douhet's book is a lucid and well-reasoned work. There was sufficient reiteration to make his ideas stick in the mind of the reader and enough foreboding to satisfy the most ardent prophet of doom. Many statements were obviously correct and these served to mask the flaws. He prophesied that future wars would be won in a few days by the country that possessed the necessary air power. This was to be achieved by aeroplanes dropping high explosive to destroy buildings, incendiaries to burn the ruins and poison gas to prevent firefighting. In this way total destruction of the target was assured. He also forecast bacteriological attacks, though this point was not pursued.

He assumed that worthwhile targets were generally concentrated in areas of about 500 m diameter. These targets were to be totally destroyed by ten aeroplanes each carrying 2 tonnes of bombs, to be delivered uniformly over the target area from a height of 10,000 ft by trained crews. His calculations pre-suppose complete accuracy, even scatter and no faulty ammunition, a tall order even now, 60 years later. The optimum unit size was thus ten aeroplanes. Defence against air attack was basic; the enemy was to be destroyed on the ground.

Douhet specified a force of 1,000 bombers, able to obliterate 50 targets a day. Land and sea forces were to be defeated from the air, their lines of communication, bases and supplies all having been destroyed within the first few days. Given that his proposed force was capable of the requisite level of destruction, he may just have been right. Target priorities were to be determined by the air force and as a rule no action was to be undertaken in support of the surface forces. To this end the air force was to be independent of the other services.

The General did consider the possibility of the enemy taking defensive measures, but appeared to largely discount them. Anti-aircraft fire he regarded with contempt, with some justification considering the contemporary state of the art. More surprisingly fighter defence was also discounted for two reasons. The first was the difficulty of interception. It would have been necessary to set up a warning system covering the length and breadth of the defending country. The sightings would then have been sent to a central control unit for analysis and they would have produced a plot showing the approximate speed, height and course of the raiders. By the time a defending fighter unit was sent off in pursuit, about ten minutes would have elapsed, and a further ten or 15 minutes would have been lost in gaining altitude. By this time the raiders could have changed course and been anywhere within an area of no less than 1,600 square miles. Whether the defending fighters found the raiders thus became a matter of pure luck. And Douhet's 50 squadrons, flying dogleg courses, would have quickly swamped the system even on a clear day.

However, there still existed the chance of a lucky interception. This was to have been countered by heavily armed escort aeroplanes. Douhet explains: 'Great speed in an aeroplane is always attained at the expense of carrying capacity. So in planes of great carrying capacity we must be content with a moderate speed. . . . The bombing plane then should be a plane of moderate speed, since protected by combat planes it need not flee or dodge the attacks of the enemy and thus sacrifice load to speed. What determines victory in aerial warfare is firepower. Speed only serves to come to grips with the foe or to flee from him, no more. A slower heavily armed plane able to clear its way with its own armament can always get the best of the faster pursuit plane.'

Douhet wanted his heavy escort aeroplanes to have a slightly better speed, ceiling and radius of action than his bombers, but added: 'There should on the whole be very little difference between one type of aeroplane and the other, which implies that combat planes, like bombers, ought to be capable of carrying a substantial load. . . . This increase in the carrying capacity of the combat unit should be made use of for increasing fire power and if possible, armour protection. . . . A plane designed and constructed along these lines would, on the face of it, be so superior in intensity of fire power as to outmatch any pursuit ship now existing.'

To summarise, Douhet wanted a bomber which carried 2 tonnes of guns, gunners and armour plating in lieu of bombs. This would have given him up to six gunners per aircraft. After the enemy air force had been destroyed, these machines would have been converted back into bombers. In an extended version of *The Command of the Air* written in 1927, he took the obvious next step of specifying that all the aircraft were to be of one type and called battleplanes.*

The British Royal Air Force under the influence of Lord Trenchard was more completely committed to the concept of independent action than any other and came closest to Douhet's ideal. They were not, however, willing to totally abandon the concept of fighter defence, and the force was rebuilt with two bomber squadrons to each fighter squadron. Also showing Douhet's influence were the Italian Regia Aeronautica and the French Armée de l'Air. This was most noticeable in the design of some French aircraft, the large slabby *multiplace de combat* types which appear to show the influence of Douhet's multi-role theory. Not affected were the Americans, Russians and Japanese who retained their air arms as appendages of their surface forces. The new German Luftwaffe when it emerged was somewhere in the middle, basically geared to the needs of the army but with an independent striking capability. One suspects that Hermann Goering would have preferred to be totally independent, but the overall commitment to the blitzkrieg concept forced him to ride both horses at once.

Given that most of the bombers were likely to get through and that they were capable of doing considerable damage when they did, it seemed a good idea to have an effective strategic bomber force. Though Douhet's predicted level of destruction was far beyond the technology of his time, there appeared a distinct possibility that wars could be won by bombarding and thus demoralising the civilian population. Consequently some sort of defence had to be attempted and the only possible means was the defensive fighter aeroplane. The Royal Air Force in particular concentrated their efforts to counter the threat of the bomber and as will be shown in the next chapter, forgot many of the lessons of the previous conflict in the process.

---

* Sixteen years later the Americans converted B-17 bombers into YB-40 gunships. They were a failure.

Chapter 4

The great leap forward

The late 1920s and early 1930s saw great technical advances in aviation. Engines increased in power and the use of the supercharger enabled them to develop greater power at high altitude. The adoption of the monoplane layout reduced drag, as did the retractable undercarriage and the enclosed cockpit. Variable pitch propellers were fitted, giving greater efficiency. All these innovations improved speed and enabled greater heights to be sought than were attainable in World War 1. Armament was increased to give greater firepower. But for fighters the most important advance of all was the development of the radio telephone. For the first time it became possible for pilots to talk to each other in the air and to receive instructions from the ground.

Today we take radio telephony for granted, and it is hard to realise the enormous improvement in fighter tactics that it made possible. The ground control organisation could direct the fighters to an unseen enemy. The formation leader could give detailed orders to his pilots in flight and attacks by numbers of formations could be co-ordinated from outside visual distance of each other. Perhaps most important of all rapid warning of a surprise attack could be given.

Initially radio telephony had its problems. Speech was distorted and it helped greatly if the pilot had some idea of what the message coming through was about. Much practice in listening was necessary. With time the radio sets were improved, but listening errors were still possible. About this time the practice of using code-words came into being as a kind of unmistakable verbal shorthand. For instance, the Royal Air Force used the word, 'bandit' for an enemy aircraft and 'bogey' for an unidentified aircraft. Radio call-signs were issued to the fighter squadrons, originally in the form of flower names. This was changed when a certain squadron commander refused point-blank to identify himself as 'Pansy Leader'.

By the mid-1930s the spectre of war was again looming. The extravagant theorising of the previous decade had cast doubt on the true role of the fighter. The technical advances described earlier had benefited the bomber also, and the performance advantage traditionally enjoyed by the fighter had become marginal. A time lag of just three minutes in reaching the bomber's reported position would have placed the intercepting fighters several miles astern, involving a long chase to catch up. This was clearly unacceptable, but the only alternative was for the fighters to fly standing patrols. No country possessed enough fighters to do this effectively. An efficient early warning and reporting system was therefore of the highest priority.

Given an effective control system, the problem then became two-fold. Could the defending fighters stop the bombers? and would they have to tackle escorting fighters? To the first question the answer was clear: the bomber was able to inflict heavy damage, so the attempt had to be made. The answer to the second question was equally clear to those nations whose borders adjoined a potential enemy; their fighters would have to combat enemy fighters. To the Royal Air Force, separated from potential enemies by many miles of sea, it appeared that an anti-bomber force was the main priority. At the time, the idea of a single seat, single engined fighter with sufficient range to escort the raiding bombers appeared out of the question.

However, on July 21 1936, a Spanish Nieuport NiD52 shot down another Spanish machine of the same type, marking the beginning of an unbroken nine years during which the skies of the Northern Hemisphere were never quiet.

The Spanish Civil War was an ideological conflict between fascism and communism. As such it proved an ideal testing ground for the leading exponents of both creeds with Hitler's Germany and Mussolini's Italy aiding the fascists, and Stalin's Russia helping the communists. The first German fighters to arrive in Spain were Heinkel He 51 biplanes. These were handed over to Spanish pilots who achieved little, a state of affairs which led to the German instructors taking over and flying operationally. The initial Italian contingent comprised Fiat CR 32 fighters flown by Italian volunteer pilots from the outset, legality being maintained by their transfer to the Spanish Foreign Legion. The communists, or republicans as they preferred to be known, flew a mixture of aircraft, mainly of French design. Their pilots were a mixture of volunteers from a dozen nations, lacking training and organisation. Against the disciplined German and Italian flyers they were able to achieve little. Then in October 1936, help arrived from Russia in the form of Polikarpov I 15 and I 16 fighters flown by Russian volunteer pilots.

In general, the air war over Spain was fought in direct support of surface forces. Air combats were frequent and at first differed little from the encounters of the Great War. The main difference came with the introduction of fast monoplane bombers, the Russian SB 2, the German Dornier Do 17 and Heinkel He 111 and the Italian Savoia-Marchetti SM 79. To intercept these, fighter pilots needed very early warning or a large degree of luck. Some indication of the difficulty of interception is given by the Italian loss ratios. Only 8 per cent of the SM 79s delivered to aid the Spanish were lost as opposed to nearly 25 per cent of the CR 32s.

The Polikarpov I 16 was at that time the most modern fighter in service in the world. A low-wing monoplane, it could attain 280 mph in level flight and climb to 16,400 ft in a little over six minutes. Against the German and Italian biplanes it was a formidable opponent, but as a fighting machine it had some serious faults. It was a stubby aeroplane barely 20 ft long and with a wing span of less than 30 ft. The inertia moments about all three axes ie, pitch, yaw and roll, were small which led to severe instability at low speeds and high altitudes. Only the most experienced and confident pilots could use the I 16 to its full capability.

On the nationalist side, the He 51 was outclassed by both types of Russian fighter, although the CR 32 was sufficiently agile to hold its own in a dogfight. Armed with two 12.7 mm Breda SAFAT machine-guns, it had more punch

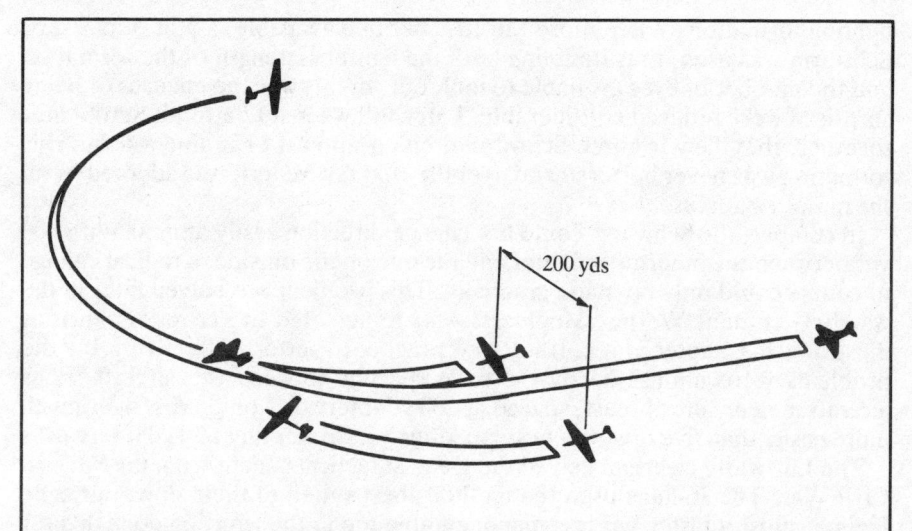

Fig 15 The sandwich manoeuvre.

The Rata attacks an Me109 which breaks outwards. If the Rata follows, the second Me109 drops in on its tail.

than its opponents. This gave it a theoretical edge in a head-on attack and the greater range and weight of fire of the heavy machine-guns, enabled it to open effective fire earlier than the 7.7 mm armed Russians. However, this advantage seems marginal at a closing speed exceeding 150 yds a second.

In the spring of 1937 one of the all-time great fighter aircraft arrived ready for use in Spain. The Messerschmitt Me 109 was first assigned to the 2nd Staffel (flight) of Jagdgruppe 88, commanded by Oberleutnant Gunther Lutzow. The circumstances surrounding the arrival of the Me 109 were destined to totally alter fighter tactics although the initial delivery was a mere six aircraft. Further supplies were slow in coming and the servicing problems associated with a new type making its operational debut, ensured that the number of aircraft available was always low. Lutzow and his successor, Oberleutnant Joachim Schlichting were thus faced with the problem of how best to use the new fighter in such small numbers. Prior to this, the smallest fighting element had consisted of three aircraft, flying in Vic or echelon. The number of Me 109s available rarely permitted this and the practice arose of flying in pairs. Through experiment it gradually became apparent that the best way to use a pair was to fly them in-line abreast about 200 yds apart. The advantages of this were three-fold. By concentrating their search inwards, each pilot could watch the blind spots of the other pilots behind and below him. If one aircraft was attacked from behind, the pilot could break away outwards. His companion could also break in the same direction and if the attacker followed through, he would find the second Messerschmitt on his tail. If the lead Me 109 launched an attack, the number two was well placed to drop in behind and cover him, enabling the leader to concentrate all his attention on his attack in the knowledge that he would be warned of any approaching danger.

It can be seen that the loose pair, or Rotte was far superior to any previous fighting formation. When more Me 109s became available, a pair of pairs, or Schwarm was used, thus doubling both the fighting strength of the formation and the number of eyes available to look-out. In this way the chances of being surprised were reduced considerably. Later still when a 12 aircraft Staffel flew together, they flew in three Schwärme, either abreast or in line astern. This formation was never bettered and over the next few years it was adopted by all the major air forces.

In combat, the Schwarm could not change direction easily at first. With 600 yds between the innermost fighter and the one on the outside, a radical change of course could only be made gradually. This problem was solved later in the war by Leutnant Werner Moelders, who re-invented the crossover turn as illustrated in Chapter Three. It still took practice to perform effectively, but the problems were minimised by the wide spacing between the aircraft. Four aircraft in near-line abreast, spaced at 200 yd intervals, could cross over much more easily than five or seven in stepped-up Vic formation at 30 yd intervals.

The Luftwaffe clearly received the greatest tactical benefit from the Spanish Civil War. The Italians used the methods best suited to their slow, but agile Fiats, against a faster but less manoeuvrable foe in the whirling dogfights for which they were well suited. They were satisfied with the results obtained. The Russians, had to a degree, been forced to adopt dive and zoom attacks owing to the turning ability of the Fiats. They also observed the Germans in action and adopted a four aircraft formation of their own. But as their aeroplanes were not equipped with radio, the spacing between aircraft was rather closer. In 1938 it was recommended that the entire Russian fighter force adopt the four aircraft *zveno* composed of two pairs (*pary*). But many of those who had fought in Spain vanished in Stalin's purges and the recommendation was never carried out.

Meanwhile, many thousands of miles to the east, China and Japan were indulging in an unseemly brawl. A brief clash in 1932 was followed by five years of uneasy peace, which in mid-1937, exploded into war. The Japanese, with their excellent aeroplanes and vastly superior training, quickly gained the upper hand. A Russian volunteer force was assembled to aid the Chinese, but it made little difference. The heaviest air fighting took place in April 1938 and while there can be little doubt that the Japanese got the better of these exchanges, the victories claimed seem exorbitant. For example on April 10, a dozen Type 95 fighters led by Major Teranishi, took on about 30 Polikarpov I 15s, later claiming that 24 were destroyed during a half hour battle. Three weeks later, 30 Japanese fighters took on 80 Chinese over Hankow, claiming 51 victories, for two admitted losses. Overclaiming has always been a feature of air combat, but even allowing for the all-round superiority of the Japanese aircraft and pilots, these claims should be treated with some caution.

The following year, Japan clashed with Russia and the air fighting was more intense than at any time previously. In four months the Japanese claimed 1260 victories, the Russians 660. It is interesting to compare these figures with the admitted losses on both sides which were: Japan, 168; Russia, 207. Even more interesting is that the same Japanese source gave a detailed list of losses which add up to 223!

During the course of the fighting, the Russians had introduced the I 16 type 17. This had 9 mm armour protection for the pilot and the lightly armed Japanese fighters found it difficult to shoot down. The Russians used dive and

The great leap forward

zoom tactics against their agile opponents with great success. The I 16 was armed with two 20 mm ShVAK cannons and a couple of hits from these could seriously damage the lightweight Type 96 and 97 fighters.

The effect on many Japanese pilots was salutary. The design philosophy embodied in their fighters had always been manoeuvreability before all else. To achieve this, weight had been kept to a minimum. Armour, self-sealing tanks and even radios had been left off. Anything that detracted from the ability to turn as tightly as possible was omitted. But now, many pilots wanted their machines to be faster even at the expense of agility. They wanted self-sealing fuel tanks. They wanted greater hitting power with 12.7 or 20 mm guns. Some even wanted hit-and-run tactics adopted as standard, as Major Douglas had advocated 20 years earlier.

To the Japanese High Command, this was little short of heresy. To them a fighter was an aeroplane that fought. By this they meant an aeroplane that outmanoeuvred its opponent and shot it down. Manoeuvreability made the aircraft less vulnerable to enemy bullets and thus less likely to be shot down. However, with pilots who had achieved an apparent kill ratio often exceeding

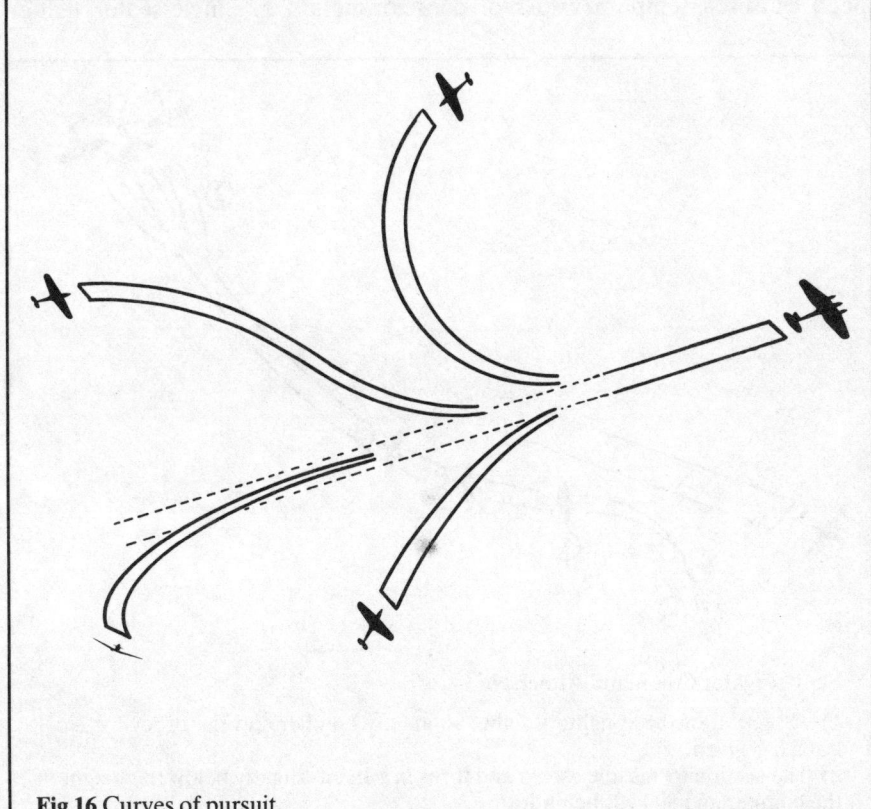

Fig 16 Curves of pursuit.

Typical curves of pursuit, illustrating both the effect of gravity on the path flown and the tendency to take up the astern position too early.

10 to 1, it is understandable that the Japanese commanders preferred their men to stick to tried and tested methods.

We have seen what kind of benefits were derived by the participants in Spain and China. Only three of the world's major air forces had not taken part. The United States stood aloof and isolationist. But for Britain and France, the stormclouds of war were gathering. France felt securely sheltered behind the supposedly impregnable Maginot Line while tactically, the Armee de l'Air was ready to take up where it had left off in 1918. The basic fighting element was the three aircraft *patrouille* and dogfighting was still considered possible.

As we saw in the previous chapter, the Royal Air Force was preparing to meet an altogether different threat. The British bombers were to raid Germany in tight formation, driving off the defending fighters with the concentrated fire of their power-operated multi-gun turrets. It was only to be expected that German bombers would attempt to do the same, and that this would constitute the main threat. The prospect of dogfighting was not taken very seriously, as the 1938 Training Manual, Chapter VIII, *Air Fighting Tactics* illustrates: 'Manoeuvre at high speeds in air fighting is not now practicable, because the effect of gravity on the human body during rapid changes of direction at high speed causes a temporary loss of consciousness. . . . Single-seater fighter

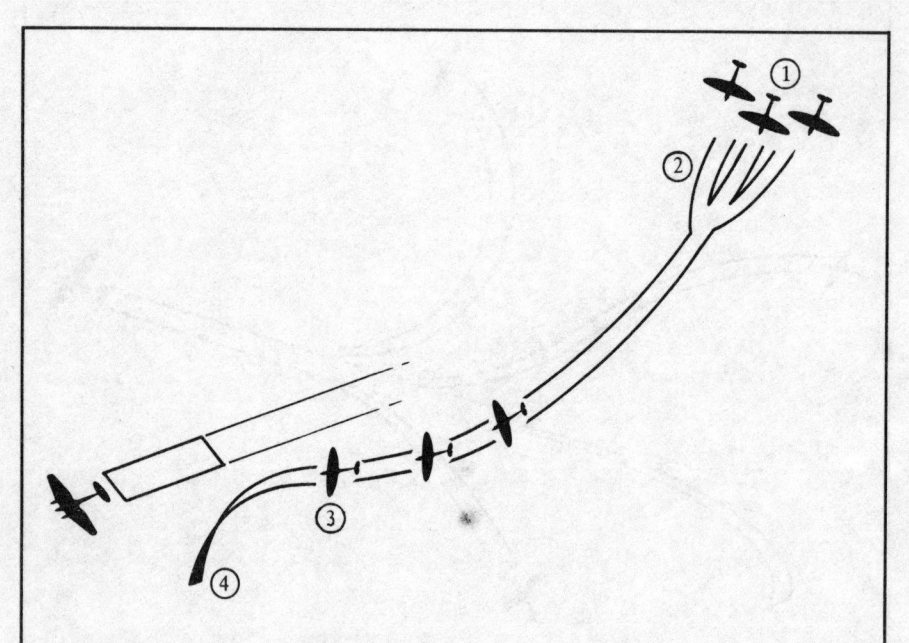

Fig 17 Fighter Command Attack No 1

1) A section of three fighters sights an enemy bomber and the order for No 1 Attack is given.
2) The section forms line astern and turns in pursuit, slightly below the height of the bomber and 800 yds behind.
3) The leading fighter closes to 400 yds and opens fire.
4) The leader breaks away, outwards and down. The other two fighters in the section close and fire in turn before following.

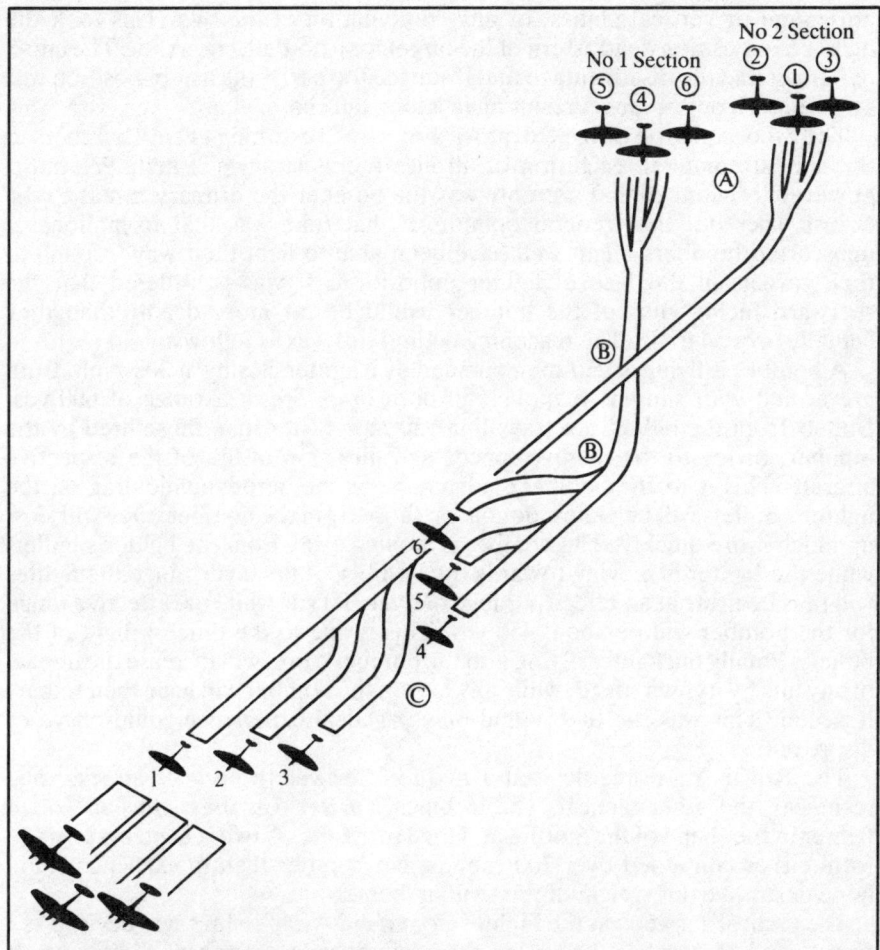

Fig 18 Fighter Command Attack No 2.
1) Two sections of fighters sight an enemy bomber formation and the order to attack is given.
2) Both sections form line astern behind the bombers and slightly lower. No 1 section takes the right-hand flank bomber while No 2 section lines up on the left-hand flank bomber, but remains 200 yds back from the leading section.
3) The order to commence the attack is given and each section forms echelon inwards, one behind the other. After the attack, No 1 section breaks to starboard and down; No 2 section breaks down to port.
No 3 Attack is identical but against a larger number of bombers. Each section forms echelon inwards to fire at as many bombers as possible.

attacks at high speeds must be confined to a variety of attacks from the general direction of astern.'

The astern attacks used the 'curve of pursuit'. The fixed gun fighter, unless it started its attack from directly behind and level with its quarry, tended to hold the target in its sights during the approach, thus describing a curving path in the horizontal or vertical planes, or any combination of the two. This took the fighter to a position dead astern of the target for a no-deflection shot. The curve of pursuit had the disadvantage that if started too early, the astern position was attained well out of range, resulting in a long tail chase.

The preoccupation of the Royal Air Force with downing enemy bombers to the almost complete exclusion of all else seems strange at first. We must, however, remember that not only was the bomber the primary threat to the British Isles but that general opinion at that time was that formations of unescorted bombers might well have been able to fight their way through to their targets in the face of fighter opposition. It was considered that the rearward facing guns of the bomber would be far more deadly than they actually proved to be. The reasoning behind this was as follows:

A bomber is flying at 250 mph pursued by a fighter closing at 300 mph. Both are armed with similar weapons and both open fire at a range of 600 yds. Bullets from the fighter are travelling 550 mph faster than those fired by the bomber, owing to the relative speeds and direction of fire of the respective aircraft. This is to the bomber's advantage as the aerodynamic drag on the fighter's bullets will be almost double on those from the bomber; they will slow up much more quickly. The bomber is moving away from the fighter's bullets while the fighter is moving towards the bomber. At 600 yds range the fighter will thus be firing at an effective range of over 700 yds while the effective range for the bomber will be about 450 yds. This is due to the time of flight of the bullets. Finally the fighter, flying into the bomber's fire, will increase the impact of any hits by its own speed, while any hits on the bomber will have their impact lessened. This was the theory and only practical experience could prove or disprove it.

The Royal Air Force devised a two-fold answer to bomber attacks, one technical, the other tactical. The technical answer was the eight gun armed fighter in the shape of the Spitfire and the Hurricane. A two second burst of fire from either contained over 300 rounds. No bomber then in existence could hope to survive this weight of fire striking home.

The tactical answer was the Fighter Command Attack which was devised as a formal and efficient way of using the basic fighting section of three aircraft against bomber formations. Fighter Command used the three machine section as its smallest unit, two sections made up a flight and three flights a squadron consisting of 18 aircraft, although squadrons rarely flew with more than two flights at a time.

No 1 Attack was for use against a single bomber. On sighting the enemy, the leader would order 'stand by for No 1 Attack'. His section would slide neatly into line astern behind him and the leader would position himself 800 yds behind the bomber and slightly lower. Then came the order 'No 1 Attack, No 1 Attack – Go'! The leader would then close the bomber in a gentle climb and open fire at 400 yds range. On completing his attack, he would break out and down at which point the second aircraft in the section would move into firing position, followed in due course by the third.

No 2 Attack was for use by two sections of fighters against three bombers. The order to stand by for No 2 Attack was given and the leading section of fighters formed line astern. The second section then dropped back, still in Vic formation, with the leader flying directly astern of the third aircraft of the leading section. The leader of the first section would select a bomber on the

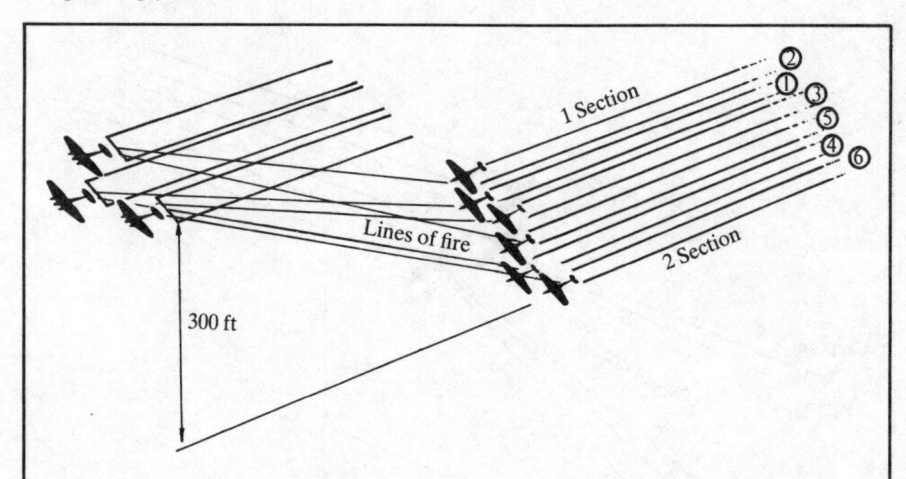

Fig 19 Fighter Command Attack A.

Two sections of Defiants fly in flat Vics abreast, taking station about 300 ft below the bombers. The range is determined by the 'no-allowance' angle for the speed of the aeroplanes and the muzzle velocity of the guns. The Defiant could not traverse its turret to fire directly ahead and so the two section leaders lined up directly behind the outside bombers in the formation. This was responsible for the intricate system of crossfire shown.

flank of the enemy formation as his target and take up a position 800 yds astern and slightly lower as in Attack No 1. When the leader of the second section identified the first section leaders target, he moved into position 1,000 yds astern and slightly below the bomber on the opposite flank with his section sliding into line astern automatically. When everyone was nicely in position, the order 'No 2 Attack – Go!' was given. The leading section then formed an echelon inwards and closed to 400 yds before firing. The second section also moved inwards in echelon formation and followed up the attack in their turn. After attacking, the section leaders broke away outwards and down, their sections following in line astern.

No 3 Attack was similar to No 2 Attack, but against larger numbers of bombers. The principle of the section leaders attacking the flank bombers was retained, as was the inward echelon. All three attacks had one advantage; they reduced the collision risk to a minimum for the fighters. However, one feels that a further order is missing from the manual. 'On the count of three, the enemy will be shot down!'

The quality most lacking in the fighters of the late 1930s was endurance. If bombers were to be opposed by fighters they would need escort fighters to protect them. If contemporary single engined fighters lacked the range to do the job, then perhaps a twin engined fighter might manage.

This idea seemed to germinate simultaneously in several countries. The German Messerschmitt Me 110 first flew in 1936, its close contemporaries were the French Potez 631, the Dutch Fokker G 1 and the American Lockheed P-38. Russia started the Samolet 100 although this ended up as the Pe 2 bomber. While not as manoeuvrable as their single engined counterparts, they lacked

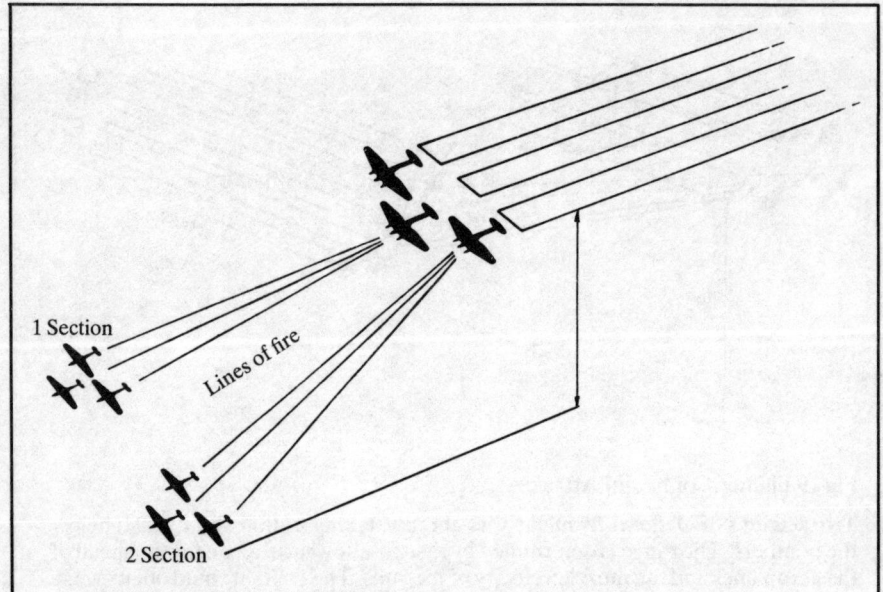

Fig 20 Fighter Command Attack B.

The Defiants fly in two Vics 300 ft below the bombers, but ahead of them. The angle is determined by the blind area of the return fire. In contrast to Attack A, the Vic concentrated its fire on one bomber.

little or nothing in speed and the vulnerable tail area was guarded, with the exception of the P-38, by a gunner. They carried heavy armament and could operate over relatively long distances. The only major air powers not to subscribe to the fashion for heavy fighters were the Japanese and Italians, both firmly committed to manoeuvrability, and the British, whose heavily armed bombers could look after themselves. True, the British produced a compromise by converting the Blenheim bomber into a fighter, but it was a half-hearted attempt and doomed to failure.

Obsessed by the need to destroy unescorted bombers, the Royal Air Force did manage to produce one two-seater fighter. The Boulton Paul Defiant was designed to destroy bombers by flying in formation with them in such a position that the defending gunners were unable to bring their weapons to bear. The Defiants could then pick off the bombers at their leisure with their four machine guns mounted in a power operated turret set behind the pilot. No forward firing guns were fitted, which removed temptation from the pilot who might otherwise have tried to start his own private war.

Two fighter attacks were written for the Defiant, both dealing with two sections of fighters against three bombers. In Attack 'A', the Defiants took station in close Vics 300 ft beneath the bombers. They then pulled forward, holding their fire until the 'no-allowance angle' for the weapon and the airspeed was reached. The no-allowance angle was the point where the forces exerted by the slipstream balanced the trajectory of the bullet as described in Chapter One. Each Defiant aimed at a particular bomber in the formation so that each bomber was under fire from two fighters.

Attack 'B' was more interesting. On sighting the enemy both sections dived and positioned themselves 300 ft below, ahead and to port and starboard of the bombers respectively. The leading section took the lead bomber as their target while the second section concentrated on a flank machine.

The greatest problem of using fighters in a defensive role was to get sufficient numbers to the right place at the right time. During the Great War most air activity had taken place over the battlefield. Consequently it had been a relatively simple matter to find the enemy. The air defence of the British Isles posed quite a different problem. Raiders approaching across the sea gave little warning before crossing the coast. It took 20 to 25 minutes for a fighter squadron to take off and reach the bombers at 18,000 ft. Laden bombers cruised in formation at about 180 mph and could have been up to 75 miles inland before the fighters reached an attacking position. Many valuable targets were much nearer the coast than this and the problem of defending them seemed insoluble. Then came a great leap forward in the ability of fighters to fulfill their defensive role. Radio-location, or radar as it has since become known, enabled the defenders to look far out to sea. For the first time fighter squadrons could be alerted in time to meet raiders as they arrived, thus increasing the capability of the defence many times over.

Early radar was far from perfect, an accurate assessment of height or numbers was impossible, but it could and did tell the defenders that unwelcome visitors were on the way, their approximate height to within a couple of thousand feet either way and whether they were few or many. Radar could also detect the raiders' direction of flight, and with practice, their approximate speed. But most important of all it provided up to half an hour's warning of their arrival.

Chapter 5

The storm breaks

The Second World War began on September 1 1939 when Germany invaded Poland. The Luftwaffe delivered a series of heavy strikes on Polish airfields which only succeeded in destroying non-operational aircraft. The Polish Air Force had redeployed their combat units to secret locations a few days earlier thus avoiding destruction on the ground. Outnumbered and outclassed they fought hard, but to little avail. On the ground the battle went against them; the early-warning posts were quickly over-run, as were the supply routes and finally the airfields themselves. Britain and France declared war on Germany but failed to exert sufficient pressure to halt the invasion. Russia invaded from the east and Poland was swiftly subjugated. Europe then settled into an uneasy quiescence which became known as the Sitzkrieg or Phoney War.

The Phoney War was a strange period during which the opposing armies did little more than lob the occasional shell at each other. In the air a few reconnaissance machines snooped around and the occasional bombing raid was launched against naval targets. No land targets were attacked for fear of retaliation. Sometimes these raids were intercepted by fighters but in the main these encounters were no more than skirmishes. Only along the Franco-German border did fighters meet one another and some vicious dogfights erupted, one of the largest occurring on November 6.

Nine Hawk 75s of Groupe de Chasse II/5 were escorting a reconnaissance Potez 631 on the frontier when they were bounced from above by about three times their number of Me 109s. The French pilots were not taken by surprise and turned on their assailants, shooting down four over French territory and claiming another four probables. These were all subsequently confirmed from German records as having crashed or force landed in Germany. The sole French loss was one Hawk which crash landed in France; the pilot was unhurt.

This fight is interesting on several counts. The Germans had the initiative and launched the attack. As we saw in the previous chapter, German fighting formations were the most advanced in the world at the time. The German Me 109 was to become one of the all-time great fighters, while the American built Curtis Hawk was doomed to oblivion. Nor were the German pilots inexperienced; their leader, Hauptmann Hannes Gintzen was the top-scoring fighter pilot in the Polish campaign. The question arises, why did Jagdgruppe 102 take such a beating?

Part of the answer lay in the qualities of the opposing aircraft. The German fighter was an early model, the Me 109 D, only a few of which were built.

Slightly faster than the Hawk 75 in level flight, it was not as manoeuvrable, particularly in the rolling plane. The Hawk 75 could bank into a turn much faster and hold a tighter turn. The French fighter was fitted with a constant speed propellor which enabled its engine to run much more efficiently than the Messerschmitt. This conferred distinct advantages in both acceleration and climb. Finally the German fighter was outgunned because the Hawk 75 had twice the firepower. The Me 109 carried a 20 mm cannon but technical problems prevented its operational use and its armament was thus reduced to two small calibre machine-guns. Against modern fighters these were ineffective. All in all, the French aeroplane was the superior machine in a dogfight. Their surprise attack having been thwarted, the German pilots stayed to fight and paid the penalty. Had they been flying the much more potent Me 109 E, and used dive and zoom tactics, the tables would almost certainly have been turned.

Meanwhile, the Royal Air Force had been rethinking. A memorandum issued by Fighter Command in November accurately predicted a future event: 'The possibility cannot be excluded however, that the enemy might over-run the Low Countries at a very early stage of the war, and by using aerodromes or refuelling grounds in Holland and Belgium, might be able to send over fighter escorts with his bomb raids (on England)'.

To counter this previously unthinkable possibility, the memorandum had little to offer in the way of constructive suggestions. The onus of solving the problem was passed down to the pilots themselves with the words: 'I want all concerned to be thinking ahead . . . and (at the discretion of Commanding Officers) to carry out simple tactical experiments, so as to be prepared for various eventualities'.

The extent to which Douhet's theories had permeated Royal Air Force thinking was also exposed: 'A possibility of the future is that the escort fighter will be a modification of the bomber type, in which the whole bomb load has been discarded in favour of guns, ammunition and armour. It would not be necessary that it should have a performance better than the bombers which it is escorting, since it would not have to manoeuvre except in conjunction with its own bombers. We must be prepared for its appearance sooner or later.

Within a few weeks, the theoreticians had taken a couple of bad knocks. The Vickers-Armstrong Wellington was the most formidably armed bomber of its day. With twin .303 calibre Browning machine guns mounted in hydraulically operated turrets in the nose, tail and in a retractable ventral 'dustbin' amidships, it had been thought that the concentrated fire of a formation of Wellingtons would be sufficient to drive off enemy fighters. On December 14 a dozen Wellingtons attacking German shipping in the Jade estuary were intercepted by the Me 109s of the II Gruppe of Jagdgeschwader 77, and lost five of their number. Four days later, 22 Wellingtons approached Wilhelmshaven in perfect weather. They were intercepted by large numbers of Me 109s and 110s and suffered heavily. The German pilots were not so committed to the stern attack as were their British counterparts and attacked from all angles. This proved effective as the combat report of Hauptmann Reinecke of Zerstörergeschwader 76 showed: 'The Me 110 is easily capable of catching this English type. This provides scope for multiple attacks from any quarter, including frontal beam. This attack can be very effective if the enemy aircraft is allowed to fly into the cone of fire. The Wellington is very inflammable and burns readily.'

This encounter was a disaster for the British; twelve bombers were shot down and a further two crash-landed on reaching England. The German losses were two Me 109s shot down and several 109s and 110s damaged. The superiority of the fighter over the heavily armed bomber was now firmly established. To survive in daylight the bomber needed fighter protection, unescorted it could only operate under cover of darkness.

The Western Front quietened down during the winter, partly due to the appalling weather and little of note occurred until the middle of spring. Then in quick succession, Norway and Denmark were occupied by German forces and the German army launched an all-out assault through neutral Belgium and Holland. The task of the Luftwaffe was two-fold; support of the army and neutralising the opposing air forces. The Dutch and Belgian Air Forces were swept aside in the first few days and the Allied air defence was left to the Armée de l'Air assisted by a handful of Royal Air Force Hurricane squadrons.

Lacking an effective early warning system, the defenders fought at a disadvantage as their airfields were bombed and strafed. The German army swept into France and many French fighter units were diverted to strafe the invading armoured columns in a vain attempt to delay them. This meant that there were fewer fighters available to oppose the Luftwaffe, thus assisting the Germans to attain air superiority. As the German juggernaut rolled inexorably on, the French Air Force, lacking leadership at the higher command levels, became demoralised.

In the heavy fighting that took place during this period, the Royal Air Force squadrons learned much. Unescorted German bomber were often encountered and it was found that the Fighter Command attacks worked well enough. But with German fighters in attendance they were suicidal. The German fighter pilots also had lessons to learn, despite their experiences in Spain and Poland, as the following account of an action fought on the morning of May 13 shows: Sergeant James Lacey was patrolling the Sedan area at 20,000 ft when he spotted two German aircraft below, a Heinkel He 111 bomber at 10,000 ft apparently escorted by a Me 109 about 5,000 ft higher. He hestitated for a moment, the natural reaction of a law-abiding citizen about to commit his first act of vandalism. The book said attack from astern at full speed. Opening his throttle, he pushed the nose of his Hurricane down and hurtled towards the unsuspecting German fighter. With the speed gained in his mile-high dive, he closed the distance so rapidly that he was unable to bring his sights to bear and went straight past the Messerschmitt.

The German pilot, intent on guarding the Heinkel, failed to see the Hurricane and Lacey turned and clambered back into position for another attempt, easing himself gently into position behind the 109. His opponent was a small aeroplane; from end on at 250 yds it looked an impossible target. Lacey edged closer. From 100 yds he still felt unsure of his ability to hit it and so he crept still closer. At 50 yds it appeared a satisfyingly large target and he opened fire. His bullets struck home and the German fighter went down, mortally stricken. Full of new-found confidence, Lacey went down after the Heinkel which he also shot down.

This combat demonstrated that many of the lessons of the First War were still relevant. It was essential to keep a sharp look-out and seek the best position

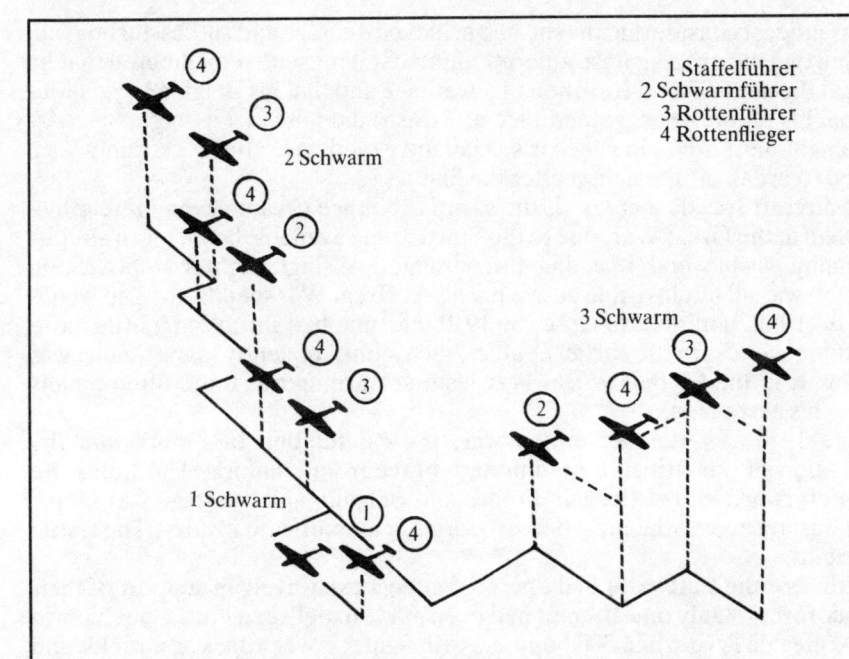

Fig 21 A typical Staffel formation, plan view.

1 Staffelführer
2 Schwarmführer
3 Rottenführer
4 Rottenflieger

The usual Staffel-formation as seen in the picture was an ideal marching formation, giving more space to each aircraft with greater relaxation for the pilot, higher flexibility in case of changing direction (cross-over turn) and finally much better observation possibilities for everyone. Instead of always keeping his attention to a tight formation, each pilot in this loose unit could look around for attacking enemy fighters. By changing space and staggering, this formation could easily be changed, especially in case of bomber support or close support to Stuka-units.

rather than go charging in. Sergeant Lacey's initial plunge could easily have been disastrous, taking him below a faster opponent. The idea was to get in close to deliver a fatal burst with the first few rounds.

Much more professional was the first victory of Adolf Galland who later became one of Germany's greatest aces. Flying in company with Leutnant Roedel, he encountered eight Hurricanes west of Liege. The German fighters were about 3,000 ft higher and attacked immediately. Galland's combat report reads: 'The enemy was attacked from a superior position above and astern. The first burst with machine-guns and cannon hit the enemy aircraft. When I broke away Leutnant Roedel fired and scored hits. The enemy machine spiralled down and I followed, firing from a distance of between 50 and 70 m. Parts of the aircraft were observed to break off and it spun down into the clouds. Ammunition used: 90 cannon shells; about 150 machine-gun bullets. The Hurricanes appeared poorly trained and failed to support each other.'

Galland immediately went in pursuit of another Hurricane and shot it down as well. He was later to comment on this action that the best fighter pilot needed both an excellent weapon and luck and that he had had both. If this remark seems modest considering that he had achieved a classic and successful bounce, scoring two victories against superior numbers, it must be remembered that he started the action from a position of advantage and that his Belgian adversaries (whom his report wrongly identified at British) did not react as aggressively as they might have done, in which case Galland would have almost certainly been forced to break off the action after the first pass.

As aircraft speeds increased, the surprise bounce became even more effective than in the Great War, due to the shorter time available between an aircraft becoming visible and reaching firing range. A single fighter approaching head-on was all but invisible at two miles. At Great War speeds, the gap would take over half a minute to close; by 1940 this time had shrunk to a little more than ten seconds. In the earlier conflict, the victim frequently knew that he was in a fight; in the Second World War his first warning was more often bullets hitting his aeroplane.

June 1940 saw Italy enter the war, the capitulation of France and the evacuation of the British Expeditionary Force from Dunkirk. The Luftwaffe moved forward into airfields in France and Belgium and the stage was set for what was to become the most decisive series of air battles in history. The Battle of Britain.

Hitherto, the Luftwaffe had operated almost exclusively in support of their surface forces. Only one attempt had been made to deliver a knock-out blow to the Armée de l'Air when 300 bombers with fighter cover attacked airfields and aircraft factories in the Paris area. Operation Paula, as this attack was known, was not a great success. Now the Luftwaffe was faced with an altogether different task; the subjugation of the Royal Air Force. This was necessary in order to carry out an invasion of England, the success of which would be entirely dependent on the ability of the German airmen to shield the invasion fleet from the British Navy. To do this, air opposition had to be eliminated.

Fighter Command of the Royal Air Force was in a strong position. Until this time the advantage in air war had always lain with the attacker, it being largely a matter of luck whether the defender could arrive in the right place at the right time in sufficient numbers. But now with the invisible eye of radar scanning the skies, the advantage of the initiative was greatly reduced. The fighter defences of Great Britain were divided into four areas called Groups, each with its own command system. No 10 Group covered the West Country and South Wales, No 11 Group the Home Counties, No 12 Group the Midlands, North Wales, part of East Anglia and part of Northern England, while No 13 Group covered the remainder and Scotland. Each Group was sub-divided into Sectors. No 11 Group which was to bear the brunt of the forthcoming battle, contained no less than seven Sectors. Each Sector contained a Sector airfield after which the Sector was named, plus subsidiary airfields and operated a maximum number of four squadrons of day fighters. The maximum of four squadrons per Sector was determined by a device code-named 'Pip-squeak', which was operated by one aircraft in each squadron. 'Pip-squeak' transmitted a signal for 14 seconds in every minute, on which ground stations took bearings. This enabled the Sector Controller to keep track of his squadrons in the air but limited tracking to four squadrons at a time unless they flew in pairs.

The radar stations were situated on the coast and could only operate in a seaward direction. Behind them was a network of observation posts equipped with visual and aural detection aids. Reports from both were transmitted to

The storm breaks 57

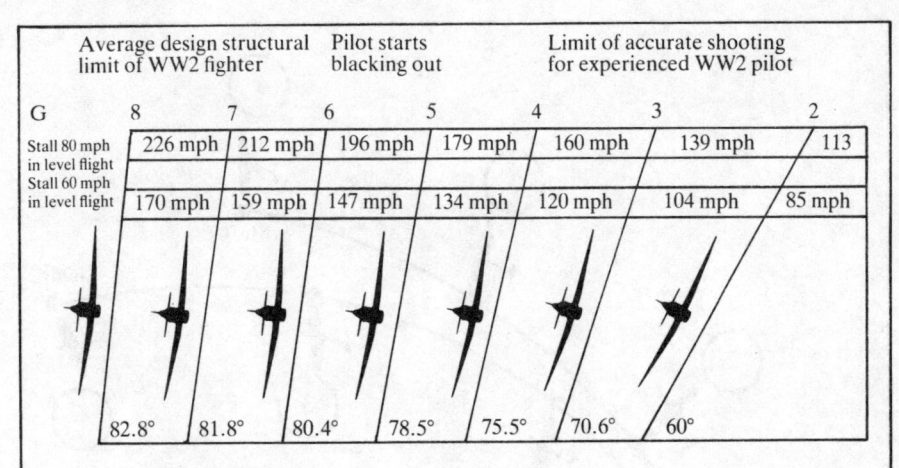

	Average design structural limit of WW2 fighter			Pilot starts blacking out		Limit of accurate shooting for experienced WW2 pilot		
G	8	7	6	5	4	3		2
Stall 80 mph in level flight	226 mph	212 mph	196 mph	179 mph	160 mph	139 mph		113
Stall 60 mph in level flight	170 mph	159 mph	147 mph	134 mph	120 mph	104 mph		85 mph
	82.8°	81.8°	80.4°	78.5°	75.5°	70.6°	60°	

Fig 22 Turning ability.

The centrifugal force caused by a tight turn is usually measured in multiples of the force of gravity, or 'G'. The number of 'G's in a turn is directly related to the angle of bank. This is calculated as:

$$n = \frac{1}{\cosine \emptyset}$$

where n is the multiple of G and Ø is the angle of bank.

An aeroplane in a 2G turn needs double its normal minimum lift to keep flying. The stalling speed increases by the square root of the 'G' in the turn. Its initial speed thus determines how hard an aeroplane can turn.

It can be seen that the fighter with the lowest stalling speed (usually the lowest wing loading) has an advantage in turning in the lower speed ranges. For aerodynamic reasons, drag increases in a tight turn. A fighter with sufficient acceleration to overcome the increased drag can sustain its turn. Lacking sufficient acceleration, the fighter will (a) lose speed, (b) lose height to maintain speed, (c) slacken its turn.

Fighter Command Headquarters at Bentley Priory where they were cross-checked, and the 'filtered' information was transmitted simultaneously to both the Group and the Sector Stations concerned. The Group Controller then allocated squadrons to intercept raids and the squadrons were scrambled by their Sector Controller and directed to meet the threat.

There was unfortunately, a time lag of about six minutes between the first radar observation and the plot appearing on the map. In terms of distance this was about 18 miles and the Controller had to make appropriate allowance. The maximum distance at which a large formation could be seen was rarely more than six to eight miles. On a cloudy day formations could easily pass each other unseen. The task of a Sector Controller was not easy. It may appear from the foregoing description that Sectors were geographically circumscribed defensive areas. However, this was not the case. Interceptions could be made outside Sector boundaries and even outside Group boundaries without difficulty. The Sectors were locations of convenience, arranged to facilitate control of the squadrons in the air.

This was the organisation which the Luftwaffe had to crack. Lacking a comparable system, they could only guess at its effectiveness. In the event they

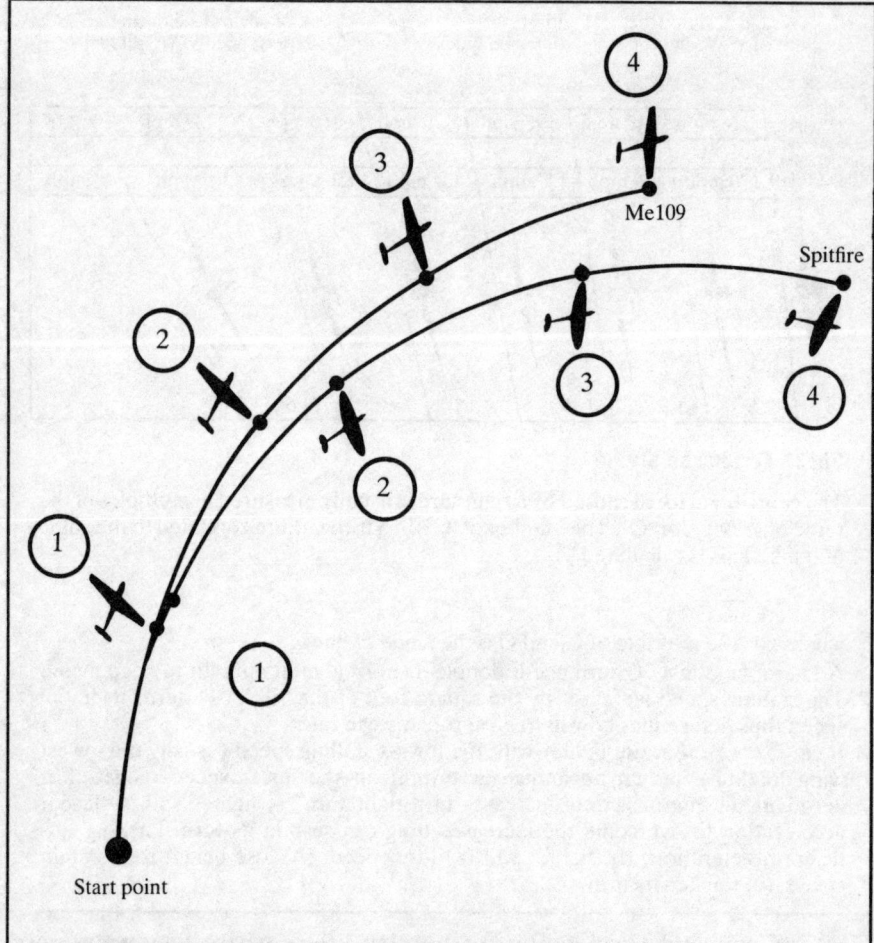

Fig 23 Turning radii, Spitfire I versus Me 109E.

Some idea of the comparative turning abilities of the Spitfire I and the Me 109E is illustrated. It should, however, be remembered that the advantage always lay with the aircraft which had the initiative.

misjudged badly. The British system had two main weaknesses. The 300 ft high towers of the radar stations could not be concealed and the essential early-warning equipment was vulnerable. The operations rooms from which the squadrons were controlled were also all above ground and sited on the Sector airfield. To lose either the early-warning system or the ground control would have been bad; to lose both would have been disastrous. Yet no serious attempt to destroy either was made. Flushed with success after victories on the Continent, the Luftwaffe was confident in its ability to destroy Fighter Command either in the air or on the ground and made little attempt to be subtle in its methods.

Tactically the German fighter pilots were superior. Their experience in Spain had, as we have seen, enabled them to develop flexible fighting formations

The storm breaks

based on the pair with the wingman guarding the leader's tail. This had been reinforced by their peace-time training which included practice dogfights of up to Staffel strength per side as part of the syllabus. A Staffel consisted of 12 aircraft and three Staffeln made up a Gruppe with each Gruppe also having a Stabskompanie or staff flight of four aircraft. Three Gruppen made up a Geschwader, the largest single fighter unit which also had its own Stabskompanie of four machines. The Geschwader rarely operated as a unit; the Gruppe of up to 40 fighters was much more frequently used. The typical Gruppe formation consisted of the three Staffeln in line astern stepped up and back like the steps in a staircase.

By contrast, Royal Air Force fighter squadrons were based on the Vic of three and 12 aircraft to the squadron formation, although larger numbers were sometimes used. Experience in France had demonstrated the dangers of being bounced from astern and to counter this, weavers were introduced on many squadrons. Weavers consisted of one, two, or even a section of three aircraft flying above and behind the rest of the squadron, zig-zagging along as a rearguard. Using weavers created difficulties. During a full throttle climb, the weavers were unable to weave without lagging behind. In level flight the weavers had more ground to cover and used fuel faster. After about half an hour their concentration weakened.

In addition, when the squadron was bounced they were the first to come under fire. Few squadrons had any fighting experience and their peace-time training had, apart from the Fighter Command Attacks, consisted of one-versus-one encounters. These bore little resemblance to the real thing and were really only a test of pilot skill. Each pilot could give his undivided attention to his opponent and thus did not have to retain an awareness of what was going on around him. Furthermore, both men were from the same squadron and flew the same type of machine. No thought was given to tackling an adversary flying an aircraft with different characteristics where different tactics might be necessary. The sole requirement was the ability to outfly the other man.

Much has already been written about the respective merits of the opposing fighters. A brief look at the respective merits of the best of either side will suffice here. The Spitfire I and the Me 109E were well matched for speed below 20,000 ft, the Spitfire having a slight edge at lower altitudes. Above 20,000 ft the German fighter became progressively better. The Me 109s acceleration was better at all heights and both its zoom and sustained climb were superior, although not by much. The Spitfire's rate of roll was better at low speeds, although this advantage progressively diminished at speeds exceeding 350 mph. Its turning ability was markedly better than the Messerschmitt, particularly at low level. As this point is always raised in any discussion of these two fighters, perhaps we should quantify the difference. A maximum rate turn carried out at 12,000 ft at a true air speed of 240 mph with both aircraft shuddering on the brink of a stall gives the following figures: Radius of turn – Spitfire 609 ft, Me 109 783 ft. Rate of turn – Spitfire 33 degrees per second, Me 109 26 degrees per second.

Both aircraft would be forced to lose height to avoid stalling and if the Me 109 tried to stay with the Spitfire in a turning contest, the combat would develop into a downward spiral. In practice this would almost never occur; one or other of the combatants would have an initial speed or positional advantage. It can, however, be seen that the Spitfire had a clear advantage over the Me 109 in the turn and if assailed from behind could quickly swing out of the line of fire, whereas the German fighter had no such option available. Should the Me 109 try to turn away, the Spitfire could cut the corner with ease and gain a firing position. One final point should be stressed. Pilot ability was the most important factor and unless the man in the cockpit could fly his machine to its limit, the excellence of his aeroplane would avail him little against a skilled and determined opponent.

The opening phase of the Battle of Britain began with attacks on coastal targets and convoys. Defence was difficult in the narrow part of the English Channel as the reaction time was reduced to a few minutes. By the time a defending squadron had arrived on the scene, the bombers had often unloaded and gone home. Fighter Command was forced to resort to the wasteful and inefficient practice of flying standing patrols of three or six aircraft. When an attack came, the patrols were often swamped by the fighter escort. The situation was made worse by the Luftwaffe flying fighter sweeps in the vicinity of the raiding force. Fighter Command squadrons hurrying to the relief of the outnumbered convoy patrols were often surprised by these sweeps and suffered heavy casualties. On July 7, No 65 Squadron were bounced near Folkestone by the free-hunting Me 109s of Jagdgeschwader 27 and lost three out of six Spitfires. If these sweeps could be positively identified in time they were left strictly alone but radar could not tell the difference between fighters and bombers. Royal Air Force squadrons sent to intercept found themselves greatly outnumbered and often with a height disadvantage. Orders were issued to intercept only if bombers were present and the German fighter sweeps, failing to bring the enemy to battle, gradually ceased.

The next phase of the battle was aimed directly at Fighter Command. In mid-August heavy attacks were launched at airfields and radar stations. Of

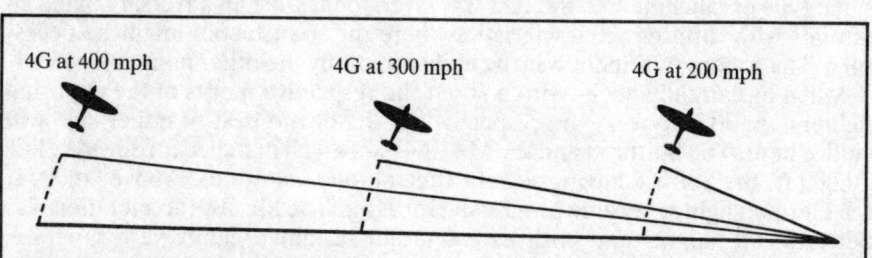

Fig 24 Radius of turn.

The radius of turn is determined by the speed and the angle of bank of the aeroplane. This is calculated:

$$R = \frac{V^2}{G \tan \emptyset}$$

Where R is the radius of turn in feet.
V is the speed in ft per second.
G is gravity (32.3 ft per second, per second).
$\emptyset$ is the angle of bank.

Therefore a 4G turn is not constant but varies with speed. The diagram also shows that the angular rate of turn (measured in degrees per second) varies as well.

these, the raids on the radar stations were the more serious threat and situated as they were on the coast they were vulnerable. Although much damage was caused, little apparent effect was discernible to the Luftwaffe and the attacks were quickly discontinued. Had an all-out series of raids been mounted against them, there seems little doubt that the early warning system could have been badly disrupted, with disastrous results for the defenders.

Attempts to knock out the British fighters on their airfields were less than successful. The Luftwaffe relied for its information on high flying reconnaissance aircraft. During quiet spells, as many as four or five sections of British fighters were scrambled to intercept these snoopers. To avoid interception the camera planes were forced to fly at great heights. When the photographs were enlarged, the film was found to lack definition. The Germans could tell which airfields were in use but not the type of aircraft using them. Consequently many heavy raids were directed at airfields not used by Fighter Command. This represented a considerable waste of effort by the Luftwaffe.

The German fighters had their problems. Starting with a considerable numerical superiority they discovered that the much vaunted Me 110 could not hold its own against Spitfires and Hurricanes. The heavy fighter needed fighter protection. When British fighters appeared, the Me110 units were often forced to form defensive circles for mutual protection and could no longer carry out their primary task of bomber protection. The burden of escorting the bombers fell more and more on the Me 109s. Thus the number of effective fighters available was drastically reduced. The term defensive circle' was dropped from the Luftwaffe repertoire on the direct orders of Reichsmarschall Hermann Goering; in future it was to be called the offensive circle'. However, this change in terminology passed un-noticed on the other side of the Channel.

Bearing in mind that the Spitfire could out-turn the Me 109 with ease, as could the Hurricane at medium heights. It becomes obvious that the Germans were at a disadvantage in a turning flight. This they countered by using dive and zoom tactics. They would plunge out of the sun, fire, then accelerate straight back up. For maximum effect they needed to range ahead and to the sides of the bomber formations, breaking up the British fighter squadrons before they could engage. The German commanders, alarmed at the mounting bomber losses, decreed that they should be heavily escorted but while the Me 109 was a first class attacking aeroplane, it was not so good for defensive work. It was comforting for the German bomber crews to see their escorts weaving about nearby, but it reduced the effectiveness of the fighters considerably. The main deficiency of the Me 109 was its short range. The bombers could go only where the fighters could accompany them and this was not very far; North London for the Jagdgeschwadern based in the Pas de Calais; Southampton and Portland for those in Normandy.

The defenders had a different set of problems to solve. The controller had to be certain that the plot on the board was a genuine raid rather than a feint. When the squadrons were scrambled they rarely had time to gain an altitude advantage. Much of their time was spent gaining height with the enemy already in sight. They were almost invariably outnumbered. And their task was to destroy bombers and if possible avoid combat with fighters.

A memorandum on the subject of fighter tactics written by Squadron Leader 'Sailor' Malan shortly after the Battle makes interesting reading: 'I am of the opinion that climbing for height underneath enemy fighters over Base, Biggin Hill, is both a dangerous and stupid practice, and believe that the only safe and efficient way of gaining height is to climb in a direction which gives the squadron its height well out of harm's way, bearing in mind the direction of the sun and the existing weather conditions.

'Furthermore, it is found that the modern fighter is a difficult machine to climb at its most efficient climbing speed above 15,000 ft, and that a spiral climb takes considerably longer than a straight or zig-zag course. Experience has proved that to gain height efficiently above 20,000 ft in a Spitfire requires a fair amount of concentration on the instrument panel, particularly when climbing on a turn (which in itself is inefficient) thereby not allowing for an adequate look-out for enemy fighters above, and it is therefore considered inadvisable to have more than one leader concentrating on gaining height for the squadron. From the above it can be seen that it is inadvisable to split the squadron into two flights.

'In conclusion, it is my considered opinion that the safest and most successful method of gaining altitude, when operating from bases east of London, is to climb the squadron in three sections "line astern" shaping the course according to the position of the sun and weather, but making sure that height is being gained away from the enemy fighters and climbing on a zig-zag course the whole time.'

A little reading between the lines is called for here. Malan's reference to operating in the three sections is a direct indication of the fighting formation that he had earlier introduced to No 74 Squadron. His squadron were flying in sections of four, each comprising two pairs, the classic leader/wingman. Probably the first leader in Fighter Command to experiment with pairs in the Second World War, had been Flight Lieutenant Robert Stanford Tuck when in temporary command of No 92 Squadron at the time of Dunkirk. But to Malan must go the main credit for forming a viable squadron fighting formation using the pair as the basic unit. It was still inferior to the German Staffel formation, but it was a great improvement on previous British formations. Once they had attained their altitude, all aircraft weaved gently to allow the pilots to watch the blind spot astern, the three sections writhing across the sky like a trio of serpents. As the word spread, more and more British squadrons adopted Malan's formation.

The vulnerability of both the Vic formation and the spiral climb were amply demonstrated on August 18. Twelve Hurricanes of No 501 squadron were gaining height near Canterbury when they were sighted by III Gruppe of Jagdgeschwader 26. Oberleutnant Gerhard Schoepfel, leading the Gruppe now takes up the story: 'They were using the English tactics of that period, flying in close formation of threes, climbing in a wide spiral. About 1,000 m above, I turned with them and managed to get behind the two covering Hurricanes which were weaving continuously. I waited until they were once more heading away from Folkestone and had turned northwest and then pulled round out of the sun and attacked from below.'

The two weavers were dispatched with one quick burst each from close range and Schoepfel slid gently into position behind the rear Vic of Hurricanes. A further short burst and another British fighter fell from the sky. 'The Englishmen continued on, having noticed nothing. So I pulled in behind a fourth machine and took care of him but this time I went in too close. When I pressed

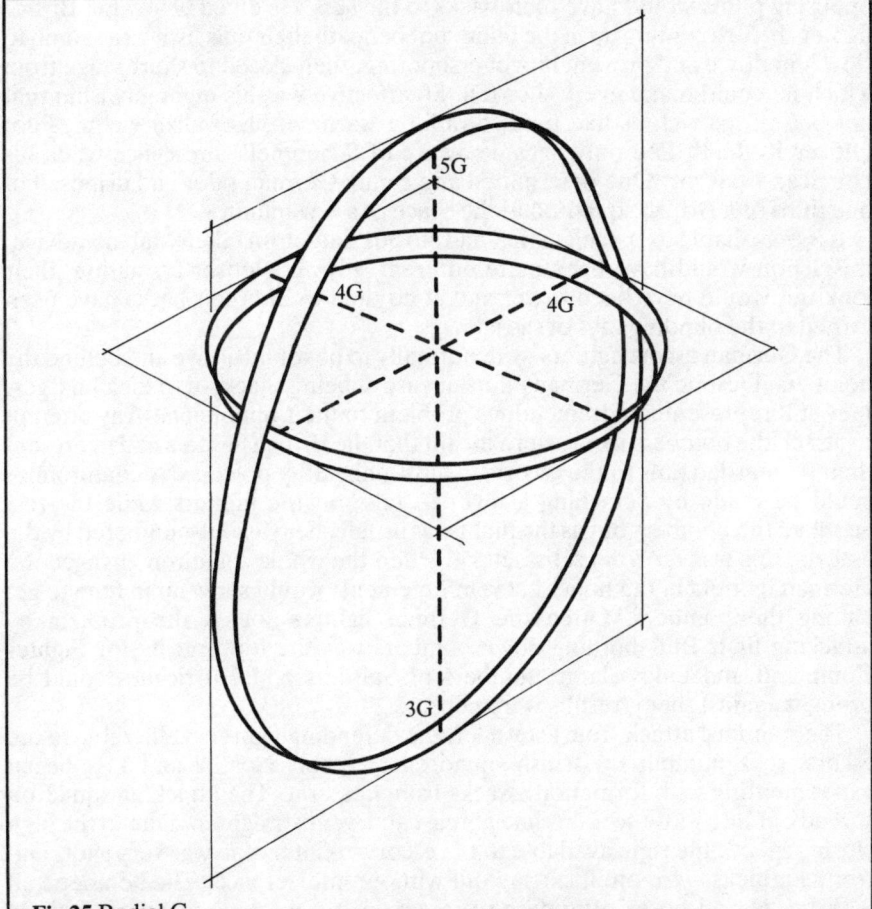

Fig 25 Radial G.

All previous calculations refer to turns in the horizontal plane. An oblique or vertical turn is affected by gravity. Gravity affects turning ability by plus 1G when pulling over the top and minus 1G when pulling out at the bottom. The 4G at 300 mph envelope shown is therefore not spherical but egg-shaped.

the firing button the Englishman was so close in front of my nose that pieces of wreckage struck my propeller.'

With oil from his fourth victim obscuring his vision, Schoepfel broke away and dived for home. At this his Gruppe, which had remained aloft to cover him, came spilling down on the remaining Hurricanes and an inconclusive dogfight took place.

Schoepfel's attack had been classic. Had he led the Gruppe down to attack they would have had no top cover. Had he split the Gruppe and left half behind as top cover the Germans would have been outnumbered in the ensuing dogfight. Either way the large attacking formation would have stood a greater chance of being detected than his solitary Messerschmitt. Instead he went down alone, taking full advantage of the fact that at some point in any spiral climb the opposing pilots would have their backs to the sun. He dived below the British fighters before coming up in the blind spot beneath their tails, using the climb to slow him down and prevent him overshooting, then closed to short range from which he could make every shot tell. So effective was his marksmanship that not one of his victims had time to radio a warning. His fourth victim, Pilot Officer Kenneth Lee only became aware of Schoepfel's prescence when his Hurricane was hit. One determined and canny German pilot had disposed of one third of a British squadron in the space of a few minutes.

It is reasonable to speculate that had No 501 Squadron taken Malan's advice, this action would have been quite different. Flying a looser formation, their look-out would have been better and at no time would their backs have been turned to the blinding rays of the sun.

The German escort fighters were normally to be found above and behind the bombers. Despite the German pilots unease at being shackled to their charges, they still represented a tremendous problem to their opponents. Any attempt to attack the bombers from astern meant that the British fighters had to present their unguarded tails to the escorts, a most unhealthy practice. A compromise could be made by detaching a flight to take on the fighters while the rest attacked the bombers but as the flight was usually heavily out-numbered by the escorts, this was far from satisfactory. Often the whole squadron engaged the German fighters in the hope that reinforcements would show up in time to get among the bombers. Often the German fighters solved the problem by attacking first. But shooting down bombers was the top priority for Fighter Command and unless large numbers of Spitfires and Hurricanes could be brought against them, results were poor.

The standard attack from astern left the defending fighters vulnerable to the escorts so a number of British squadrons, notably Nos 32 and 111, began experimenting with formation attacks from head-on. The attacking squadron spread out into loose sections line abreast and went straight in. Due to the high closing speed, the time available to the escorts to intervene was very short and frontal attacks were often carried out without interference. The bombers, all with big glazed noses offering no protection to the crew, were particularly vulnerable to this form of attack, there being, as Dornier pilot Wilhelm Raab wryly remarked, 'not even a molehill to hide behind'. A determined head-on attack often broke up the bomber formation, after which they could be picked off one by one.

Head-on attacks were by no means reserved for bombers. In fighter versus fighter engagements they were often unavoidable. If attacked from astern, fighters broke hard into their assailants. Given sufficient time they could turn through 180 degrees to face their opponents, or in the confusion of a dogfight, two fighters would turn towards each other. Either way a head-on attack became inevitable. With closing speeds often exceeding three hundred yards a second it then became a contest of marksmanship and nerve. The first pilot to break away both surrendered the initiative and gave his opponent a free shot. The secret was to keep straight on and keep shooting to force the other man to break first. But if he was equally determined, the result could be traumatic, as Flight Lieutenant Alan Deere of No 54 Squadron discovered during a low-level scrap with Me 109s of Jagdgeschwader 51 near Deal: 'About 3,000 yds directly ahead of me and at the same level a Hun was just completing a turn preparatory to re-entering the fray. He saw me almost immediately and rolled out of his turn

Fighter Pilot Tactics 65

Above The rotary engine as fitted to the Sopwith Pup, was very compact and allowed the pilot to be positioned close behind it. Thus all heavy weights were positioned close to the centre of gravity. This conferred outstanding manoeuvrability at the expense of performance, which was limited by the shortcomings of the rotary engine (*Flight International*).

Below The long stationary engine, clearly shown here, gave excellent performance at the expense of manoeuvrability. The SE5A was one of the most successful fighters of the Great War and was used by many of the great air fighters, including McCudden and Mannock (*Flight International*).

Above A Spitfire I of No 66 Squadron at dispersal at Gravesend, Kent, during the Battle of Britain. A legend since the summer of 1940, its achievements overshadowed those of the more numerous Hurricane, seen in the middle distance. The Hurricane is from No 501 Squadron (*Alfred Price*).

Left Pictured here as Marshal of the Royal Air Force, Sholto Douglas was a protagonist of performance rather than manoeuvrability. As a young squadron commander in 1917/18 he made a great contribution to British tactical thinking. During the Second World War, he succeeded Lord Dowding as head of Fighter Command at the end of 1940, where he was largely responsible for initiating the large fighter sweeps which carried the war to the Luftwaffe (*IWM*).

Fighter Pilot Tactics 67

Above The most famous German fighter of the Second World War was the Messerschmitt Me 109. The Me 109Es shown here are from 6 Staffel, Jagdgeschwader 27 and the four aircraft Schwarm can be clearly seen. This photograph was taken by the leader, Oberleutnant Julius Neumann. A day or two later Oberleutnant Neumann's Me 109 was hit in a dogfight and he force-landed on the Isle of Wight (*Alfred Price*).

Right Hauptmann Joachim Marseille was the highest scoring fighter ace in the desert air war. His flying abilities and marksmanship can rarely have been equalled. He was probably the first exponent of the high speed and low speed yoyos (*Alfred Price*).

Above When the FW 190A made its debut over Northern France it gave the Spitfire V a very hard time. Its astonishing rate of roll and its ability to 'brute force' around a tight turn made it a formidable adversary. Later variants were given very heavy armament and armour protection to deal with the massed American bomber formations but the extra weight reduced its ability as a fighter. The example shown here is a bomber destroyer of Jagdgeschwader 3 (*Alfred Price*).

Below General of the Fighter Pilots Adolf Galland addresses a conference. Galland started the war as a fighter pilot, and was still flying fighters during the final days, although a Lieutenant-General. A great pilot and a sound tactician (*Alfred Price*).

towards me so that a head-on attack became inevitable. Using both hands on the control column to steady the aircraft and thus keep my aim steady, I peered through the reflector sight at the rapidly closing enemy aircraft. We opened fire together and immediately a hail of lead thudded into my Spitfire. One moment the Messerschmitt was a clearly defined shape, its wingspan nicely enclosed within the circle of my reflector sight, and the next it was on top of me, a terrifying blur which blotted out the sky ahead. Then we hit.'

Incredibly the collision was a glancing one and Deere coaxed his battered Spitfire back to crash land in a Kent field. The fate of the German pilot is unknown; two Me 109s failed to return from this sortie. It is likely that he was one of them.

Flight Lieutenant Deere's determination to carry the attack through becomes evident from his using both hands on the control column. In combat, pilots normally flew with their right hand on the stick and their left on the throttle. This gave them a slight left-hand bias and they broke more readily to the left as they were able to exert more pressure on the stick by pushing to the left with their right hand than they could by pulling to the right. Many collisions were avoided during head-on attacks because of this bias the natural tendency was for both pilots to break left at the last split-second and thus miss each other. Another factor directly due to the left-hand bias, was that pilots could peer over their left shoulder more easily than their right. Their look-out to the right rear was thus potentially less efficient and an attacker was less likely to be detected from this angle.

As the battle progressed, the German bombers were given more fighter protection. Me 109 units now flew high cover over the raids and together with the close escort these made the bombers even more difficult to get at. Fighter Command countered with a slight change of emphasis. Shooting down bombers remained the primary task of the defending fighters but positive steps were taken to counter the German fighters.

'The general plan was to engage the enemy high fighter screen with pairs of Spitfire squadrons from Hornchurch and Biggin Hill half-way between London and the coast, and so enable Hurricane squadrons from London Sectors to attack bomber formations and their close escorts before they reached the line of fighter aerodromes east and south of London. The remaining squadrons from London Sectors that could not be despatched in time to intercept the first wave of the attack by climbing in pairs formed a third and inner screen by patrolling along the lines of aerodromes east and south of London. The fighter squadrons from Debden, Tangmere and sometimes Northolt, were employed in wings of three or in pairs to form a screen south-east of London to intercept the third wave of the attack coming inland, also to mop up retreating formations of the earlier waves. The Spitfire squadrons were redisposed so as to concentrate three squadrons at each of Hornchurch and Biggin Hill. The primary role of these squadrons was to engage and drive back the enemy high–fighter screen, and so protect the Hurricane squadrons, whose task was to attack close escorts and then the bomber formations, all of which flew at much lower altitude.'

This plan, devised by Air Vice Marshal Keith Park commanding No 11 Group, would have worked well had the picture of the attacks built up by the reporting network been clear cut. Unfortunately this was rarely the case. The extra time needed to concentrate the squadrons was often lost due to the

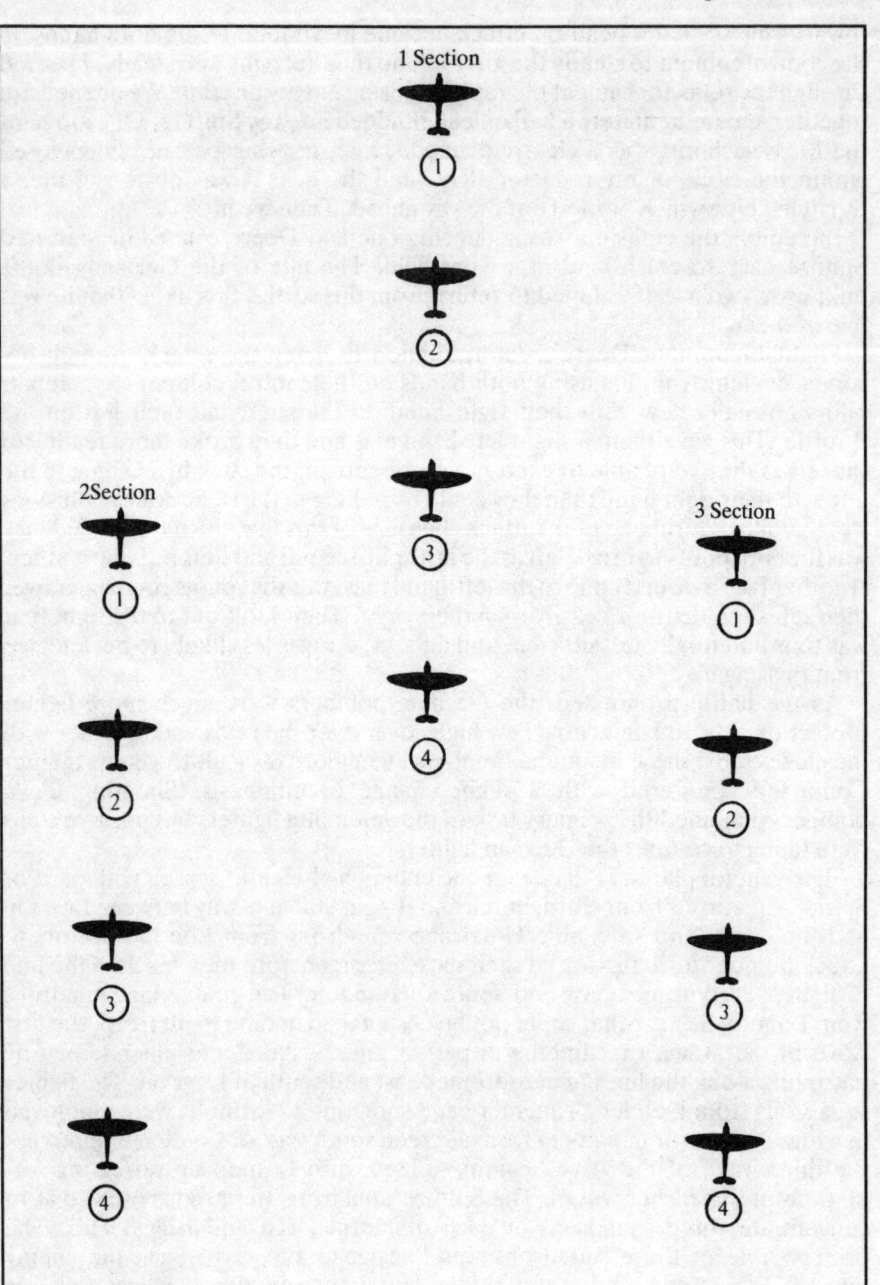

Fig 26 'Sailor' Malan's Formation.

This formation, while inferior to the German Staffel, was a great improvement over the Vic and remained in widespread use by the Royal Air Force for the following three years.

resultant uncertainty in the minds of the controllers. There has been a tendency to accuse the Luftwaffe of inflexibility during the Battle of Britain. The Fighter Command Commander-in-Chief, Sir Hugh Dowding commented in 1941: 'I must emphasise, throughout, the extreme versatility of the German methods both in the timing and direction of their attacks, and in the tactical formations and methods employed'.

Thus it can be seen that the short-comings of the reporting system, coupled with deliberate German attempts to confuse the defenders left Fighter Command little time to form large formations in order to meet force with force. The weather also was a factor. Difficulties were encountered in attempting to join up two or more squadrons in cloudy weather, as was noted in a No 11 Group report dated October 1.

Large formations were becoming a controversial issue in Fighter Command at about this time. Squadron Leader Douglas Bader, commanding No 242 Squadron argued that it was bad for morale to be constantly outnumbered and that squadrons should always form wings before engaging the enemy. He argued that a large formation attacking at one time would be more effective than the same number of aircraft arriving piecemeal. To test Bader's theory the No 12 Group Commander, Air Vice Marshal Trafford Leigh-Mallory formed the Duxford Wing, first with three, then with five squadrons. In practice it was less than successful. Even with the advantage of being able to form up and gain altitude in the peaceful skies of Cambridgeshire, it took so long for the aircraft to get under way that the squadrons frequently failed to make contact. When they did the results were not outstanding. In big fighter battles a law of diminishing returns seems to operate. Casualties are in direct inverse proportion to the number of fighters involved. The reason for this is not hard to find. In a small engagement with a dozen or less participants an experienced pilot can retain a general awareness of what is happening and react accordingly. In a large dogfight of up to a hundred aircraft this becomes impossible. Confusion arises, as does the collision risk. Both reduce efficiency. With many aircraft whirling around in a small area, positive identification becomes more difficult and many pilots have been shot at by their own side. As we saw in World War 1, survival became of prime importance to the individual pilot in a confused situation; shooting down the enemy was secondary. This was equally true in World War 2 and would still be the case today.

Two further phases marked the battle. Dissatisfied with the results of their attempts to reduce Fighter Command by attacking their airfields, the Luftwaffe switched their attention to London. This gave the defenders a valuable breathing space. No single airfield attack had been really devastating but the cumulative effect had reduced efficiency. Had these attacks continued, Dowding would have had little option but to pull his fighters back to airfields north of London, beyond the range of the Me 109s and therefore out of reach of the bombers. Long after the war, Keith Park was asked why he made no use of the other, ie, non-fighter airfields in his area to ease the pressure. He replied that only the established fighter airfields had good communications and without them, all he commanded was his desk at Uxbridge. This third phase worked in favour of the defenders as we have seen. The British fighters rose to defend their capital; the German fighters failed to destroy them.

The fourth phase was not critical for the defenders. Bombs were hung on the Me 109s which made fast hit-and-run raids at high altitude. These were extremely difficult to intercept and Park was forced to fly standing patrols to have any chance of catching them. The bomb load carried was too small to have any chance of achieving anything and this phase was really just a side-show.

To summarise, the Luftwaffe had failed in their aim of knocking out Fighter Command. While the British radar and reporting network remained intact they stood little chance of doing so. More British fighters were shot down by German fighters than vice versa but the rate of exchange was not enough to be decisive. Even discounting the superior German fighter tactics and formations, this was probably inevitable, as the Germans generally had both height and the initiative. The greatest German tactical blunder was to shackle many of their fighters to the bombers in the close escort role, which greatly reduced their effectiveness. But this was only obvious with hindsight.

Fighter Command had achieved their aim. They had succeeded in inflicting unacceptable casualties on the German bomber units, and had remained intact as an effective fighting force despite all the Luftwaffe could throw at them. Tactically they had learned much and had come a long way since the days of the Fighter Command attacks. Forewarned by the scanning eye of radar, they had fought a classic defensive battle. Was any other option open to them? It has been suggested that they should have carried the fight to the enemy and that a single devastating strike on the German fighter airfields could have been decisive since the Germans had no early warning system. This was precisely what the Germans expected. Their aircraft were carefully dispersed and camouflaged and their makeshift airfields bristled with anti-aircraft guns. The price of such a strike would have been very high and the loss of trained pilots disastrous. Not only that, the German bombers, based inland, would have escaped unscathed.

Chapter 6

The conflict widens

As 1940 drew to a close, the German assault on Britain changed from daylight to night raids. Activity during the day diminished and this state of affairs continued into the early months of 1941. Occasional German reconnaissance aircraft were intercepted and a few fighter clashes took place over the Channel. However, the renewal of the German daylight offensive, which Fighter Command expected, failed to materialise. By now Hitler's eyes were firmly turned eastwards and many Luftwaffe units were being transferred in readiness for the forthcoming invasion of Russia although the Royal Air Force had no means of knowing this.

Air Chief Marshal Sholto Douglas, Sir Hugh Dowding's successor as Chief of Fighter Command, seized the opportunity to gain the initiative. Under his direction, a policy of 'leaning forward into France' was instituted. The purpose of this policy was five-fold as laid down in 'Tactical Memorandum No 14'. Firstly, to destroy enemy aircraft. Secondly, to force the enemy to increase his fighter strength in the west at the expense of other vital fronts and thirdly, to dislocate transport and industry. The fourth objective was to obtain moral superiority and the fifth, to build up and maintain a high standard of efficiency in the squadrons under his command. To achieve these aims various types of offensive operations were introduced but the two which most directly concern us were the Rodeo and the Circus.

The Rodeo was a fighter sweep with one or two wings of 36 aircraft apiece trailing their coats across the skies of occupied Europe much as German fighters had ranged across southern England the previous year. And with the same result; the German fighters stayed on the ground and left them to it.

The Circus was also basically a fighter sweep, but in order to bring up the German fighters, it included a handful of bombers. As the Circus was to account for the majority of fighter sorties flown by Fighter Command over the next few years, a look at its early organisation is of interest.

First in at high altitude came three Target Support Wings each consisting of three squadrons of Spitfires. Their task was to sweep the sky clear of opposition along the route of the main force and over the target. One Target Support Wing flew the same course as the bombers, overtaking them on the way. The other two wings came in from different directions, thus making it difficult for the Luftwaffe to concentrate their forces. On arrival in the target area, all three wings split into sections of four and flew around until the bombing attack was completed.

The meat in the sandwich would typically consist of half a dozen Blenheims or occasionally Stirlings at about 12,000 ft. These aircraft carried bombs but were really only bait. The surrounding mixture was disproportionate, consisting of nine or ten squadrons of Spitfires and Hurricanes disposed in wings as follows:

The Escort Wing consisted of three or sometimes four squadrons. The Close Escort Squadron typically flew in two sections of four, each section about 1,000 yds out on the bomber's flanks. Each section was followed by a pair, the pairs weaving in cross-over turns as a tail guard. They flew level with the bombers or 500 ft higher. Their brief was to protect the bombers by countering enemy attacks, but under no circumstances were they to become embroiled in a fight. Understandably, this was the most unpopular position in a Circus, as these pilots were often shot at but had little chance of hitting back. Slightly astern and 1,000 ft higher, came the Medium Escort Squadron flying in Malan's formation, with three sections of four in-line astern. This squadron was free to attack any German fighter attempting to get at the bombers. Then came the High Escort Squadron, astern and a further 1,000 ft above, deployed in six pairs in line astern, with the pairs deployed in a flat arc nearly line abreast. The High Escort was constrained to stay in position and give top cover to the Close Escort Squadron as far as possible. The Low Escort Squadron was an early addition to the Escort Wing, flying the same formation and spacing as the Close Escort Squadron but 1,000 ft below the level of the bombers.

Sitting above the Escort Wing, came the Escort Cover Wing, normally of three squadrons, the lowest of which positioned itself astern of and a thousand feet higher than the highest squadron of the Escort Wing. The remaining two squadrons positioned themselves at 1,000 and 2,000 ft vertical spacings respectively, stepped up into the sun. The highest squadron acted as top cover while the two lower squadrons were able to engage the enemy as opportunity offered.

Still higher flew the High Cover Wing, again consisting of three squadrons, stepped up into the sun from the Escort Cover Wing at intervals of 1,000, 2,000 and 4–5,000 ft. Once again the two lower squadrons were free to engage the enemy while the top squadron held the roof up. Thus the direct escort for half a dozen bombers consisted of 120 fighters.

This was not all. Over the French coast, timed to meet the bombers on their return journey were two or three squadrons of the Forward Support Wing, their height determined by the altitude of the German fighter formations. This wing remained on patrol for several minutes after the main force had passed, brushing the Germans off their tails. Finally in mid-Channel ready to reinforce where necessary, was the Rear Support Wing, generally two squadrons strong at medium altitude.

These massive efforts involving a total of nearly 300 fighters to protect a handful of bombers sound impressive, but what in fact did they achieve? Royal Air Force fighter losses were considerably higher than those of the Luftwaffe, a fact that was masked at the time by the overclaiming which has always been a feature of air warfare. With most British pilots who baled out of their stricken aircraft becoming guests of the Führer for the duration, the comparative losses of trained flyers were even more one-sided. Thus it can be seen that of the five objectives laid down in Tactical Memo No 14, the first was counter-productive, the second failed completely, the third had but marginal effect, the fourth was achieved to a degree and only the fifth aim was successful.

Fighting efficiency, by dint of constant practice, was improved and mainly due to the initiative of Wing Commander Douglas Bader commanding the Tangmere Wing, the Luftwaffe style 'finger four' formation was widely adopted by Fighter Command. Trial and error played their part. Initially, when the 'finger four' was bounced, the two pairs broke in opposite directions. This was excellent practice when bounced from astern by a Rotte, as only one pair could be followed and the attackers would soon have been in danger from the other pair if their onslaught was continued. However, in the crowded skies of France in 1941, it was more likely to be a Staffel than a pair coming down and to break in opposite directions was unsound. Not only was the formation broken up, but for a few seconds the pairs lost sight of each other. This was rectified by all aircraft breaking in the same direction using the cross-over turn, the outside men going high, the inside men low. In this way, the formation cross-cover was maintained and the four aircraft remained a cohesive fighting unit.

The Luftwaffe were reduced by now to two Geschwadern in France. Jagdgeschwader 2 Richthofen commanded by Major Walter Oesau, and Jagdgeschwader 26 Schlageter, led by the redoubtable Oberstleutnant Adolf Galland, fought hard and well against the incursions of the Royal Air Force. Always outnumbered, they retained the initiative of when and where to strike and succeeded in giving rather better than they got. Because it was more important that they remained effective fighting units, the German fighters never offered battle on an all or nothing basis, but sought to inflict damage at the least cost to themselves. It was not the Fatherland they were defending, and the puny bombing forces used were hardly able to inflict serious damage on the German war effort. Consequently the German pilots restricted themselves mainly to quick hit-and-run: attacks making intelligent use of cloud or sun to work their way into position for a fast diving attack, straight in, then on past and down, climbing back up at a distance to repeat the dose.

A variation on this form of attack was to dive behind the bombers, pulling hard up into them from below. It was to counter this ploy that the fourth and lowest squadron of the Escort Wing was introduced. These attacks were timed to coincide with other German formations nibbling at the flanks of the higher Spitfire squadrons, thus distracting them. Occasionally, a Schwarm of Me 109s would ease their way into the Circus as though they had every right to be there. Oberstleutnant Galland described one such occasion in which the nephew of Reichsmarschall Goering met his end: 'On that fateful November 13 (1941), I flew with Peter Goering as his accompanying aircraft against a formation of Blenheim bombers which were heavily protected by fighters. On our climb we passed near this hellish goods train. We were overtaking British fighters right and left. This was so incredibly impertinent that it succeeded. This young enthusiastic pilot had never seen so many Spitfires at such close range. When we were about 200 yds from the bombers, I called out to him "Let them have it Peter!" He was flying about 50 yds to my left. After the first bursts of fire, his plane suddenly dived vertically. No one was behind him.'

In this daring attack Galland used the element of surprise to take him through the fighter escort by approaching from an unexpected angle. His shallow climb gave him sufficient speed to overhaul the bombers and their attendant fighters. This account is an excellent example of the futility of attempting to protect bombers by packing fighters tightly around them. Galland's brilliantly audacious attack clearly took the escorting fighters by

Fig 27 Ambush on June 2 1942.

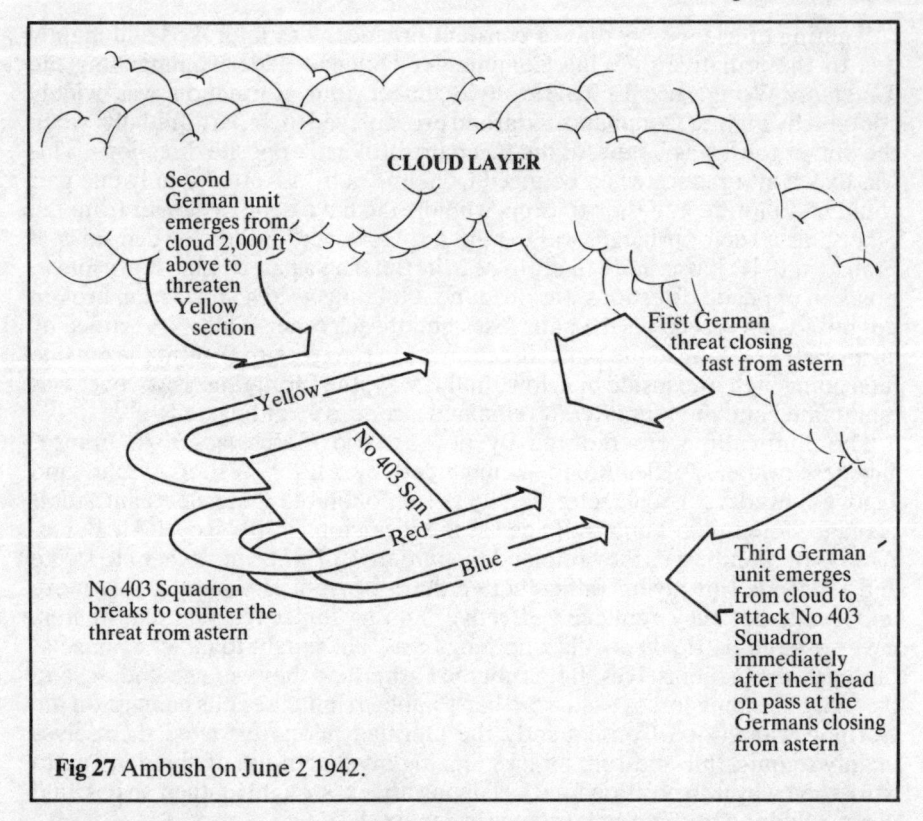

surprise and left them insufficient time to accelerate in pursuit before he reached the bombers. It was only foiled by capricious fate: Leutnant Goering was almost certainly shot down by return fire from the Blenheims.

A frequent Fighter Command complaint in 1941 was 'why doesn't Jerry stay and fight.' This was quickly silenced in 1942 when large numbers of Focke Wulf FW 190s entered service. The new German fighter outclassed the Spitfire V in almost all aspects. Its level speed, climb, dive and acceleration were all superior and its rate of roll was incredibly fast, enabling it to change direction very rapidly. Only in the turn did the Spitfire retain the advantage, with its lighter wing loading. Even this was suspect, as the FW 190 could turn very tight by using 10 degrees of flap and using its sparkling acceleration to overcome the extra drag. Accounts exist of FW 190s out-turning Spitfires, the best known of which, is related by Johnny Johnson in his book *Wing Leader*, when he tells of the occasion a FW 190 gave him a very hard time over Dieppe.

Armed with this outstanding fighter, the German pilots stayed and fought as never before. An exceptional action took place on June 2 1942 when the North Weald and Hornchurch Wings joined forces for a Rodeo over the German fighter base at St Omer. The top squadron of the formation was No 403, led by Squadron Leader Alan Deere, flying at 27,000 ft. The first part of the sweep was uneventful, but on the return trip, a dozen German fighters were spotted directly astern and closing fast. No 403 Squadron were flying in three 'finger fours'. Red Section was leading with Blue and Yellow Sections slightly behind to left and right respectively. Deere called the break and Red and Blue Sections turned hard left to face the German attack while Yellow Section pulled up and to the right. Halfway around the turn, Deere glanced across at Yellow Section only to see another gaggle of FW 190s emerging from a thin cloud layer 2,000 ft above. A brief head-on pass at the original formation which pulled up and over and a third batch of Germans came down from Deere's right. As Deere commented later: 'Never had I seen the Germans stay and fight it out as these Focke Wulf pilots were doing. In Messerschmitt 109s the German tactics had always followed the same pattern – a quick pass and away, sound tactics against Spitfires with their superior turning circle. Not so these FW 190 pilots, they were full of confidence.'

This carefully laid and precisely executed trap, which showed a high standard of ground controlling, was a disaster for No 403 Squadron. Eight out of 12 aircraft were lost.

The Spitfire V squadrons were given a hard time by their new adversary. When a FW 190 was captured intact, comparative trials were flown in order to devise the best methods of countering it. The Spitfire pilot was recommended to maintain a high cruising speed in the combat zone to lessen the chances of being bounced. He was reminded of his superiority in the turn, although as we have seen earlier, this was doubtful. As a method of evasion he could enter a shallow dive if the FW 190 was seen in sufficient time. If the pursuit was continued for any distance he could be caught, but as each ten seconds the chase was prolonged was worth a mile or more in terms of distance covered, it was worth the attempt. The real answer came in July 1942 when the Spitfire IX entered service. This more potent version closely matched the German fighter in speed and climb and reduced its superiority in diving and acceleration. Only in rate of roll did the FW 190 maintain a distinct advantage.

The defence of Malta is one of the greatest epics in the annals of air warfare. An unsinkable aircraft carrier well placed to halt the flow of Axis supplies to North Africa, it was inevitable that it should come under heavy attack. While Royal Air Force fighters held a measure of air superiority, bomber squadrons and naval units were based on the island and the Italian supply convoys suffered heavily. With the loss of air superiority, they had to be withdrawn before they were destroyed, and Rommel's supplies could pass unhindered.

At its nearest point, Malta is about 40 miles from Sicily. Warning time of an incoming raid was therefore short; about 15 minutes or less. This was to a degree offset by the small size of the island, after all, there could be no doubt of the target! The early attacks were made by the Regia Aeronautica. The Italian fighters were in the main Fiat CR 42 biplanes with some Fiat G50 and Macchi MC 200 monoplanes. They flew in Vics and their tactical ideas were basically find the enemy and then out – turn him until a shooting position was attained. Their aircraft were slow and lacked firepower and were generally outmatched by the defending Hurricanes.

Alarmed by the mounting shipping losses, the Luftwaffe moved into Sicily in force at the end of 1941 and the defence of Malta became much harder. This is not to denigrate the fighting qualities of the Italian pilots, but equipped with inferior aircraft, they were not as effective as the German fighter units flying Me 109s.

The air fighting over Malta was on a smaller scale than in the other major theatres and it was perhaps inevitable that Royal Air Force tactics evolved

Direction of search

Fig 28 Royal Air Force formations over Malta.

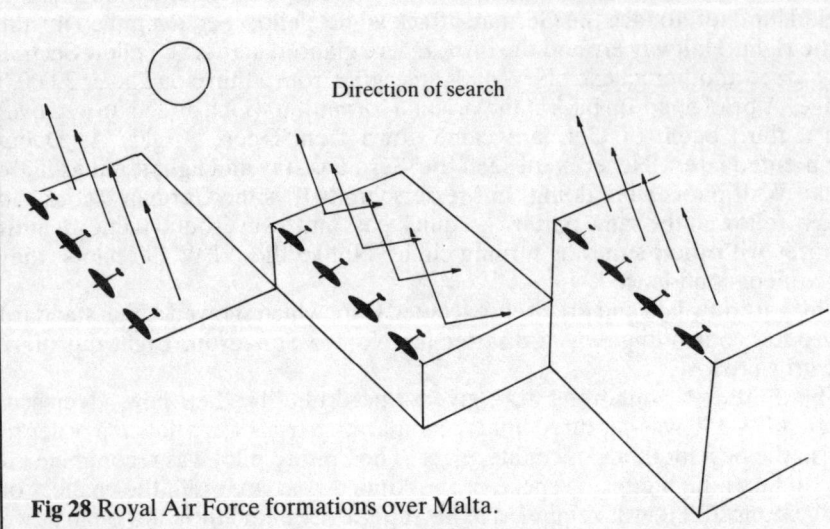

1) Line abreast stepped down into sun. With all aircraft searching inwards all blind spots were covered. Stepping the sections down towards the sun made it difficult for an attacking formation to remain unseen.

2) Flat Vic. Very similar to line abreast.

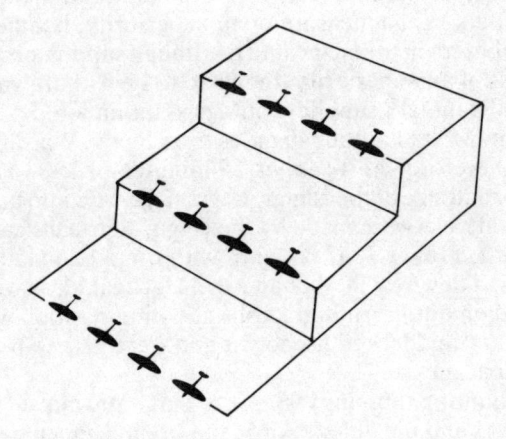

3) Sections line astern stepped up and back. This formation required less practice and although sections used the cross-over turn the sections themselves did not need to cross-over.

more rapidly than elsewhere. With the short notice available, every second was crucial. The British fighters took off and climbed hard south into the sun and away from the oncoming raid. When sufficient altitude had been reached, they turned and came storming back over the island with the sun behind them.'

Pilot Officer Reade Tilley spend many months on Malta flying Spitfires. An American in the Royal Air Force, he transferred to the United States Army Air Force at the end of 1942 and wrote a tactical paper called *Hints on Hun Hunting* which set down his accumulated experience for the benefit of his compatriots. While some of it was peculiar to the Malta campaign, much was relevant to air combat in any theatre and as a result it was adopted by the Royal Air Force as Tactical Bulletin No 15. Tilley's first point stressed the necessity of rapid take-off of the utmost importance on Malta as this passage shows: 'When fighters are scrambled to intercept an approaching enemy, every minute wasted in getting off the ground and forming up means 3,000 ft of altitude you won't have when you need it most. Thus an elaborate cockpit check is out. It is sufficient to see that you are in fine pitch (propeller setting) and that the motor is running properly. Don't do a Training School circuit before joining up. As you roll down the runway take a quick look up for the man off ahead of you: when you have sufficient indicated air speed give him about six rings of deflection (of the gunsight) and you will be alongside in a flash. Don't jam open the throttle and follow along behind as it takes three times as long to catch up that way. If you are leading, circle the drome close in, throttled well back, waggling your wings like hell (for identification). The instant you are in formation get the cockpit in "fighting shape"; trimmed for the climb, oxygen right, check engine instruments, gun button to fire. Now you are ready for action.'

Tilley's next point was the tactical formation. He favoured the fours in-line abreast formation, similar to the German Schwarm but with all aircraft abreast instead of staggered as in the finger four. A Fighter Command Tactical Memorandum issued in November 1942 gave more formation variants than Reade Tilley and for that reason is mentioned here. 'The formation which is now used in Malta and which for nearly a year has achieved so much success is "line abreast" with aircraft flying in fours line abreast at intervals of 150/250 yds. Where possible the three fours of the squadron keep together. They may fly sections line abreast stepped down into sun, a flat Vic, or line astern, stepped down. The advantages of the line abreast formation are obvious. There are no stragglers. With everyone searching inwards, everyone's tail is covered. When attacking bombers, everyone can help themselves to a target, and the return fire is split more effectively. It is easier to reform after attacks than any previous formation. Flying formation can be done at greater speeds than previously and fuel consumption is more uniform. If an outside aircraft drops back for any reason, the leader has only to turn into it without throttling back, and it automatically comes into formation.'

To return to Reade Tilley: 'Red Section leads with the Squadron Commander at Red one. Red three, the second in command, flies next to the Squadron Commander on his left he will take over the lead in case the Squadron Commander's radio fails or he has to leave the squadron because his aircraft is unserviceable'.

An apparently minor detail but very important. Prior to this the second in command led a different section. Chaos reigned when he tried to take over the lead, which could only be sorted out by radio, and for a minute or two the squadron was effectively leaderless while it re-organised. The cross-over turn was used by sections as well as within sections as Reade Tilley pointed out: 'When the leader turns, White and Blue Sections will cross over at full throttle. The section the leader turns towards will usually cross under, the others over. In order to be in position when the turn is completed, the leaders of White and Blue Sections have to be quick and precise. Within the sections each pilot will cross over.'

As can be imagined, considerable practice was necessary to perfect this manoeuvre. Radio discipline was dealt with next. 'The Squadron Leader is the only man who uses the RT for transmission when the squadron is in pursuit of the German. There is no need for you to say anything, just keep your mouth shut and reflect on the ground controller's messages to the leader. So keep your eyes open and your mouth shut until you spot the enemy, then your moment has come. The procedure: make your voice purposely calm, slow and unexcited: "Hello Red leader; 109s at 4 o'clock above" or "Red three to Red leader; aircraft at 9 o'clock our level." Sometimes the enemy aircraft are not seen until they are actually attacking. *The the message must be instantaneous and precise.* If it is incoherent or garbled because you are excited, the man being attacked may get a cannon shell instead – and first. The *proper* procedure: "109s attacking Red section" or if you see one man being fired at "Look out Red four", or "Red four break"; any one of these messages spoken clearly is perfect. Just be sure you designate the man being attacked correctly. The one sure way to lose friends and help the enemy is to give a panic message over the RT at the critical moment. "Look out, there's a 109 on your tail!" said in a screech, is usually sufficient to send every Spitfire within a radius of 50 miles into a series of wild manoeuvres. There is no call sign used so every pilot in every squadron responds automatically. Far better to say nothing at all and let one pilot be shot down than to break up several formations for Jerry to pick off at his leisure.'

No fighter pilot who wanted to live long could afford to ignore the sun. It could be a friend or a deadly enemy, depending on how it was used. 'Always note the bearing of the sun before taking off; then, if you get in a scrap miles out at sea or over the desert and a cannon shell prangs your compass, you may be able to save yourself a lot of unnecessary walking or paddling. Never climb down sun. If it is necessary to fly down sun, do so in a series of 45 degree tacks. If circumstances permit, always climb up sun. If a German is hiding in it, he can make only one head-on pass at you, then you can turn smartly and jump him out of the sun thus foxing him at his own game. If you are patrolling an objective, split your force into two sections and patrol across sun. The sections will fly more or less "line abreast", but with the up-sun section out in front just a bit. Vary the length of the legs you cover and gain and lose altitude all the while. If the Germans spot you first, this will make it more difficult for them to time an attack to get you on the turn; and always make the turns *in to* sun. When flying low over water or desert, adjust your height so that you can see your shadow on the surface, then watch the water for other shadows sneaking up behind yours, as they may harbour an unfriendly feeling towards you.'

Cloud could also prove to be friend or foe. 'Cloud is greatly over-rated as cover for offensive fighter operations. It is of most use to a fighter pilot who is in trouble. If you are shot up or the odds are impossible, it is great stuff to hide in.

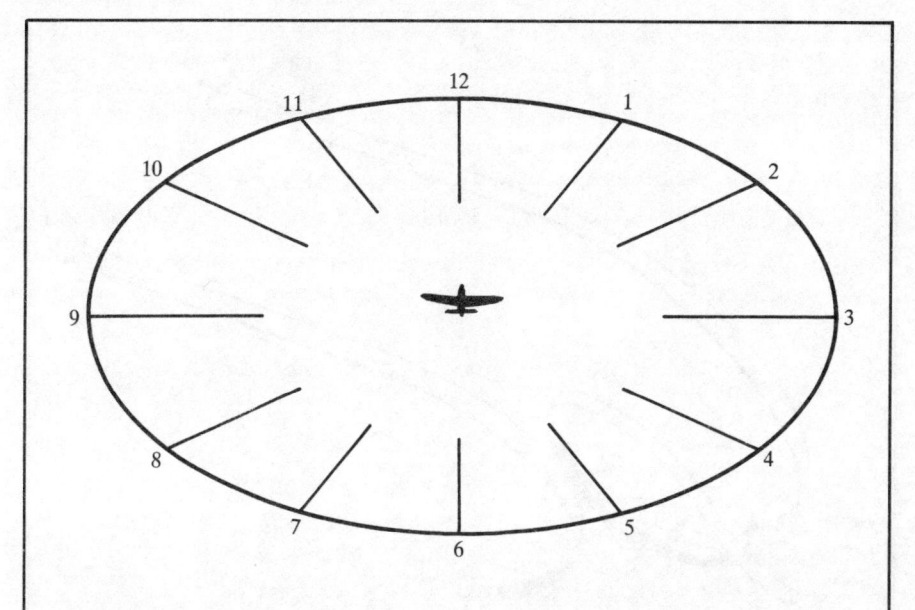

Fig 29 The clock code.

Sightings of unidentified or hostile aircraft were reported by using the clock code. The pilot imagined that his aircraft was in the centre of a giant clock. 12 o'clock was straight ahead; 3 o'clock to his right, and so on. Unidentified aircraft at the right-hand front at a higher level would be reported as 'Bogeys 2 o'clock high!'

Layer cloud is most useful as you can pop in, or dive out below to take a look. Remember that it is not healthy to maintain a straight course when there are gaps in the cloud. If you are being pursued turn 90 degrees in every cloud you pop into; if it seems in order, a quick 180 about may put you in a position to offer some head-on discouragement to the pursuer along the way. Never fly directly on top of layer cloud, as you stand out like a sore thumb to an unfriendly element, even those as far as 10 miles away, if they are slightly above you. On days when there is very high layer cloud, fly halfway between it and the ground in order to spot fighters above you. High layer cloud is perfect for defensive fighter work, because you can see the enemy formations and distinguish between fighter and bomber long before they can see you.'

Finally Reade Tilley deals with combat. 'When stalking the wily Hun, bear in mind that he seldom puts all his eggs in one bucket but usually splits his aircraft into several groups, each group stacked up-sun, 3,000 to 5,000 ft. Keep an eye on the sun; you will be safer. The Germans are masters at using stooge decoys who would probably be as helpless as they look, if half the Luftwaffe was not keeping a jealous eye on them from the sun. Enemy aircraft do not fly alone, they fly in pairs or fours. If you can just see one, have a damn good look round for his pal before you go in to attack . . . and remember *look out behind*.

'When you attack, a series of two or three second bursts with new aim and angle of deflection each time is most effective. Don't cease attacking just because the enemy aircraft is beginning to smoke or a few pieces fall off; then is

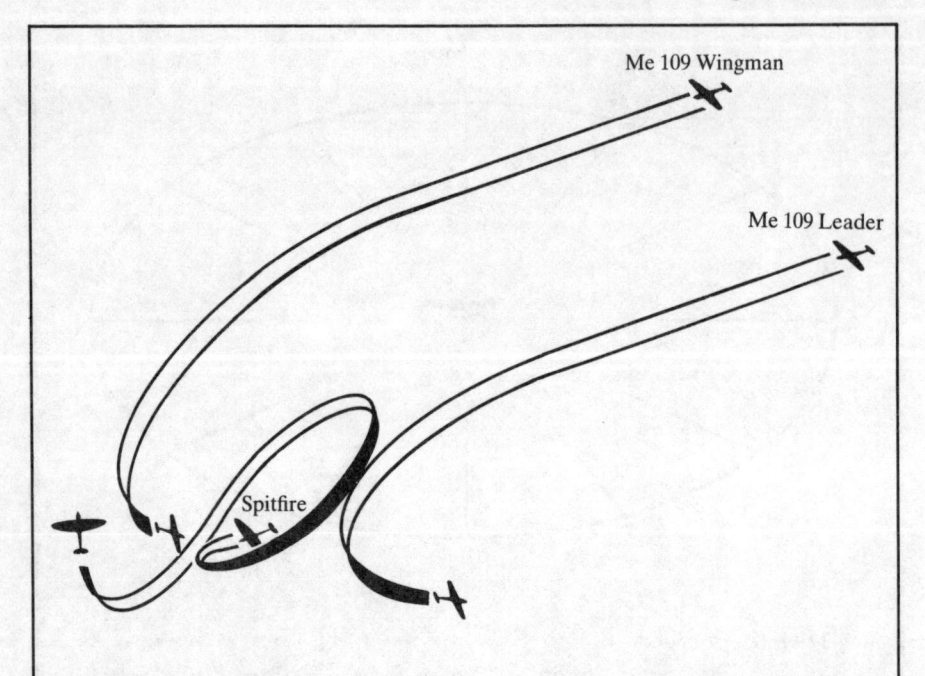

Fig 30 Beating the box.

'The Spitfire pilot's timing has to be near perfect. He has to make his move sharply and get his burst in with plenty of deflection ahead of the enemy leader and be going over and down before the enemy gets within effective range. His unobtrusive throttling back, in addition to giving him greater manoeuvreability, has spoiled the timing of his attacker who finds he is closer to the Spitfire than intended when he initiates his dive, which means he has to get his nose down faster than he intended. Then, just as he's getting ready to fire, he sees tracer out in front of him and realises he's looking at the wrong end of the Spitfire. These small diversions tend to put him off a little and when in range he's got a snap shot only . . . If he missed, the attacking enemy wingman coming straight in at high speed was faced with the problem of overshooting, with the Spitfire disappearing rapidly under his wing. It was unlikely that the German wingman could bring his sights to bear.' Colonel Reade Tilley, December 1980.

the time to skid out for a good look behind, before closing in to point blank range and really giving it to him. When actually firing at an enemy aircraft you are most vulnerable to attack. When you break away from an attack *always* break with a violent skid just as though you are being fired at from behind – because maybe you are!

'A tactic the 109s are very keen on is known as "Boxing". 109s come over top and split into two groups, one on either side of you. Suddenly one group will peel down to attack from the beam. You turn to meet the attack, the other group come in and sit on your tail. If you are leading a section or squadron you can fox them easily by detailing half your force to watch one side and half the other. When you are alone and two box you, it's easy providing you work fast.

As the first one starts his dive, chop the throttle, yank the nose around, fire a quick squirt in front of him, then skid into a sloppy half roll, keep the stick well back, and pull out quickly in a skidding turn. The second 109 will have lost sight of you beneath his wing. You should be in a good position to pull up and give him a burst at close range. This procedure applicable in Spitfire versus 109. Not recommended when your plane is the less manoeuvrable.'

The one versus two encounter sounds confident and aggressive but then it was deliberately written that way. In fact, it was a desperate last ditch manoeuvre which might or might not get the Spitfire pilot out of a very tight corner and was only attempted when no other possibilities existed. Reade Tilley, who retired from the United States Army Air Force with the rank of Colonel, recently confirmed this: 'It's sole purpose was to save your ass!' as he pithily put it. 'If you could spoil their first attack they might decide to go someplace else!'

Hints on Hun Hunting contained most of the essentials of air fighting. It is interesting to note that German fighters also began to fly line abreast fours during 1942, replacing their finger four type Schwarm.

Meanwhile, on the Russian front, drastically different tactics were being used. Germany had invaded Russia in June 1941 and in a massive attack on the Soviet airfields, destroyed over 1,800 aircraft on the first day, most of them on the ground. Bereft of effective air cover, the Red Armies suffered massive defeats and the German forces began their triumphant march eastwards. The Russian fighter units were forced to resort to desperate measures. Their aircraft were inferior to the German Messerschmitts, their pilots poorly trained and their tactical ideas almost non-existent. On the second day of the campaign, a Me 110, a Ju 88 and a He 111 all fell to ramming attacks. All three Russian pilots were flying the obsolete Polikarpov I 16 and two of the three survived the attack. In all, about 200 ramming attacks on German machines were recorded. It was not quite as suicidal as it seemed, Lieutenant Boris Kobzan downed no less than four Germans in this manner. The precedent had been set long before. On August 26 1914, Lieutenant Peter Nikolaevich Nesterov had sent his unarmed Morane M crashing into an Austrian reconnaissance machine. Both aircraft fell in flames. Now as the general situation worsened, ramming became a patriotic duty, as the much publicised report of Junior Lieutenant Talalikhin, describing his action against a Heinkel He 111 west of Moscow, shows: 'I managed to hit the bomber's left engine and it turned away losing height. At that moment my ammunition ran out and it occurred to me that although I could still catch it, it would get away. There was only one thing for it – to ram. If I'm killed, I thought, that's only one, but there are four fascists in that bomber. I crept up under its belly to get at its tail with my propeller, but when I was about ten yds away, a burst of fire hit my machine and shot my right hand through. Straight away I opened the throttle and drove right into it.' Talalikhin baled out of his I 16 successfully and was made a Hero of the Soviet Union the following day.

As the war dragged on, the Soviet Air Forces were rebuilt and learned their tactical lessons well, abandoning the three machine section for the *pary* (pair) and *zveno* (four) as had been recommended after the Spanish Civil War. However, in direct contrast to the western European theatre, almost all the air fighting was carried out in direct support of the ground forces. Thus most air combats took place at a comparatively low level. The Messerschmitts often had an altitude advantage, but the Russian fighters partially countered by flying

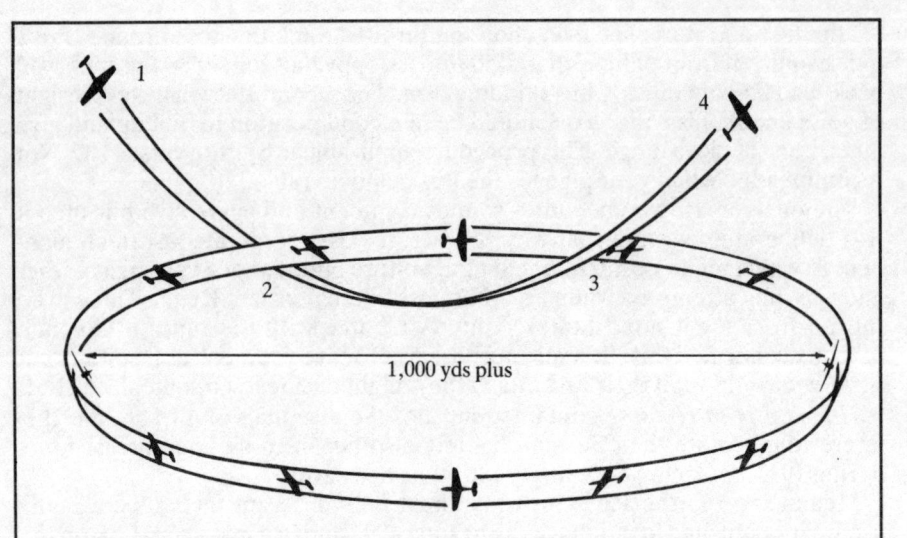

Fig 31 Marseille's answer to the defensive circle.

1) Marseille dives steeply past the circle.
2) Pulling out hard, he selects his victim and zooms up to attack. From this direction he is concealed beneath the nose of the fighter covering his victim.
3) Closing to point-blank range he fires a split-second burst.
4) The speed of his zoom carries him high above the circle, well placed to attack again.

It should be stressed that the judgement and timing demanded by this form of attack were far beyond the ability of the average pilot.

everywhere in the combat zone at full throttle. This used fuel faster and considerably reduced their range, but made them more difficult to bounce as it increased the time available to spot the German fighters coming in.

In many ways the North African campaign was fought in similar conditions to those in Russia. There were wide open spaces, poor or non-existent early warning systems and operations carried out almost entirely in support of the ground forces. The equipment of the Royal Air Force was not the best, because until the spring of 1942, all Spitfires were held back in England. While the opposition was Italian, the Hurricanes and Curtiss Tomahawks and later Kittyhawks held their own, but when the Luftwaffe arrived with their latest model Me 109Fs, the British and Commonwealth fighters were given a hard time.

One of the most remarkable fighter pilots of the war was Oberleutnant Hans-Joachim Marseille of Jagdgeschwader 27. Marseille was an exceptional flyer and one of the few pilots to master the art of deflection shooting, claiming 151 victories over the western desert between April 1941 and September 1942. Incredible though this may seem, a high proportion of his victims can be confirmed with the help of Allied records.

With the exception of the Spitfire V which arrived in the spring 1942, and in small numbers, the Allied fighters were completely outclassed by the Me 109F and later the 109G. If German fighters were sighted, the Hurricanes and

The conflict widens

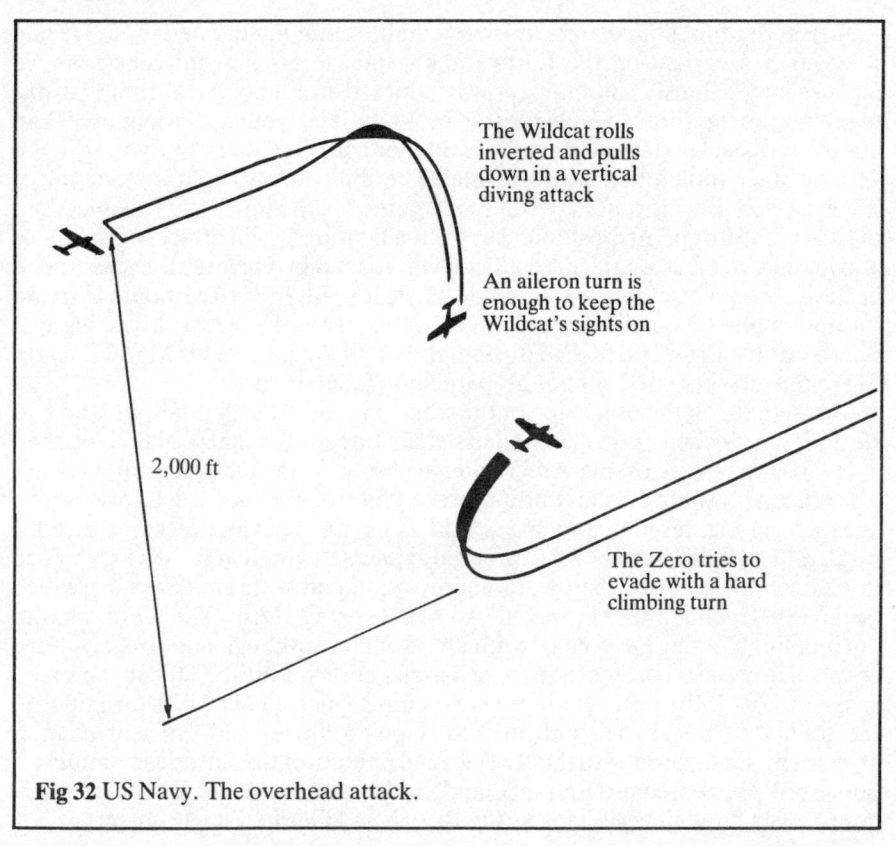

Fig 32 US Navy. The overhead attack.

- The Wildcat rolls inverted and pulls down in a vertical diving attack
- An aileron turn is enough to keep the Wildcat's sights on
- 2,000 ft
- The Zero tries to evade with a hard climbing turn

particularly the Curtiss fighters, often formed defensive circles. As has been mentioned earlier, Fighter Command had found the circle a hard nut to crack in 1940. The German pilots found it equally difficult to tackle in 1941 and 1942. That is, with the exception of Marseille.

On June 6 1942, Marseille's Staffel of Jagdgeschwader 27 encountered a dozen Tomahawks of No 5 Squadron, South African Air Force, who formed a clockwise defensive circle at 5,000 ft. A defensive circle was a pretty large thing. The aeroplanes would be banked at about 70 degrees and thus be pulling about 3 Gs. Speed was probably in the region of 250 mph. The diameter of the circle was nearly 1,000 yds and the fighters would be spaced around the circumference at roughly 250 yd intervals. The individual fighters could turn much harder, but this was about the limit for holding formation. Each fighter in the circle was well placed to cover the tail of the aircraft in front. Marseille climbed above the circle, dropped the nose of the aircraft and came hurtling down past the South Africans. Pulling hard upwards in a zoom climb, he selected a victim and attacked in a climbing turn to the right. Closing to 50 yds, he straightened out and gave a quick burst as the Tomahawk disappeared beneath his nose. The stricken fighter streamed smoke and fell out of the circle. The aircraft covering it had been unable to see the Messerschmitt until the last second, owing to the steep angle of bank. Marseille soared upwards and levelled out to select his next victim.

No less than six Tomahawks fell to Marseille's guns in this one action. He had discovered a variant on the Luftwaffe's standard hit-and-run tactics. As we have seen previously, hit-and-run was adopted to nullify the turning advantages of the Spitfire and Hurricane in 1940. The young German ace had discovered a way to hit and stay in position for a further attack by fighting in the vertical plane rather than the horizontal. The ability to turn tight is a function of speed as well as wing loading. The speed gained in the initial dive enabled him to zoom rapidly up into position, carry out a lightning-swift attack and be away above the circle before the defenders could react. Having lost his excess speed in the subsequent climb, he was able to turn tightly over the South African formation and be quickly in position to attack again. However, Marseille was not to survive the war. He died on September 30 1942, when his Me 109 caught fire in the air. He baled out but his parachute failed to open.

Meanwhile, on the other side of the world, a war of a very different kind had started. On December 6 1941, air units of the Imperial Japanese Navy launched a devastating attack on the American naval base at Pearl Harbour in Hawaii. The stage was set for a war without precedent, fought over 1,000s of miles of ocean from scattered island bases and from the heaving decks of aircraft carriers. The fighter units of the Imperial Japanese Navy had gained experience in China; furthermore they were mainly equipped with an aeroplane which became a legend, the Mitsubishi A6 M2 Type O Zero. The Zero was an outstanding fighting aeroplane, with a reasonable although not excessive turn of speed, excellent acceleration (over 5 mph per second at 15,000 ft in the speed range of 120–150 mph), very low wing loading which enabled it to turn tightly, the ability to sustain a climb at a very steep angle, and efficient cannon armament. Compared with the short legged fighters of the European nations, it possessed phenomenal endurance and could stay in the air for six or seven hours, over three times as long as the British and German single-seaters.

The Japanese Navy pilots used a three aircraft battle formation (*shotai*) developed in China, an offset 'line astern' with roughly 100 yds intervals between machines. Three *shotai* made up a nine aircraft *chutai*, a ragged looking formation with all pilots except the leader, weaving. It would never have won prizes at air displays, but was loose and flexible. Japanese air discipline was excellent as the Americans found out at the Coral Sea battle in May 1942. Their formations tended to split into single aircraft when attacked and more often than not found themselves pursued by at least three Zeros. Japanese tactics were based on hit-and-run, which was rather surprising in view of the dog-fighting capability of their mounts. The *shotai* would form line astern for the attack and pull back upstairs after firing.

Opposing this formidable force was the United States Navy, whose fighter arm was equipped in the main with the F-4F Wildcat. Whereas from the end of World War 1, just about every air force in the world had trained their fighter pilots to seek the no-deflection tail shooting position, the US Navy had from 1922 onwards, emphasised the use of deflection shooting. This was carefully practiced on drogue targets and with gun cameras. In the F-4F, the pilot sat up high above a short down-slanting engine cowling, which enabled him to aim even at very high deflection. By contrast, the long noses of the European fighters often completely obscured the target.

Four basic textbook attacks were used, the overhead, side, opposite and astern approaches. The overhead attack required that the attacker positioned

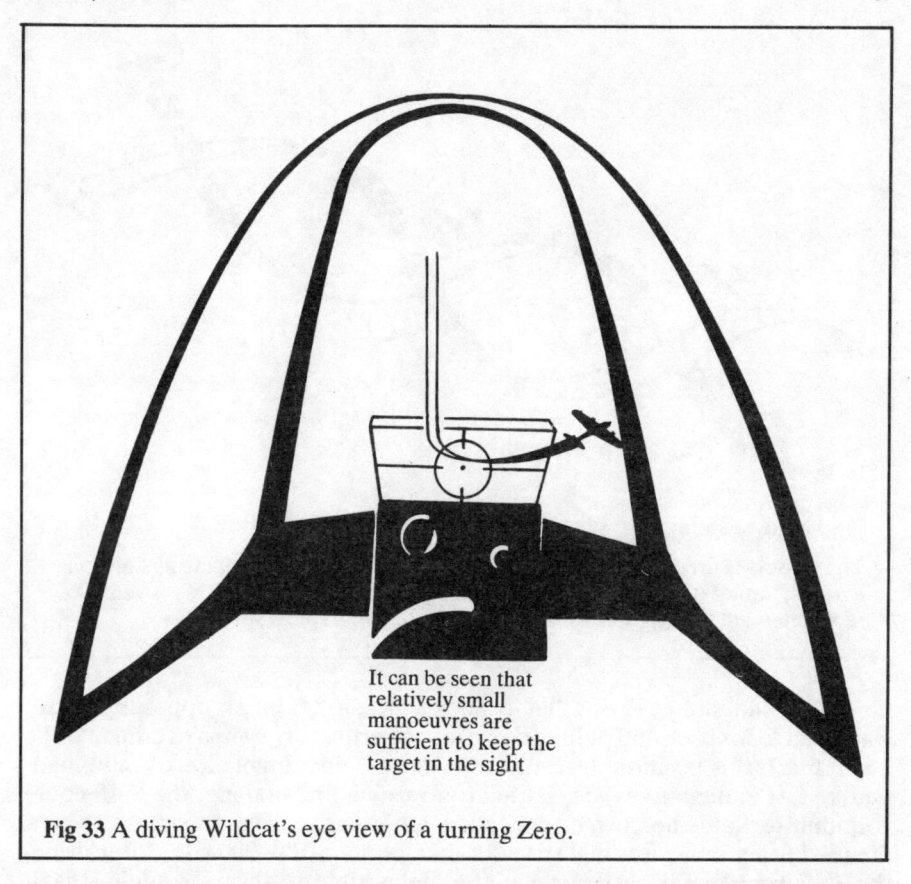

It can be seen that relatively small manoeuvres are sufficient to keep the target in the sight

Fig 33 A diving Wildcat's eye view of a turning Zero.

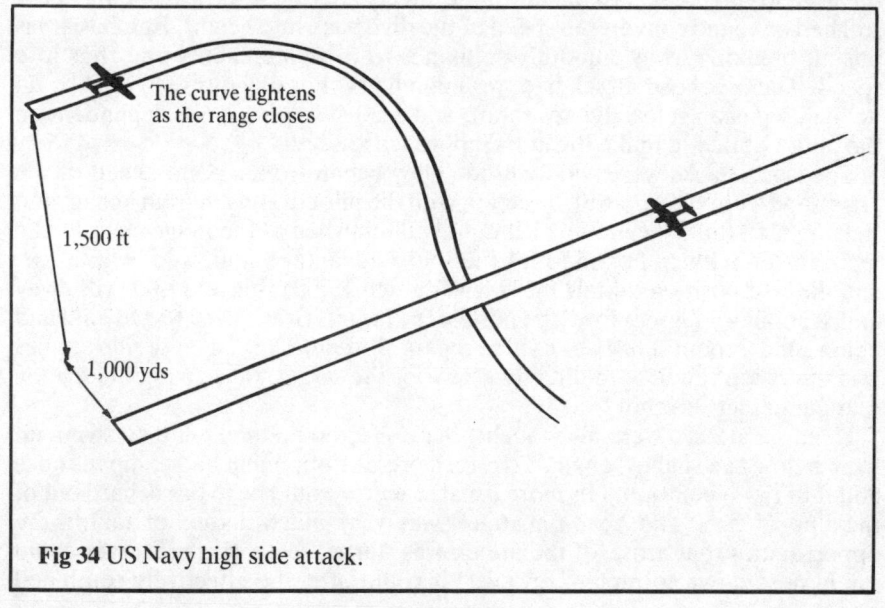

The curve tightens as the range closes

1,500 ft

1,000 yds

Fig 34 US Navy high side attack.

Fig 35 The scissors.

The scissors is used to force an opponent to overshoot. Although not as simple as it looks; timing is critical, the more manoeuvrable fighter should always win. Not recommended for a fighter with a considerable initial speed advantage.

himself ahead and at least 2,000 ft above the target, on an opposite course, rolling on to his back and pulling down into a vertical dive when overhead. If he could reach this position unseen, not even the redoubtable Zero could manoeuvre fast enough to evade. By aileron-turning or spiralling, the F-4F could continue to hold the correct deflection quite easily. The maximum recommended firing range was 400 yds with the optimum 100–200 yds. After firing, the F-4F would break past the tail of the enemy aircraft, always assuming that it still had one, and convert the speed of the dive back into height. Emphasis was put on breaking away smoothly so as not to dissipate energy and thus lose speed. The overhead attack had two main flaws. For obvious reasons it could not be used against low flying aircraft, and against fighters it was dependent on the pilot's ability to make the initial approach unseen.

The side attacks were widely used. They began from a point ahead of the target and from the opposite direction with the pilot turning in from abeam and starting with full deflection which rapidly diminished as the range closed. The high side attack was favoured for the speed advantage conferred by altitude, and the best position to start the run was about 1,500 ft higher, 1,000 yds away and at about 45 degrees from the nose of the target. Breakaway was behind and below, and a zoom climb was used to regain altitude. The danger in side attacks was the risk of ending up directly astern of the target, thus giving the enemy rear gunner a good shot.

Head-on attacks were also taught, the preferred method being to swing up from below at a shallow angle. To return fire, the opponent had to dip his nose and thus risk a collision. His more usual reaction would be to break hard out of the line of fire. The head-on attack was very much a case of taking the opportunities that arose. If the attack was started too early, the target could safely nose down to reply. However, it could often be effectively combined with the scissors, one of the basic fighter manoeuvres which is still taught today. The scissors is a series of turn reversals aimed at forcing an attacker to overshoot, while giving him only fleeting high deflection shooting chances. There was little future in scissoring with an aircraft superior in manoeuvreability. However, if a Zero had been delivering an attack from above a Wildcat, its manoeuvreability would be comparatively reduced by its speed and the Wildcat might well be able to hold its own through a couple of reversals. A reversal would often result in the two aircraft approaching each other head-on; if the Wildcat had managed to get a bit lower than its opponent, it was then well placed for a head-on pass.

The Wildcat was outclassed by the Zero. It was slightly slower at most heights, with a much lower initial climb rate, comparatively sluggish acceleration and totally unable to compete in a turning match at speeds below 200 mph. The standard Japanese method of evasion was to haul into a steep climbing turn to the left, which the Wildcat was unable to follow. A pursued Wildcat could only hope that a friend would come and brush the Zero off his tail. On the rare occasions that the speed of the participants exceeded 250 mph the Wildcat could evade, due to the one serious weakness of the Japanese fighter. The Zero, built for incredibly tight turns, possessed a large wingspan and enormous ailerons. As speed increased the ailerons stiffened and at 290 mph or over, movement became almost impossible. The pilot of a Wildcat could start a diving turn, then when the Zero was committed to following, he would aileron turn in the opposite direction and pull out, leaving the Zero unable to follow.

Prior to the Pearl Harbour attack, many US Navy fighter squadron commanders had met and discussed tactics with operationally experienced Royal Air Force pilots. One major result was the almost universal adoption of the four aircraft division flying in two pairs. Encounters with the Zero soon made it clear that the only chance of redressing the performance balance lay in morale and teamwork. Lieutenant Commander James Flatley commanding fighter squadron VF 42, told his pilots: 'Let us not condemn our equipment. It shoots the enemy down in flames and gets most of us back to our base.' These words appear to indicate that American morale was slightly shaken by the performance of the Zero.

Lacking a better fighter, the American pilots were forced to rely to a great extent on teamwork. Lieutenant Commander John S. Thach commanding fighter squadron VF 3 had given much thought to fighting the Zero. One of the first US Navy Squadron commanders to adopt the four aircraft division and the fighting pair, he made an even more significant tactical breakthrough when he decided to fly the pairs abreast, spaced at a distance apart determined by the speed but typically about 3–400 yds. A cross look-out was kept on each other's tails, and the first section to see an attack coming in on the other pair, broke hard towards them. On seeing the first pair break inwards, the second pair would immediately break towards them, the pairs scissoring with each other. A Zero dropping on the tail of one section could follow his evading target around and be faced with a head-on attack from the other two, or break off his attack in a straight line, giving them the opportunity to reverse their turn and possibly get a fleeting shot. Either way it was an excellent counter to the bounce, and it did not require a radio warning. Thach called his brainwave the Beam Defence Manoeuvre, but widely adopted later by the US Navy, it became universally known as the Thach Weave.

The carrier battles of the Pacific contained problems unknown to land-based units. On return from a mission, the airfield could have moved 100 miles from the take-off point. The number of aircraft on board a carrier was limited by space and replacements could not arrive from the depot overnight. The striking power of the carrier was determined by the number of torpedo and divebombers it carried which limited the amount of space available for fighters. Consequently there were never enough fighters to go round. The ships needed protection and fighters had to be held back for defence, which limited the number available to escort the bombers. Escorting bombers was a dilemma. The low-level torpedo attack needed to be synchronised with the dive bombing attack to split the defences as much as possible. But with divebombers at 15,000 ft cruising at about 160 mph and the torpedo bombers anywhere between sea level and 6,000 ft, cruising nearly 40 mph slower, an adequate fighter escort was clearly out of the question. Thirty or more bombers often had to share between six and ten fighters between them.

The Americans had one great material advantage over the Japanese; their ships were equipped with radar and were thus far less dependent on the flying of standing patrols over their fleet, whereas the Japanese were obliged, in the combat area, to keep at least one *shotai* of three fighters per carrier aloft, a further *shotai* spotted for immediate launch, with a third at a lesser state of readiness. Without radar they were dependent on visual sightings and had no equivalent of the US Navy fighter control system. Never did this weakness cause more havoc than at Midway in June 1942, when a very badly co-ordinated American attack smashed the Japanese carrier force.

First to attack were the American torpedo squadrons from *Hornet* in their lumbering Devastators. The defending Zeros had a field day, and 25 out of 29 Devastators were lost. Next in came torpedo squadron VT 3 from *Yorktown*, escorted by the Wildcats of Lieutenant Commander Thach's VF 3. They were engaged by approximately 40 Zeros, all that were aloft at the time. When the Dauntlesses from *Hornet* and *Yorktown* arrived over the scene, the Japanese combat air patrol had been drawn to low level, thus giving the dive bombers an unopposed run. The fleet carriers *Akagi*, *Kaga* and *Soryu* were all fatally hit during this attack, leaving only *Hiryu*, of the original main strike force, still afloat.

Yorktown's strike was fairly typical of the inadequate fighter escort of the period. The Dauntless divebombers were launched first, closely followed by the Devastator torpedo bombers, which immediately set course. The Dauntlesses orbited overhead for 12 minutes before following. Finally came Thach's short-ranged Wildcats. After about 40 minutes, the Dauntlesses had caught up with the slow Devastators far below, and the Wildcats had overtaken both. Thach detached two Wildcats flown by Machinist Tom Cheek, and Ensign Daniel Sheedy, to escort the torpedo bombers, 1,000 ft above and just astern of them. Thach, with Lieutenant Nacomber and Ensigns Bassett and Dibb, adopted a central position at 5,500 ft, nearly 10,000 ft below VB 3. Unfortunately, Macomber, Bassett and Dibb had only recently joined the squadron and had never practiced the beam defence manoeuvre. In fact, only Dibb had even heard of it. This, as we are about to see, caused complications.

The *Yorktown* force was first spotted by the cruiser *Chikuma* which let fly with its main armament, alerting the Zeros already airborne. The Zeros came storming over, quickly shot down Bassett and smashed Macomber's radio.

The right-hand section turn hard into the attacked section, passing beneath them

Zero bounces the left-hand section from high astern

3–400 yds

Having scissored, the American fighters resume their original course with the positions of the sections reversed

The Japanese pilot has two choices. He can follow his target round and be attacked head on by the other American section or he can break the attack

The attacked section break hard towards the other section

Fig 36 Beam defence manoeuvre (Thach Weave).

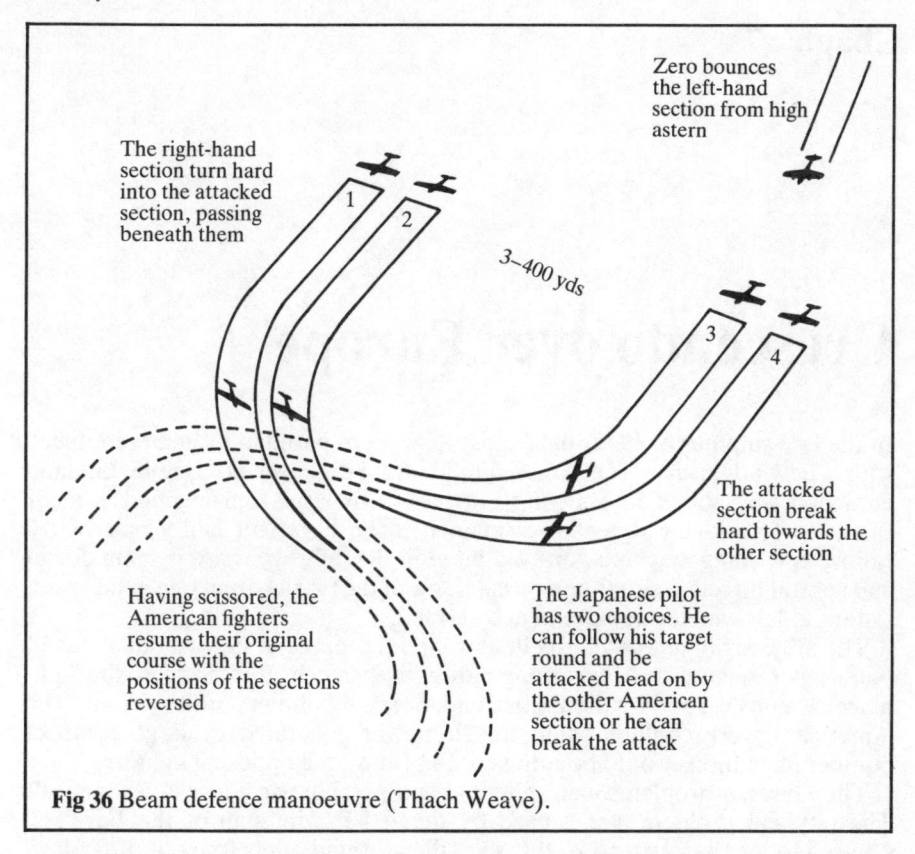

They then formed an orderly queque above and behind the Wildcats and launched a succession of high astern attacks. Instinctively, Thach tried to assume the beam defence position to counter, but Macomber's damaged radio prevented communication. Expecting Macomber to be pre-occupied in evading an attack, Thach pulled hard away into the beam defence position only to have Macomber frantically scramble back into close formation. Thach gave up and ordered Dibb out to the flank, a move which produced immediate results when Dibb was bounced and he and Thach, immediately scissored. The Zero followed Dibb round to be met head-on by Thach who passed under Dibb and opened fire, sending the Mitsubishi fighter down in flames. The action lasted 20 minutes in all, the Wildcats sustaining little further damage and claiming four enemy aircraft shot down. Thus was proved in action the 'Thach Weave' which prevented further losses while heavily outnumbered and allowed the Wildcats to get in some telling shots of their own. Even more important, it kept a high proportion of the Japanese defenders occupied, who otherwise might have been cutting a deadly swathe through the American bombers.

The most important tactical advance to emerge from the early air battles over the Pacific was undoubtedly the beam defence manoeuvre. This was the fore-runner of the fighting pair with two aircraft operating as mutual cover with either taking the lead as opportunity offered, instead of the shooter/cover relationship so prevalent in Europe.

Chapter 7

Crescendo over Europe

In the late summer of 1942, the Jagdgeschwadern based in France were faced with a new adversary. The American 8th Air Force was arriving in England equipped with the B-17 F Flying Fortress. This large four-engined bomber carried a formidable defensive armament. The F variant had a pair of .50 calibre Browning machine-guns mounted in the tail, two more pairs in dorsal and ventral turrets, a single gun on each side of the fuselage and one in the nose. Later models were even more heavily armed.

The .50 Browning was an excellent weapon, capable of spitting out about 14 bullets per second and its hitting power was much greater than the light machine-guns carried by the British and German bombers of the period. The Americans were confident that the firepower generated by large compact bomber formations would be sufficient to beat off the opposing fighters.

The German problems were physical and psychological as well as tactical. The physical problem was caused by the 104 ft wingspan of the Fortress. Unused to tackling aircraft of this size, the German pilots found it difficult to judge the range correctly. Consequently they tended to open fire when too far away, then break away too early. The psychological problem arose from a combination of the size of the target, the massed firepower of the bomber formations and the Fortress' undoubted ability to sustain damage while showing little apparent effect. These three factors combined to give an impression of invulnerability which was only gradually dispelled. It is interesting to note that the Japanese also gained the same impression of the Fortress.

The tactical problem proved more intractable. The standard fighter approach from 1,000 yds astern with an overtaking speed of 100 mph took over 18 seconds to close the distance down to 100 yds. Although American gunnery was not highly effective, with so many gunners actually firing, the approach from astern was fraught with danger. Mounting losses among the German fighter units could be redressed only by a new form of attack, from head-on.

On November 23 1942, the Fortresses raided the German-held port of St Nazaire. Major Egon Mayer intercepted with Jagdgeschwader 2. The four-aircraft Schwarm was dropped for this action, the three aircraft Kette was used. The bomber formations were based on multiples of three and each Kette attacked three bombers from head-on. Four Fortresses were brought down and a fifth badly damaged.

As the British had found two years earlier, the difficulty with the head-on attack was the very high closing speed. The attack started about 2 miles ahead

2 miles . . . . . 15 seconds

1 mile . . . . . 7 seconds

1,000 yds . . . 4 seconds

600 yds . . . 2½ seconds

250 yds . . . 1 second

100 yds . . . 2/5 second . . . Break

Fig 37 B 17 Attacked from head-on.

of the bombers. This gave the pilot about 15 seconds in which to select a target, aim, fire, and break away.

The Kette of three fighters was quickly dropped. When the bombers were escorted, the German pilots found that three-aircraft formations were too vulnerable. The head-on attack continued, however, with the German fighters in line astern or the entire unit spread out abreast in the 'company front' formation. The recommended procedure was to pull up and over the bombers and then from their position of advantage above, the German fighters were quickly able to launch another attack. The enormous tail fin of the Fortress posed an added collision risk and many German pilots preferred to break away below. Either they dipped the noses of their aircraft and passed close underneath, or rolled inverted and broke hard down with the Abschwung. This took them well below the bombers and valuable minutes were lost before they could regain sufficient height to attack again. However, if the bombers were escorted, this was the safest course.

The avowed intention of the American 8th Air Force was to bomb targets deep inside Germany in daylight. It soon became obvious that without escort fighters the bombers would suffer heavily. However, the Americans had no fighter with sufficient range. A temporary solution was therefore tried which would have gladdened the heart of General Douhet. The YB 40 was a standard Fortress converted into an aerial battleship. About 20 were built or converted and various combinations of armaments fitted. Reports speak of four .50s in powered nose and tail turrets, an extra dorsal turret with twin .50s or in at least one case, a 37 mm cannon, and triple gun installations in each waist position consisting of two .50 machine guns and a 20 mm cannon. Other heavy machine-guns were mounted wherever space could be found for them. No bombs were carried; the YB 40 flew solely to protect the bombers with its tremendous firepower.

The YB 40s made their operational debut on May 29 1943. Alas, they were a dismal failure and after a short and ineffective career were withdrawn from service. The weight of the extra armour plate, guns, ammunition and crew altered the centre of gravity aft. Trimming out the tail-heaviness adversely affected the flying characteristics. This, coupled with the drag of the extra guns, so degraded performance that the YB 40's had difficulty staying in formation with the bombers which they were supposed to protect. However, their ferocious firepower impressed the German fighter pilots greatly. So much so that they still reported an occasional encounter months after the YB 40 had been withdrawn from service! The concept of the flying battleship was once more laid back in the closet.

The early Fortress raids were escorted by British Spitfires. They were soon joined by the American P-38 Lightning. This large twin-engined fighter displayed many of the same short-comings against single-engined opponents as had the Me 110 in 1940 but the Americans badly needed a single-engined long range fighter for escort work.

The P-47 Thunderbolt appeared in the skies of Europe in April 1943. Initially it had little more range than the Spitfire, but additional fuel tanks that could be jettisoned, increased its radius of action. The German fighters had hitherto avoided contact until the escorting fighters were low on fuel and turned for home before setting about the unprotected bombers. The counter-move was simple. One German fighter unit was assigned to tackle the Thunderbolts. On

Fig 38

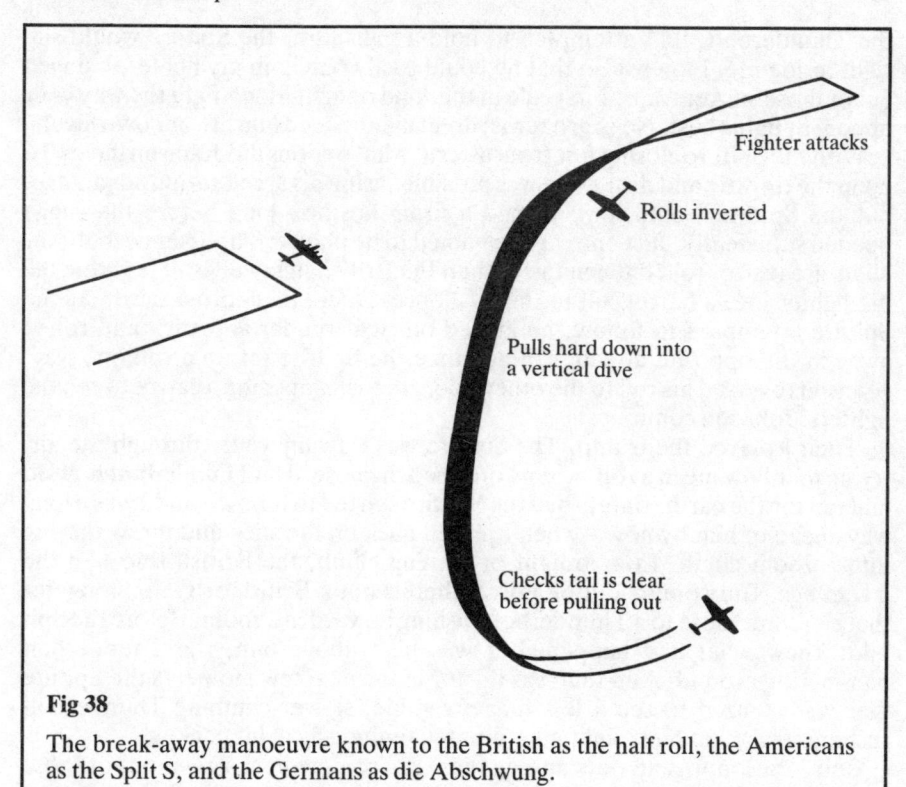

The break-away manoeuvre known to the British as the half roll, the Americans as the Split S, and the Germans as die Abschwung.

being attacked, the American pilots were forced to drop their auxiliary tanks before they could defend themselves. At a stroke they were thus deprived of their extra range.

The Thunderbolt proved to be a very successful fighter and first saw action with the 4th Fighter Group. The Group's pilots were mainly drawn from the three British Eagle Squadrons who had previously flown Spitfire Vs. They viewed their new mount with misgivings at first. It was huge. Optimised for high altitude work, the Thunderbolt had 5 ft more wingspan, a quarter more wing area, about four times the fuselage volume and nearly twice the weight of a Spitfire V. How, they asked, were they to tackle the small light German fighters in this massive aeroplane? Lieutenant Bob Johnson supplied part of the answer when on a training flight he encountered the latest version of the famous Spitfire, the Mark IX. The two pilots closed in and looked each other over. Bob Johnson had heard much about the new Spitfire and felt he had to match his Thunderbolt against it. Opening the throttle wide, he surged ahead. The Spitfire followed suit but the Thunderbolt's acceleration was better and the gap slowly widened. At high speed he hauled back on the stick and his huge fighter soared upwards, propelled by its own momentum. But as the initial impetus of the zoom climb was lost, the Spitfire, left trailing at first, caught up. In a sustained climb the British fighter was far superior and in Johnson's own words 'shot past me as though I were standing still'. Having achieved a height advantage, the Spitfire swung round, positioning itself to drop on to the tail of the Thunderbolt. 'If I attempted to hold a tight turn, the Spitfire would slip right inside me. I knew also that he could easily outclimb my fighter. I stayed out of those sucker traps. First rule in this kind of fight: don't fight the way your opponent fights best. No sharp turns; don't climb; keep him at your own level.'

With the Spitfire closing fast from astern, what options did Johnson have? To open the throttle and dive away was possible, using his acceleration advantage, but the Spitfire would have gained a firing position long before the range opened sufficiently. Just one card remained to be played. The Thunderbolt, for all its great size, rolled much faster than the British lightweight. He threw the big fighter into a barrel roll to the left, once, twice, then into a third. As the Spitfire attempted to follow, he kicked on right rudder and stick and rolled away in the opposite direction. Each time the Spitfire set up a roll one way, Johnson reversed his roll to the other side, gradually opening a gap between the fighters. Johnson continues:

'Then I played the trump. The Spitfire was clawing wildly through the air, trying to follow me in a roll, when I dropped the nose. The Thunderbolt howled and ran for the earth. Barely had the Spitfire started to follow – and I was a long way ahead of him by now – when I jerked back on the stick and threw the Jug into a zoom climb. In a straight or turning climb, the British ship had the advantage. But coming out of a dive, there's not a British or German fighter that can come close to a Thunderbolt rushing upward in a zoom. Before the Spit pilot knew what had happened, I was high above him, the Thunderbolt hammering around. And that was it – for in the next few moments the Spitfire flier was amazed to see a less maneuverable, slower climbing Thunderbolt rushing straight at him, eight guns pointed ominously at his cockpit.'

Bob Johnson was an outstanding flier. His comment, 'I stayed out of those sucker traps' is most revealing. His unknown sparring partner failed to observe the same rule. As soon as the Spitfire pilot found that he was unable to follow Johnson through the first roll (and we are discussing high 'G' barrel rolls; not pretty air display stuff), his counter should have been to pull high, circle and wait for Johnson to stop behaving like a demented bluebottle. This would have put the Spitfire beyond the reach of the Thunderbolt's zoom, with a height advantage ready to convert into speed to negate the American's level speed advantage. It is interesting to speculate on the outcome had the Englishman Johnny Johnson been flying the Spitfire.

Flying the Thunderbolt in action successfully, was therefore dependent on the ability of the pilot to use its strong points and avoid its weaknesses. Both the Me 109 and FW 190 could, like the Spitfire, out-turn and outclimb it. But whereas both German fighters could break hard downwards and leave the Spitfire trailing, if they tried this against the P-47, they were likely to achieve little more than a close-up view of a large radial engine and flame-edged wings just behind them. After diving, the German pilots often evaded a pursuing Thunderbolt with a hard turn. This frequently worked, but against Bob Johnson . . . : 'Almost at once the stream of exhaust smoke stopped; he (an Me 109) had cut his throttle and at the same moment pulled his fighter into a tight left turn. The same old mistake! The moment the smoke cut out I chopped power, skidded to my right, back on the stick and rolled inside his turn, firing steadily in short bursts. The Kraut glanced back to see a skyful of Thunderbolt wing spitting fire at him. I know he thought that I had cut inside of his own turn. . . .'

The clue here is that Johnson noticed the exhaust smoke from the Messerschmitt cease. This told him what his opponent was about to do and he was able to react instantly, using his advantage in the roll to nullify his opponent's superior turning ability.

It is a truism of the fighter world that the decisive factor in air combat is the man in the cockpit. When the P-47 made its debut, Luftwaffe pilot standards were falling. More than three years of continuous combat had stretched the ability of the training units to replace losses. German pilots were beginning to fall into two categories, veterans with 100s of hours combat experience, and novices, inexperienced and by Allied standards, undertrained.

The Americans, in contrast, were turning out fighter pilots with a very high standard of training. Many had more hours on type before entering combat,

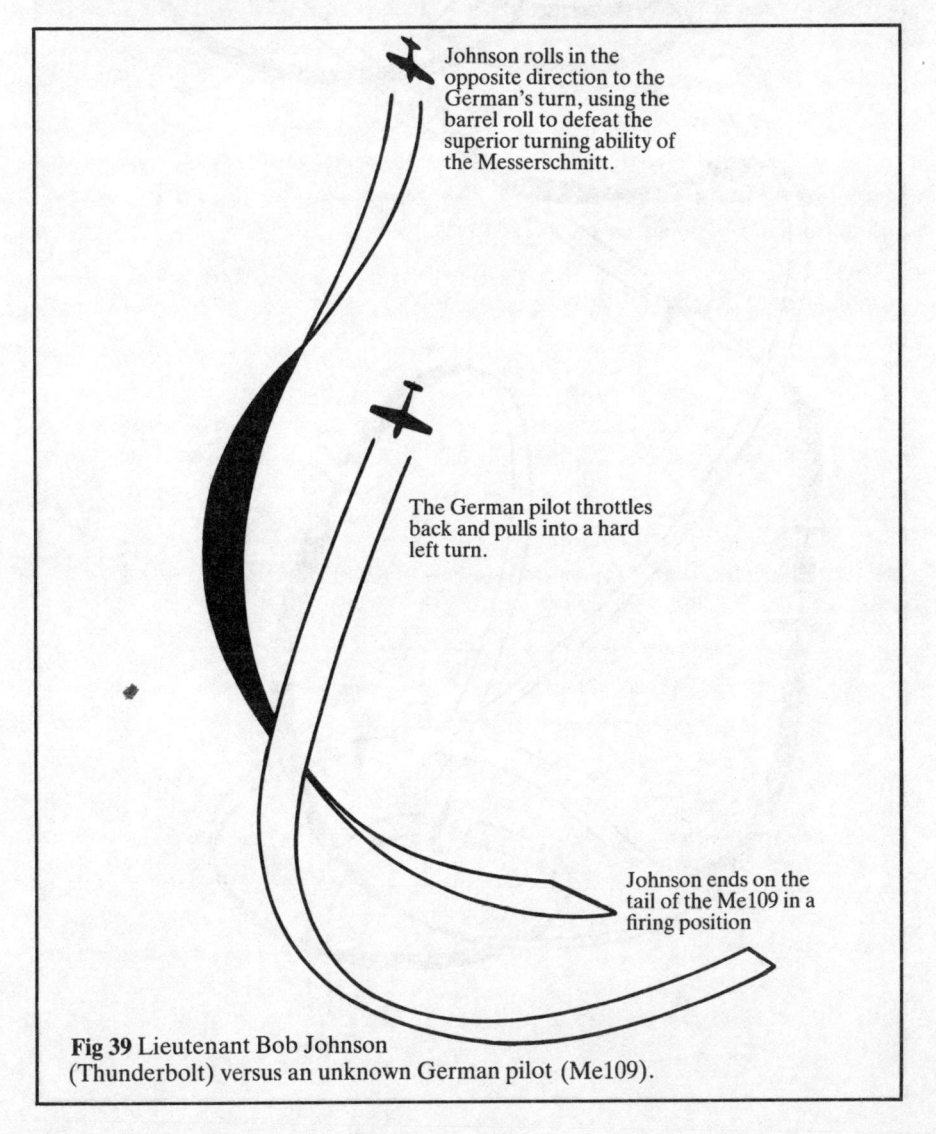

Johnson rolls in the opposite direction to the German's turn, using the barrel roll to defeat the superior turning ability of the Messerschmitt.

The German pilot throttles back and pulls into a hard left turn.

Johnson ends on the tail of the Me109 in a firing position

Fig 39 Lieutenant Bob Johnson (Thunderbolt) versus an unknown German pilot (Me109).

Fig 40

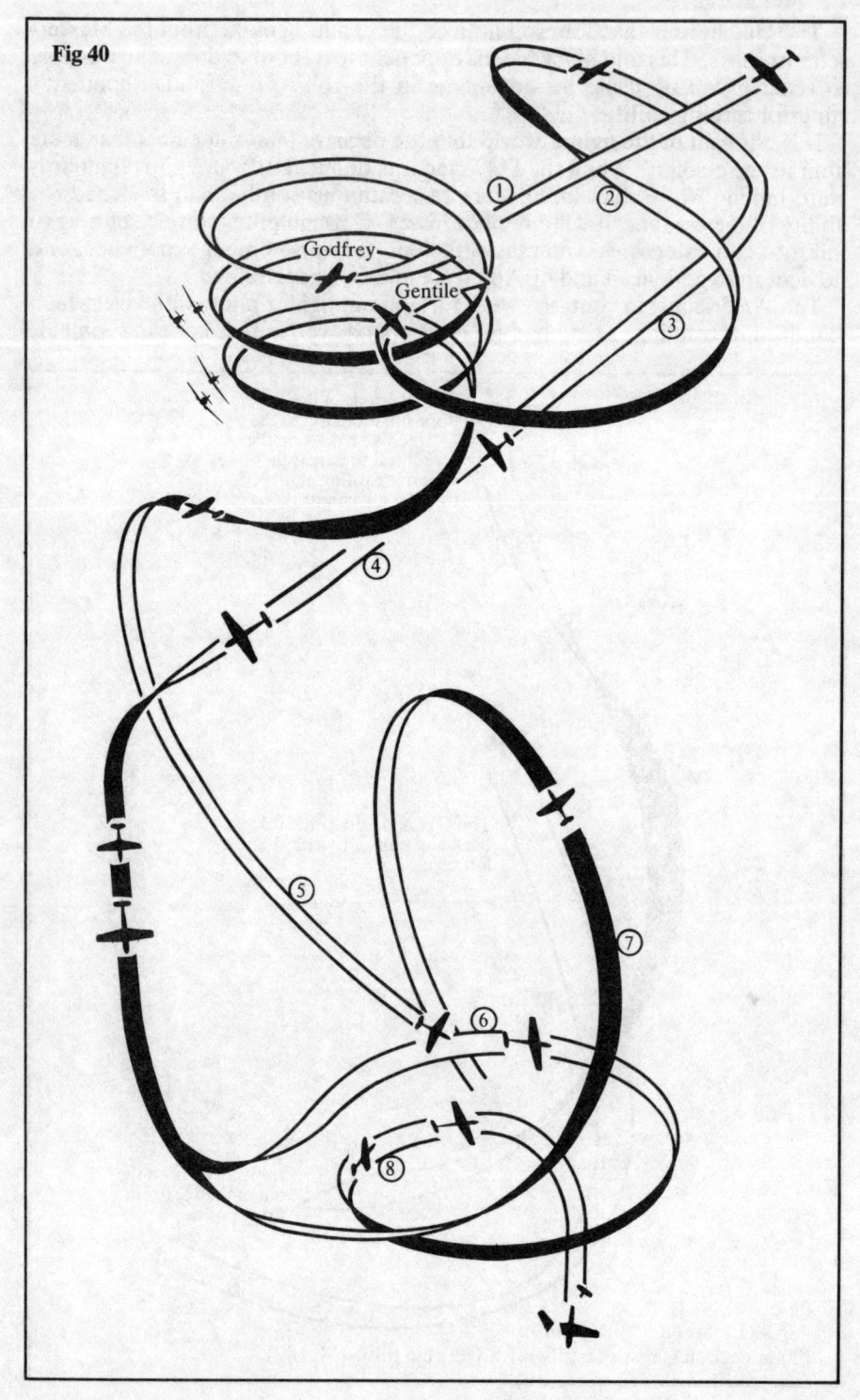

Fighter Pilot Tactics

than the Germans, (and the British) had total flying hours. They were thus more practiced and confident in their aeroplanes than their adversaries. Add to this the fact that the P-47 pilots were on the offensive and some of the reasons for the success of the Jug became clear. In the bounce, with their rapid acceleration downhill coupled with the pulverising effect of eight .50s, these aircraft were deadly. Yet well handled they could hold their own in a dogfight as well, mainly by teamwork, but to a degree by using the natural advantages which they possessed. In a defensive role the Thunderbolt would have been inadequate. Reade Tilley is to this day emphatic that had Malta been defended by Thunderbolts, rather than Spitfires, the defenders would have been annihilated. Its poor rate of sustained climb and lack of turning ability would have been fatal against the superior numbers of German fighters who almost invariably had a height advantage.

The main German concern was to stop the massive bomber raids and this could only be done by inflicting unacceptable casualties on them. Between January and June 1943 the Germans had nearly doubled their fighter strength in the west, but the bulk of these were stationed in the occupied territories or around the periphery of the Reich. However, Adolf Galland, by now the commander of the German fighter arm, disagreed with this. He advocated grouping the bulk of his forces centrally to oppose a raid in overwhelming strength. On April 17, Bremen was raided by 115 Fortresses escorted all the way by Lightnings. Galland commented: 'The defensive results were poor. Our widely drawn-out fighter forces could only get small groups of 20 to 25 aircraft to engage the enemy. They were much too weak to achieve anything decisive against the fighter-protected bomber force.'

What, in fact, were these poor results? Sixteen Fortresses were lost and 48 damaged. Fourteen percent lost and almost half the remainder damaged! On this day, the Luftwaffe had, as they were to do time and time again in the days to come, concentrated on the low squadron, the 401st Bomb Squadron, which was wiped out. Galland felt that sufficient concentration of force would be enough

---

Opposite

Fig 40 Godfrey and Gentile (Mustangs) versus Me109.

1) Me 109 bounces the two Mustangs which break in opposite directions. The German pilot follows Godfrey.
2) Gentile tries a head-on shot at the 109. He misses and the German fighter follows Godfrey through a series of tight turns.
3) Gentile reverses his turn and comes in behind the Messerschmitt.
4) The German fighter breaks with an *Abschwung* and dives vertically with Gentile in pursuit.
5) Godfrey is now the free fighter of the American pair. He dives after the Me 109 which pulls out and turns towards him, still with Gentile in pursuit.
6) The German turns away from Godfrey who drops in behind it.
7) As Godfrey takes up the pursuit, Gentile breaks upwards and awaits a further chance to attack.
8) Godfrey runs out of ammunition. He calls Gentile, who from his position of advantage above, dives down and finishes the 109

The teamwork in this combat was exceptional. As each Mustang in turn engaged the Me 109, the other sought a position of advantage ready to take over.

to completely annihilate a large raid. If this result could be achieved quickly, the American 8th Air Force would be compelled to rethink its entire strategy. On the other side of the Channel, General Ira C. Eaker, commanding the 8th Air Force wrote: 'If the growth of the German fighter strength is not arrested quickly, it may become literally impossible to carry out the destruction planned'.

The result of the Bremen raid showed that the German pilots had little difficulty in hitting the giant American bombers. The problem lay in inflicting sufficient damage to down them. German analysis showed that the average pilot scored one hit for every 50 shots fired. On average it took 20 hits from 20 mm cannon shells to shoot down a heavy bomber, while the light machine guns carried by the German fighters were of little value. Clearly greater hitting power was needed.

Experiments were carried out in dropping time-fused bombs on the tightly packed American formations. After one or two successes, this was abandoned. The difficulties of flying in formation at a pre-determined height above the bombers were too great, especially when the bombers were escorted. The bomb-laden Me 109s of 5 Staffel Jagdgeschwader 11 had intercepted the Bremen raiders on their homeward run, but not a single bomb scored.

By mid-1943, German fighters were being equipped with 30 mm cannon. Its shells were sufficiently devastating to knock down a heavy bomber with only three or four hits. Unfortunately it was a low velocity weapon and its effective range was even shorter than its 20 mm predecessor. The situation had a certain grim irony; less hits were needed but the German pilots had to come in even closer to obtain them and were thus more vulnerable to the bombers' return fire.

If the bomber formations could be split up, the defensive crossfire was much reduced and the attack from astern with its greater chance of hitting could be used. Air to air bombing had sometimes achieved this but was too unreliable. In August 1943 a different weapon was tried. This was the 21 cm rocket mortar, an army weapon which proved capable of being adapted for use with fighters. On August 17, the Me 109's of 5 Staffel Jagdgeschwader 11 took off with two of these weapons slung under the wings. Oberleutnant Heinz Knocke leading the Staffel takes up the story: 'Over Antwerp we established contact with the Fortresses accompanied by an escort of Spitfires. My stovepipes (mortars) make an engagement with Spitfires impossible for me. I do not wish to jettison them, except in case of an emergency. For the moment I shall have to wait for a chance to attack later. I trail the Fortresses, which are divided into a number of groups, all heading south-west, keeping off to the side and waiting for the moment when the Spitfires turn about in order to reach England again.

'Eventually, I have an opportunity to attack in the Aachen area. Before I am able to open fire however, my left wing is hit and the left stovepipe shot away. I can hardly hold the unbalanced aircraft on an even keel. A large hole gapes in my left wing. I am afraid that the main spar is damaged. It is possible that the wing will come off completely under too great a strain. I must avoid sharp turns, and shall try to fire my second rocket at the enemy.

'My pilots have meanwhile, discharged their rockets to good effect. Fuermann and Fest each score direct hits. Their bombers explode in mid-air. The remainder do not have any effect as far as we can tell. My own rocket also passes through the middle of the formation without hitting anything.'

Above The Zero was incredibly manoeuvrable for its time and earned a formidable reputation in the early months of the Pacific War. Its ascendancy was lost as the number of experienced Japanese pilots dwindled and the Allies introduced new and superior types (*Alfred Price*).

Below The American Wildcat was almost totally outperformed by the Zero. It was, however, a very tough aeroplane and its ability to survive battle damage, coupled with outstanding teamwork by the American Navy pilots, enabled it to hold its own (*Archiv Schiephake*).

Above The Mustang was the first really long range escort fighter. The aircraft shown is from the 4th Fighter Group and was the personal mount of Captain Don Gentile, one of whose combats is analysed in Chapter 7 (*IWM*).

Left The Me 262 was the world's first operational jet fighter. Its outstanding performance was only countered by the vast Allied numerical superiority (*Alfred Price*).

Fighter Pilot Tactics

Above Reade Tilley in the cockpit of his Spitfire Vc in Malta. The revetment behind the aircraft is partly made of petrol cans filled with sand and men from the Navy are in evidence assisting the armourers on the wing (*IWM*).

Right Pilot Officer Reade Tilley, who composed the tactical paper 'Hints on Hun Hunting', as a result of his experiences on Malta. Tilley was a pre-war racing driver. This was not exciting enough so he volunteered to fly for Finland against Russia in the Winter War. He reached London but the war ended, so he volunteered for the Royal Air Force, and flew with one of the all-American Eagle Squadrons. In 1942 he went to Malta where he saw much action. He transferred to the USAAF and retired with the rank of Colonel (*Mike Spick*).

Above A typical British fighter formation of the early part of the Second World War. Hurricanes of No 1 (F) Squadron in Vics. Serviceability appears high; 21 aircraft are in the air. During the Battle of Britain it was rare for formations more than 12 strong to be used (*Mike Spick*).

Below Oberleutnant Julius Neumann in the cockpit of his Me 109E of II Gruppe, Jagdgeschwader 27. This unit operated from Crepon and used advanced landing grounds near Cherbourg to increase its radius of action to cover Portland, Southampton and Portsmouth. For the long over-water flight a special 'over-water' paint scheme was used which can be seen here. Shortly after this picture was taken, the Me 109 was hit in combat and crash-landed on the Isle of Wight (*Mike Spick*).

Above The F89 Scorpion was designed for collision course interception to destroy bombers at night or in poor weather conditions. Here it demonstrates its awesome battery of unguided rockets. A bomber caught in the 'shotgun' pattern would have stood little chance of survival (*Northrop Corporation*).

Below The F86 Sabre was a heavier and more sophisticated fighter than the MiG 15. Generally inferior to the MiG 15 at high altitudes, its transient performance compensated for other shortcomings. In Korea the dominant factor was pilot quality (*Real Photographs*).

Above The Russian-built MiG 15 gave the West a nasty shock when it appeared over Korea. It was a simple, no-frills fighter with an exceptionally good high altitude performance (*USAF*).

Below The Mirage III achieved a fearsome reputation in the capable hands of Israeli pilots in successive Middle Eastern Wars. As a fighter it achieved nothing against the Sea Harriers of the Royal Navy in the Falklands conflict (*Avions Marcel Dassault*).

Above Successful in the Falklands, the Sea Harrier remains controversial as a fighter. Argument as to the efficacy of VIFFing continues. However, certain advantages cannot be denied. It is small and difficult to see. It has a very high thrust/weight ratio. Doubts about its ability to sustain battle damage have now been silenced (*Rolls-Royce*).

Below The F-15 Eagle is the world's most capable single-seat fighter. It is also very large and expensive. It has been operated successfully by the Israeli Air Force but little hard information has been released (*McDonnell Douglas*).

Above The F-14 Tomcat is arguably the world's most advanced weapons system. Designed for fleet defence, it is an interceptor rather than a dogfighter, with long endurance and an extremely long-range kill capability (*Grumman*).

Below The F-4E Phantom II is one of the most successful fighters of the last 20 years, and has seen action in South-East Asia and the Middle East. Over 5,000 have been built and it is in service with many air forces around the world (*Minyon Prescott*).

Equipping fighters with heavy armament had its limitations. Heinz Knocke was unable to attack until Aachen, beyond the range of the fighter escort. The rocket mortar was a very difficult weapon to use; its low velocity called for an aiming point some 200 ft above the bombers. In this action less than one in ten missiles exploded close enough to the bombers to inflict mortal damage and the fighters were still within range of effective return fire from the bombers, as the damage sustained by Knocke's 109 shows.

The engagement described occurred in the early stages of the first deep-penetration raid on Schweinfurt. Under continual attack, the bombers fought their way through and hit the target successfully. Their losses were, however, prohibitive. While the number of bombers shot down was relatively low, many of the aircraft that returned were only fit for the scrap heap. The Americans were forced to continue the search for a long range escort fighter good enough to tackle the Messerschmitts and Focke-Wulfs on level terms.

The answer was the Mustang. This small, agile fighter had the range to fly to Berlin and back. The radius of action of the Thunderbolt was also considerably increased. At first the long range American escort fighters stayed close to the bombers, working in relays. As the months passed and experience was gained, close escort tactics were modified. Other squadrons, 16 aircraft strong, ranged up and down the bomber's course, seeking out and attacking the German fighters where ever they found them. The twin engined Me 110s and 410s, which had appeared in daylight as bomber destroyers, were swept from the skies. The Germans certainly had problems. It was impracticable for them to degrade the performance of the German single-engined fighters by hanging bulky rocket launchers under the wings, since if these aircraft encountered escort fighters while so encumbered, they were sitting ducks.

The British fighters played an active, if secondary role, in the American daylight raids. They frequently provided the initial and final stages of the escort. They mounted fighter sweeps over German airfields in France and the Low Countries, thus tying down German fighters that would have been more gainfully employed elsewhere.

By early 1944, fighting formations had stabilised with the British and Americans using the finger-four while the Luftwaffe generally used fours abreast. Either formation on encountering enemy fighters, used what was long to be considered the classic fighting pair, the leader with his wingman to cover him. The reason for this is stated by Mustang pilot John C. Meyer in a report to the United States War Department. 'Mainly it's my wingman's eyes I want. One man cannot see enough. When attacked I want first for him to warn me then for him to think. Every situation is different and the wingman must have initiative and ability to size up the situation properly and act accordingly. There is no rule of thumb for a wingman.'

A fighter aeroplane is a very expensive piece of equipment but the leader/wingman relationship with one attacking and the other trailing around protecting him, would appear at first sight wasteful. In practice it was the only way to achieve effective results. Clearly the individual fighter pilot of whatever nation wanted to shoot down enemy aeroplanes and be successful. But most of all he wanted to survive. As a result, his time in combat was spent torn between two conflicting priorities, success and survival. Success could be deferred until the morrow but survival could not. And since no pilot could look in two directions at once, forward to attack and astern to defend, his concentration in attack was weakened. He needed someone to guard his tail and only when secure in the knowledge that he could not be attacked without warning, was a pilot able to focus all his attention on his target.

There were occasions when roles were reversed, as noted by the Russian Colonel Dubrov in an article published in *Aviatsiya i Kosmonautika*. If the wingman noticed the enemy first and was in a more advantageous position, the wingman attacked and his leader covered him. The next tactical step was for the pair to make co-ordinated attacks. Possibly the best example of this in published form is the action described in *The Look of Eagles* by John T. Godfrey. Godfrey usually flew paired with Don Gentile, first in Thunderbolts then later in Mustangs. Godfrey and Gentile were an exceptional team. Johnny Johnson, the top scoring allied pilot of World War 2 described them as 'the best pair ever to fight over Germany'. On the day in question they were escorting Fortresses in the target area. 'Don was the first to see the Me 109. "Johnny, at six o'clock high there's a single bandit." I looked back and there he was high above us. I gazed in disbelief as his nose dropped and he plummeted down on us. "Don, the crazy son of a bitch is bouncing us." "I know. When I yell 'Break', you break right and I'll break left." I watched as the 109 dropped closer and closer. "Break Johnny." I pulled away sharply to the right, and thought at first I had broken too late as the 109 pulled on to my tail. I tightened my turn and met Don halfway around as he tried to fire on the 109 in a head-on attack. I went around twice more with the Jerry on my tail before Don could reverse his turn and swing down for a rear attack. But this German was a smart capable flyer. As Don brought his guns to bear, he performed a split S and dived to the ground. Don and I followed him, our motors roaring in pursuit. He pulled out of his dive and banked left which brought him close to me. I followed him and fired. He wasn't one to sit still however and changed his turn to swing into Don. I followed, firing intermittently. Don meanwhile, had climbed for altitude and I kept the Jerry busy in a tight turn. As I fired, I saw flashes on his wing fuselage and even his motor, but the pilot wouldn't bale out. We were now just above the tree tops and the 109s engine was spewing smoke. I had no fore-warning that my ammunition was running out, but as I prepared for the final burst only silence came as I pressed the tit. "Finish him Don, I'm out of ammunition." Don, who had been manoeuvring above us waiting for the Jerry to break out of the turn, zoomed down in front of me and made one pass on the courageous German flyer. His shots hit home'.

In this action the leadership of the pair passed from one pilot to the other as circumstances demanded. The unengaged Mustang manoeuvred so as to resume the attack as required. This was a most effective way of using the fighting pair, but it could only be done in small scale engagements. With dozens of aircraft attacking one another in a small space of sky, it was impossible to use this leader/leader style of flying as the free aircraft of the pair would almost certainly be cut off and separated from his colleague.

In a small-scale encounter, the sequence of combat was, detect-identify-close-manoeuvre-attack-disengage. In the surprise bounce the manoeuvre phase was often omitted entirely, the attack being immediate and deadly. In a sky full of fighting aeroplanes, the sequence reduced to, look-shoot-break and frequently just look-break. These shorter sequences involved a few seconds; there was simply no time to cycle through the complicated manoeuvre patterns which were possible in small engagements.

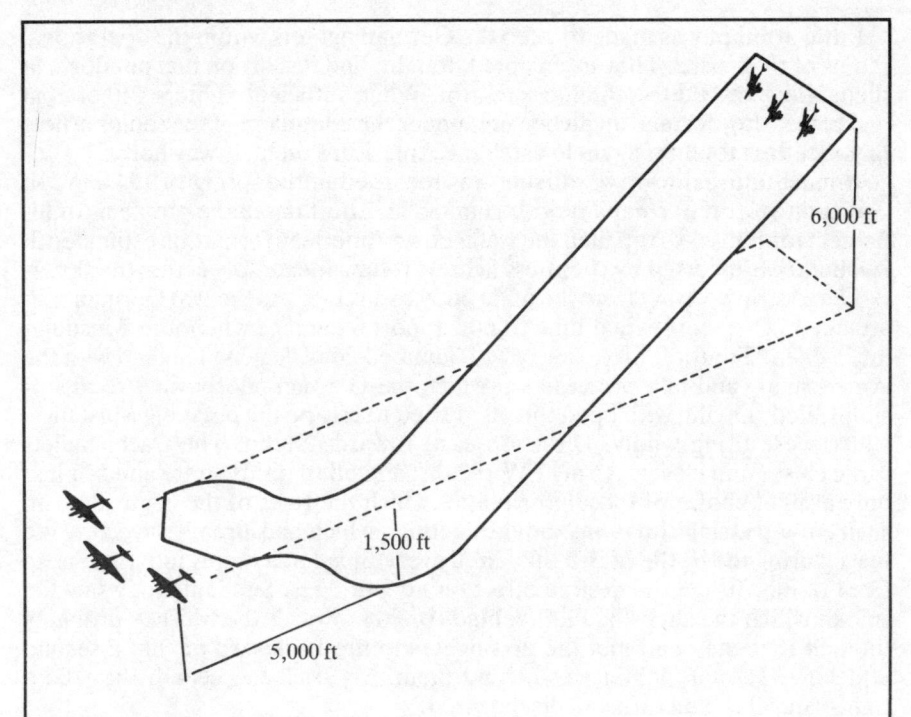

Fig 41 The roller coaster attack.

The fast shallow dive took the German jets through the escorting American fighters so fast that there was little risk of interception. However, their closing speed on the bombers was too great for accurate shooting and they were forced to 'mush off' excess speed with a sharp pull-up at the bottom of their dive.

With the advent of the new American long-range fighters the Germans were caught on the horns of a dilemma. The need to inflict unacceptable casualties on the bombers was more pressing than ever. To do this, the German fighters needed to carry very heavy armament. The weight of this armament decreased performance to the point where their aircraft were sitting ducks if caught by the American fighters, who were now likely to appear in large numbers anywhere over Germany.

The Luftwaffe answer to the problem was a compromise, the Gefechtsverband (battle formation). It consisted of a Sturmgruppe of heavily armed and armoured FW 190s escorted by two Begleitgruppen of light fighters, often Me 109Gs, whose task it was to occupy the Thunderbolts and Mustangs while the FW 190s tackled the bombers. This arrangement was excellent in theory but difficult to apply in practice. The massive German formation took a long while to assemble (as had the British Duxford Wing in 1940) and was difficult to manoeuvre. It was often intercepted by the American escorts and broken up before reaching the bombers. When the Sturmgruppe did connect they were devastating. With their engines and cockpits heavily armoured, they often braved the storm from the bombers and attacked from astern. Gun camera film shows that these astern attacks were often pressed to within 100 yds.

Little attempt was made to keep the German fighters within the operational radius of their base. They intercepted, fought, and if short on fuel put down at the nearest airfield to refuel and re-arm. When sufficient fighters gathered at one place, they formed an ad hoc unit under the command of the senior officer present, then took off again to catch the Americans on their way home.

A most unusual form of evasion was recorded in the spring of 1944. Adolf Galland took off in company with Hannes Trautloft to see the problems of his fighters for himself. Appalled, he watched an American formation estimated at 800 bombers escorted by countless fighters rolling inexorably across the sky. A B-17 had strayed away from the main body of aircraft and the two German aces attacked. They barely had time to inflict mortal damage when four Mustangs intervened. Trautloft broke away with jammed guns, leaving Galland with the Americans – and in a predicament which the German pilot vividly recalls. 'I simply fled. Diving with open throttle I tried to escape the pursuing Mustangs, which were firing wildly. Direction east, towards Berlin. The tracer bullets came closer and closer. As my FW 190 threatened to disintegrate and as I had only a small choice of those possibilities which the rules of the game allow in such embarrassing situations, I did something which had already saved my life twice during the Battle of Britain: I fired everything I had simply into the blue in front of me. It had the desired effect on my pursuers. Suddenly they saw the smoke which the shells had left behind coming towards them. They probably thought that they had met the first fighter to fire backward or that a second attacking German fighter was behind them. My trick succeeded; they did a right-hand climbing turn and disappeared.'

From Galland's account it is clear that the Mustangs could stay with the FW 190 in a dive. The reference to the German fighter threatening to disintegrate is almost certainly a sign that it had started to approach the speed of sound and was buffetting badly. The Mustangs probably experienced the same effect. They may also have been showered with spent cartridge cases and links which would give the impression of hits being scored. However, the ruse worked.

With no hope of redressing the numerical imbalance, the Luftwaffe needed a considerable improvement in the quality of its fighters. Hopes rose with the entry into service of the jet-propelled Me 262 during the last months of the war. It was 100 mph faster than contemporary piston-engined fighters and well armed with four 30 mm cannon. However, in the head on attack, the closing speed of about 350 yds per second was too high for accurate shooting. Even from astern the closing speed was too great for the short-ranged 30 mm cannon to be used to maximum effect. To overcome this the roller-coaster attack was devised. The jets approached from astern and about 6,000 ft higher than the bombers. From about 3 miles behind they launched into a shallow dive until they were about a mile astern and 1,500 ft below the bombers. This shallow but fast dive took them through the escort fighters with little risk of interception. At the bottom they pulled up sharply to 'mush off' their excess speed. On levelling out they were well placed to attack, 1,000 yds astern and overtaking the bombers at about 100 mph.

The Me 262 was difficult for its opponents to counter, but it had its weaknesses. By contemporary standards its wing loading was high (60 lb per square foot) and its rate of turn was correspondingly poor. Dogfights therefore had to be avoided. Oberst Johannes Steinhoff encountered a dozen Russian fighters early in 1945. 'I passed one that looked as if it was hanging motionless in the air (I'm too fast!). The one above me went into a steep right-hand turn, his pale blue underside standing out against the purple sky. Another banked right in front of the Me's nose. Violent jolt as I flew through his airscrew eddies. Maybe a wing's length away. That one in the gentle left-hand curve! Swing her round. I was coming from underneath, eye glued to the sight (pull her tighter!"). A throbbing in the wings as my cannon pounded briefly. Missed him. Way behind his tail. It was exasperating. I would never be able to shoot one down like this. They were like a sack of fleas. A prick of doubt: is this really such a good fighter? Could one in fact successfully attack a group of erratically banking fighters with the Me 262?'

The answer to this question was No. As has been previously noted, four out of five fighters shot down never saw their assailant. The overwhelming speed advantage of the Me 262 gave it every chance of achieving this. Therefore it was an outstanding fighter. But not in the dogfight.

What measures could the Allies take to counter the superb German jet? If they could draw it into a turning contest where its speed advantage was lost, its effectiveness was lost also. At low speeds it lacked acceleration. However, an experienced Me 262 pilot would not allow this to happen. It could be swamped by sheer numbers. On rare occasions it could be caught by a Spitfire, Mustang or Tempest where they had a considerable height advantage. The only really positive method to employ was to patrol the approaches of known Me 262 airfields and hope to catch them landing or taking off. The endurance of the Me 262 was short and on its final approach to land it was at its most vulnerable, flying slowly and almost out of fuel. A high proportion of the German jets lost were shot down in this way.

The last unit of Me 262s to be formed was Jagdverband 44. Never more than a dozen aircraft strong, it was composed almost entirely of aces under the command of General-Leutnant Galland. JV 44 generally flew in Ketten of three aircraft. German runways were just wide enough to permit three Me 262s to take off in line abreast. By using formation take-offs the time and fuel spent in forming up was reduced to a minimum.

Also in limited service during the last year of the war was the worlds first rocket-propelled fighter – the Me 163. This was an interceptor with an endurance of only a few minutes. Its one great advantage was a rate of climb that would take it to 30,000 ft in just over two and a half minutes. The bomber formations, flying at a stately 180 mph covered less than eight miles in this time. The Me 163 could sit on the ground until contrails appeared in the distance before taking off to intercept. In practice the rocket fighter achieved little. Its attack problems were much the same as the Me 262, but aggravated by lack of endurance. Nevertheless, the Me 163 was a very small aeroplane and with the motor throttled back stood a good chance of approaching its prey undetected. However, with the throttle open, it trailed dense smoke across the sky and was visible for miles. Its greatest disadvantage was the volatile nature of its fuel. Accidental explosions were commonplace and it probably caused more casualties to the Germans than to its opponents. Had it been reliable in service and possessed greater endurance, then in large numbers it would have been a force to reckon with. But without these attributes it was a failure.

As the tempo of the American daylight attacks mounted, it became clear that the German fighters were losing the Battle of Germany. August 1944 saw 22 major attacks on targets in Germany, each by hundreds of heavy bombers.

American bomber losses were 307. The Luftwaffe lost 301 fighters with 270 pilots killed, missing or wounded. This rate of exchange was disastrous for the Germans and it became clear that desperate measures were needed. The requirement was to bring down 5–600 heavy bombers in one operation. This, it was argued, would stop the American raids completely for at least a month and give both German industry and the Luftwaffe a much needed breathing space.

The only way to achieve a result on this scale was to mount a large-scale ramming attack. Ramming had been discussed since 1943 as a means of bringing down bombers. Sturmgruppe pilots occasionally rammed their opponents when all else failed; Major Walter Dahl had already survived two such attacks. Late in 1944, Oberst Hans-Joachim Herrman submitted detailed proposals for a massive ramming attack. He proposed using about 800 high altitude Me 109 Gs with guns, armour and all unnecessary equipment stripped out. Thus lightened they could climb rapidly to 36,000 ft, beyond the reach of the American escorts. High above the bombers they could pick their targets and dive, passing through the escorts too fast for effective interception to be possible.

The German pilot loss was expected to be around the 300 mark. Herrman had done his homework carefully, assessing the known results of both deliberate ramming attacks and accidental collisions. His anticipated pilot losses were no more than those of a normal month's fighting. Aircraft losses would be higher, but Germany was not short of aircraft. The effect on the American bomber force would have been catastrophic.

Fully trained fighter pilots were not to take part in the ramming attack. Volunteers were called for from the fighter training units but time was running out. The first of the ramming units, Sonderkommando Elbe did not start forming until April 1945, but this was far too late and a mere 120 aircraft eventually took off on the only mission flown. It was a dismal failure. Fifteen bombers were rammed and of these seven struggled back to England. The inadequately trained pilots had been unable to achieve worth-while results.

Chapter 8

The setting of the Rising Sun

The Battle of Midway and the bitter and protracted fighting over Guadalcanal later in the year cost the Japanese Navy many experienced pilots. The flying schools were unable to keep pace with demand; training was shortened and novice pilots were rushed to combat units to fill the gaps. Numerically the units were up to strength, but the kind of experience gained by the veterans of combat against the Chinese and Russians, could not be replaced. From mid-1943, a decline in pilot quality became evident. The aircraft were modified but the effects were fairly marginal. The Model 52 Zero appeared, its wingspan reduced to give better rolling performance, but it was still basically the same old Zero.

The Japanese Army Air Force was in slightly better shape. Their combat losses had also been high but at least their waterborne airfields had not been sunk with the attendant loss of highly trained and experienced pilots. The standard Army fighter at the outbreak of war had been the Type 97. Designed as a dogfighter, it had in pre-service trials demonstrated the ability to turn through a complete circle at 150 mph in just over eight seconds with a radius of turn of less than 95 yds. Successful over China and Nomonghan, it was by the standards of 1942 slow, vulnerable and undergunned, and was in the process of being replaced by the slightly faster Type 1 Hayabusa (codenamed Oscar by the Allies). The Hayabusa became the workhorse of the Japanese Army Air Force and with a performance closely comparable to the Zero, posed similar problems to its opponents. As the war lengthened, it was, like its naval counterpart, progressively modified and up-gunned. With the exception of turning ability, it never approached the performance of its Allied contemporaries.

Concerned by their experiences against the Russians in 1938, and influenced by European fighter development, the Japanese High Command had begun to change course. From manoeuvrability, their priorities now became speed and rate of climb. This radical change led to the Hien and Shoki which entered service from late 1942. These new fighters were closely comparable to contemporary Allied fighters in performance and wing loading, and featured some armour protection for the pilot and fuel tanks.

By mid-1943 the triumphant sweep of the Japanese forces across the Pacific had been halted and from this point onwards they fought defensively. An Allied document *Japanese Air Tactics up to May 1944* noted some fundamental changes. 'At the end of 1943, the Japanese were observed to have adopted the standard Allied fighter tactical unit of flights of four aircraft composed of two pairs. Another outstanding event during the last twelve months has been the introduction into service of the high performance single-engined fighter Tojo (Shoki). Its peformance, especially its speed, climb and dive is more nearly comparable to modern Allied fighters.

'It is with the newest and fastest fighters that the Japanese have adopted the tactical formation of two pairs of aircraft, and Tojo and Tony (Hien) especially are found employing it. The older and slower Oscar (Hayabusa) has also been reported in this formation, but some of the slower fighters still use the original three aircraft formation, which has been effective when all pilots were experienced and capable of breaking formation to go into combat independently.'

Some of the tricks used by the Japanese were stressed. The use of ruses was left to the discretion of the individual Japanese unit commander, but the following occurred often enough to merit a mention. 'Deceptive tactics of various kinds continue to be used extensively in efforts to lure Allied aircraft out of formation. Decoys with indifferent camouflage are used, which fly straight and level at about 15,000 ft while a patrol of well camouflaged aircraft waits high up. Other examples of the Japanese liking for deceits and feints are:

'(i), The staging of fake dogfights.

'(ii), The performance of aerobatics to attract attention while the attack comes in from another direction.

'(iii), A Japanese fighter on the flank of an Allied formation feints an attack while a second dives from ahead and above; then the attacker takes up the flank position and the feinter moves up ahead to repeat the same tactics.

'(iv), Japanese fighters would station themselves on either flank to draw attention while one was always up in the sun ready to attack.

'(v), Three Japanese fighters would position themselves on one flank while three were up in the sun; one would dive out of the sun and after his attack would take up a flank position, then one of the wing fighters would move up into the sun and the manoeuvre would be repeated in constant rotation'.

The last three ploys were almost certainly only used against bomber formations; it is difficult to imagine the well trained and aggressive Allied fighter squadrons tamely submitting to them. Specifically against fighters, the report noted: 'Head on attacks against Allied fighters are generally avoided, probably because the Japanese armour is still inadequate against the fire power of Allied fighters. Attacks are usually made from high astern or from above and the side. Japanese fighter pilots attempt to draw their opponents into a steep climb and into a stalling position, and then do a quick stall turn or loop back onto their opponent's tail. In order to make the most of their superior manoeuvreability, the Japanese fighter pilots often prefer to be jumped, and then execute a quick turn to get on their opponent's tail, rather than initiate the attack. . . . Their favourite evasive tactics are half rolling and diving away, or steep turns and climbs.'

Against heavy bomber formations, the head on attack was preferred although rather surprisingly the Japanese fighters seem not be have displayed the Banzai mentality so often attributed to their nation but preferred to be more cautious. The report continues: 'He can often be turned by a long burst at maximum range: his so-called suicide mania is not in evidence and there is no report of his having rammed any of our bomber aircraft or having shown any inclination to do so. He respects the fire of heavy bombers and a concentration of tracers usually affects him. This is not to imply that he lacks courage. He often presses attacks to very close range in the face of a well-flown formation, but he does this less often than against individual aircraft or against weaknesses in guns.'

This was the Allied view. What of the Japanese themselves? An official instruction to Japanese fighter pilots fell into Allied hands in February 1944. The salient points were:

'(1) Keep out of the field of fire of revolving turrets on Allied aircraft.

'Against small aircraft:

'(2) Keep clear of a cone of 30 degrees behind the tail.

'(3) Attack from the upper or lower rear or from the beam.

'(4) The Flight or Squadron Commander must always be followed, and against an Allied formation a simultaneous attack is to be made.

'Against medium bombers:

'(5) Attack from the upper rear or from the beam; use a frontal attack only in an unavoidable situation, in which case attack from above or below.

'(6) Avoid a cone of 30 degrees behind the tail.

'(7) The Flight or Squadron Commander must always be followed as to the method of attack.

'Against heavy bombers:

'(8) Attack from the front, below and towards the side or above and towards the side.

'(9) In attack, one flight alternating with one squadron will select targets as indicated by the formation leader and hamper the bomber's evasive tactics.

'(10) In the case of attacks make from left and right when one side has finished, the other will immediately take up the attack. The flight on each side will then repeat its attack.'

It can be seen from the Japanese instructions that the cautious approach noted in the Allied Paper was very real. It appears that the Japanese commanders, aware of the growing numerical and technical inferiority, were concerned to keep an effective force in being.

Items (2) and (6) are interesting as they deliberately eschew the no-deflection tail shot favoured over Europe. The Japanese fighters were generally more vulnerable to return fire than their Western counterparts. Another reason suggests itself in the following account of an action over Palembang in January 1945. Hideyaki Inayama of the 87th Sentai of the Japanese Army Air Force was pursuing a damaged Avenger divebomber. 'Six hundred yards . . . 500 yds . . . suddenly its ball turret gunner opened fire. Red tracers slipped past my Shoki, but I held my fire. 200 yds . . . I could clearly see the gunner in the ball turret. Now I was flying in the wash of my quarry and my aircraft was bounding around like a mad thing. Steadying the Shoki I fired at point blank distance. The bullets from my four 13 mm guns ripped into the Avenger, its "greenhouse" canopy bursting into fragments like leaves in a gale. . . . The Avenger rolled over onto its back and then fell away.'

Inayama's Shoki was very closely comparable in size, wing loading and general performance with the German Me 109E of 1940. By Japanese fighter standards it was a heavyweight. Yet it could be bounced about by the turbulence of a single-engined Avenger sufficiently to make shooting difficult. Inayama was an experienced pilot and could cope with the problem. An inexperienced pilot could not have aimed straight in such turbulence. And how

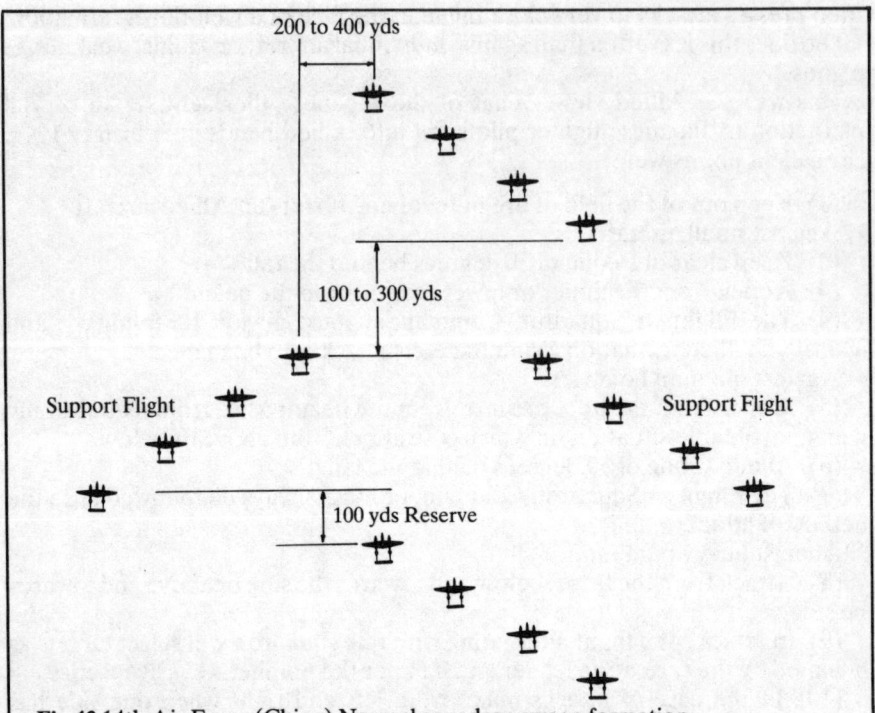

Fig 42 14th Air Force (China) Normal squadron sweep formation. Spacing limits were dictated by variations of weather and mission. The Squadron Commander led the reserve flight.

much worse would the slipstream have been on the lightweight Hayabusas and Zeroes?

Items (4) and (7) can only be accounted for by the poor quality of replacement pilots. No well trained and disciplined pilot needs an instruction to follow his unit commander.

Meanwhile, what of the opposition? The United States Navy was the main opponent. It had extensively re-equipped with the Grumman F6F Hellcat. The Hellcat was essentially a large Wildcat with improved performance all round. Trials were flown against a captured Zero Type 52. They showed that the Hellcat was considerably faster at all altitudes, outclimbed the Zero marginally above 14,000 ft and rolled faster at speeds above 235 mph. The Japanese fighter could out-turn its American opponent with ease at low speeds and enjoyed a slightly better rate of climb below 14,000 ft. The trials report concluded: 'Do not dogfight with the Zero 52. Do not try to follow a loop or half-roll with a pull-through. When attacking, use your superior power and high speed performance to engage at the most favourable moment. To evade a Zero 52 on your tail, roll and dive away into a high speed turn.'

Not all the air war in the East was fought over the Pacific ocean. The American 14th Air Force was based in China. Their fighters were mainly the twin-engined P-38 Lightnings and late models of the single engined P-40 Kittyhawk. The 14th, commanded by the ex 'Flying Tigers' boss, Claire Chennault, evolved their own combat formation which seems to have had no parallel elsewhere in the Second World War. Like all other nations, it was based on the flight of four aircraft in two pairs. Unlike them, the fours flew echeloned back from the centre of the formation. The Assault Flight led, echeloned to the right. Echeloned left and right came two Support flights, between 100 and 300 yds behind the trailing man of Assault Flight, spaced sideways 200 to 400 yds from the Assault Flight leader and 1,000 to 2,000 ft higher. Another thousand feet or so higher and directly behind the Assault Flight flew the Reserve Flight. The 14th Air Force formation was less flexible than the finger four or fours abreast flown in other theatres and is strangely reminiscent of Major Douglas' No 84 Squadron formation in 1918. It seems to have been devised for quick in-and-out strikes with all aircraft in the flight acting in unison. One innovation however, was that the Squadron Commander led the reserve flight, from which position of vantage he could keep a fatherly eye on things, ready to intervene where necessary. On the debit side, the reserve flight, including the Squadron Commander, was most likely to be bounced from above and astern, and the other flights were in no position to give rapid assistance.

As we have seen previously, the Luftwaffe experimented briefly with air to air bombing as an expedient to break up the American heavy bomber formations. The Japanese persisted throughout the war with this method of attack and had developed special bombs for the purpose as early as 1939. The German bombs relied on blast and shrapnel effect to down the bombers. The Japanese bombs worked on a slightly different principle. They were mechanically fused to explode after a set time. The explosion scattered a great number of steel pellets filled with phosphorus downwards in a cone like the pellets from a shotgun. The steel pellet penetrated the skin of the bomber, and the phosphorus, which ignited automatically on contact with the air, set alight anything inflammable that it touched.

The method of delivery also varied from the German. The attack was made from head-on and the bomb released between 1,000 and 2,000 ft above the formation. Both the weapon and the method of delivery sound more formidable than the German experiments. However, the results were not startling. Japanese air to air bombing was summarised by the *British Directorate of Air Tactics* in the words: 'Although losses have been caused to Allied aircraft by Japanese aerial bombs, they are still comparatively rare, and Japanese persistence in this type of attack cannot be said to pay good dividends. The greater danger appears to be the effect on a formation of disturbing it so that enemy fighters may be able to pick off any resulting straggler by more normal methods of attack.'

Earlier in this chapter it was noted that there were few suicide attacks up to May 1944. However, in August of that year Kamikaze methods were used when two of the huge four-engined B-29 bombers were rammed and brought down over Yawata. The Japanese Army Air Force formed Taitari (ramming) units. While ramming attacks persisted until the end of the war they never achieved sufficient results to be decisive. The American escort fighters and the massed firepower of the bomber formations ensured that they rarely got close enough to ram their targets.

Under the massive aerial onslaught of the Allies, the quality of the Japanese pilots deteriorated more and more as the veterans were lost and replaced by green novices. The Rising Sun was setting.

Chapter 9

The road to MiG Alley

The closing months of World War 2 had seen important technical advances. One was the gyroscopic computing gunsight. The pilot set the wingspan of his adversary on the gunsight and adjusted the circle of diamonds on the reflector sight until the wings of the target appeared to touch them. The sight then automatically set up the correct deflection for the shot. All the pilot had to do was track the enemy in the sight and open fire. The gyro sight enabled the average squadron pilot to score hits at angles that had previously been the preserve of the tiny minority of naturally gifted marksmen.

The 'G' suit also saw limited service. The centrifugal force of a hard turn drained the blood from the pilot's head and caused him to black out. The 'G' suit automatically constricted the lower part of the pilot's body when manoeuvring and retarded the flow of blood downwards. The pilot thus retained his faculties at up to 9G instead of the 5 to 6G hitherto, although the maximum loading at which he could shoot accurately remained about 4G.

The piston-engined fighter had reached the practical limit of its development potential. Blister shaped canopies, giving the pilot a better view to the danger area astern were widely used but otherwise its appearance had hardly altered. It flew faster and higher and climbed better than its 1939 counterpart. Its armament was much heavier. Its weight had increased greatly and its turning ability had deteriorated as a result. But with the tactics of the day stressing position and speed, the ability to turn tightly was low in the order of priorities.

The advent of jet and rocket engines was the most significant technical breakthrough. Freed from the limitations of the propellor driven piston engine, fighters reached ever greater speeds and heights. This gave rise to a new aerodynamic problem, dubbed by the popular press as the sound barrier. The speed of sound varies according to the height at which the aeroplane is flying. The variation is just over 100 mph, from 761 mph at sea level to 660 mph at 36,000 ft and above, as shown in diagram 44. Regardless of its value in miles per hour, the speed of sound is called Mach 1 and aircraft speeds are often given as a proportion of this, ie, Mach .82 or Mach 1.32. When relating this to speed over the ground, the altitude should be borne in mind.

The importance of the Mach number becomes apparent when we consider its effect on a fast-flying aeroplane at 36,000 ft. As it flies it sets up a disturbance in the air ahead, rather like the bow wave of a ship. This bow wave travels at the speed of sound, and is in effect the air beginning to move out of the way of the aeroplane. At 500 mph (Mach .76), the bow wave reaches out to 220 ft ahead of

The road to MiG Alley 121

the aeroplane. At 600 mph (Mach .91) it only reaches 88 ft ahead. The air has insufficient time to flow smoothly out of the way and is roughly forced aside. The molecules of air are compressed together. As no aeroplane is a completely uniform shape, the air is compressed in an uneven manner. Thus, at high speeds the aeroplane becomes surrounded by air of varying density due to the uneven compression. This is known as compressibility and adversely affected the handling of the aeroplane, often causing severe buffeting. As far back as 1943, fighters in a long dive had experienced buffeting but now this area, known as the trans-sonic zone, could be reached in level flight. In a fighter this was a severe handicap for the pilot, as once this state was reached he became unable

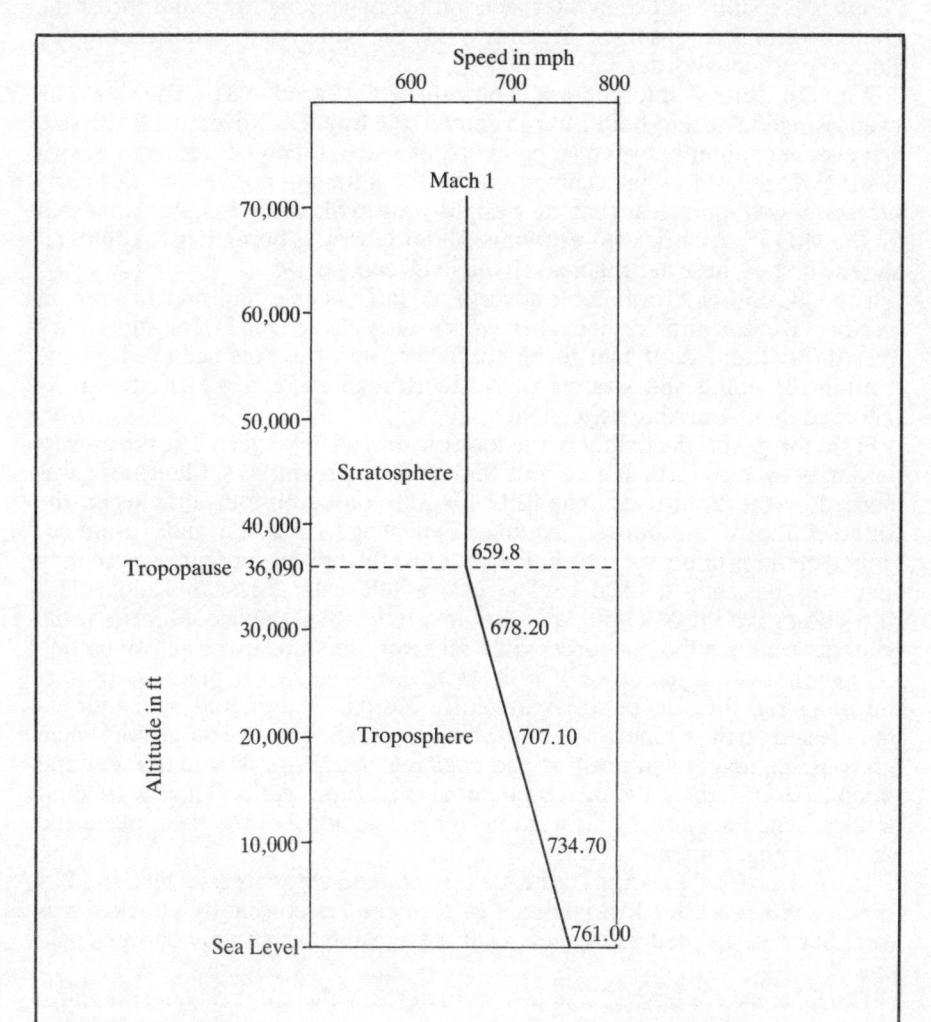

Fig 43 The speed of sound.

Based on the International Civil Aviation Organisation Standard Atmosphere, defined as: Sea level temperature 15°C; Sea level pressure 29.02 Hg; Temperature lapse 1.98°C per 1,000 ft to the Tropopause where it remains constant

to fight effectively. Nowadays, aerodynamic design has solved the problem but in the late 1940s and early 1950s little was known about it. It was appreciated that sweeping the wings back at a sharp angle delayed the onset of compressibility but that was about all.

The uneasy truce between East and West continued until June 1950, when communist North Korea invaded the American-aided south. The United Nations intervened in time to prevent South Korea being over-run, and the American Far Eastern Air Force swept the small obsolete North Korean Air Force from the sky. With total air supremacy, United Nations forces had advanced almost to the Chinese border by November. At this stage the People's Republic of China intervened in overwhelming force and thrust the United Nations troops back. By May 1951, the battlefront stabilised roughly along the original border.

With the Chinese intervention, a new shape appeared in Korean skies. The swept-winged Russian-built MiG 15 entered the fray. On November 8 1950 the first ever encounter between jet fighters took place, Lieutenant Russell Brown in his F-80 Shooting Star claimed one of the newcomers. Despite this early success, it was soon clear that the straight-winged Shooting Star was no match for the MiG 15. America's swept winged F-86 Sabre was brought in to counter it and the first of these aeroplanes arrived in December 1950.

The MiG 15 was a formidable adversary. Had it been established in strength on North Korean airfields, it could have seriously challenged UN air supremacy over the battlefield. It had to be contained, and this was achieved by the constant bombing and strafing of North Korean airfields which effectively rendered them unusable by jet fighters.

From this point, the fighter battle took on an artificial aspect. The north-west border between North Korea and the Chinese province of Manchuria was marked by the Yalu river. The MiG 15s were based on four airfields on the Chinese side of the border, Antung, Fencheng, Takushan and Tatunkou. United Nations pilots were forbidden to cross the border for fear of escalating what was basically a local conflict into a full-scale war with China. This restriction gave the MiG pilots a sanctuary into which they could retire if the going got rough, although border violations were common in the heat of battle.

From the Antung complex of airfields, the MiGs were well placed to protect the industrial and depot areas of North Korea. They could gain altitude unmolested on the Chinese side of the border, crossing to give battle only when a favourable height and position had been reached. With the aid of radar and ground control their defensive potential was formidable. Thanks to their political sanctuary, the MiGs were in complete control of the time, place and size of the engagements.

The industrial area south of the Yalu river contained targets which the UN forces could not afford to ignore. Fighter-bombers constantly attacked this area, but they needed protection against the MiGs which only Sabres could give.

The Sabres were based 200 miles south of the Yalu and their time on patrol was therefore limited. No help was available from ground radar. All the Americans could do was to put large numbers of Sabre aircraft on patrol at high altitude to cover the strike aircraft and intercept the MiG formations visually. All the natural advantages lay with the MiGs – except one. From mid-October to March the prevailing wind was from west to northwest. From 30,000 ft

The road to MiG Alley 123

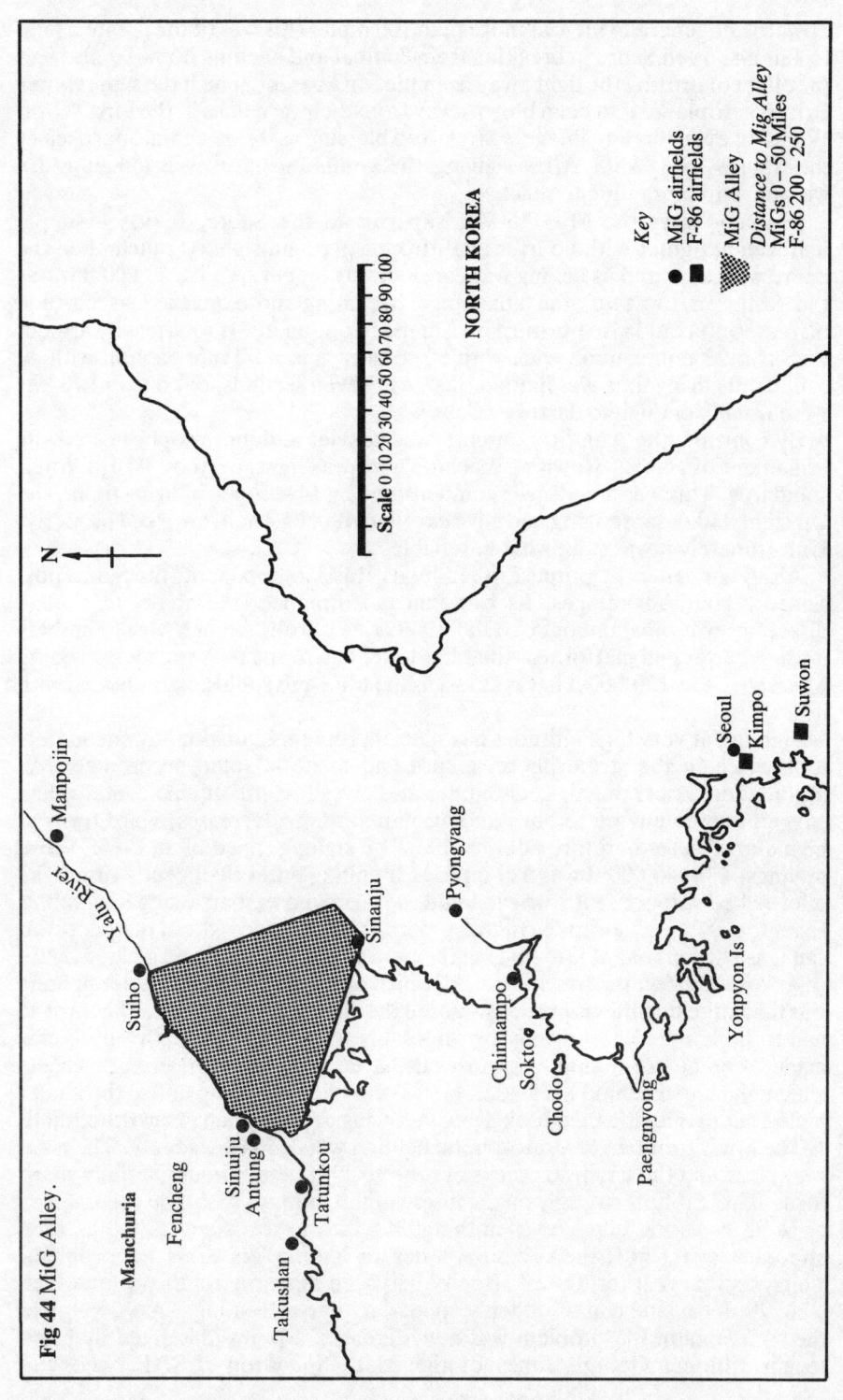

Fig 44 MiG Alley.

Key
- MiG airfields
- F-86 airfields
- MiG Alley

Distance to MiG Alley
MiGs 0 – 50 Miles
F-86 200 – 250

upwards, it generally blew at more than 100 mph. This was of the greatest help to a fuel-starved Sabre in breaking from combat and heading home. It also had the effect of drifting the fight away from the MiG bases in much the same way as British aeroplanes had been blown away from their own lines in the First World War. But even this advantage was a mixed blessing as it slowed the approach of the Sabres into 'MiG Alley', giving the communist forces a longer radar warning and more time to react.

In many ways the MiG 15 was superior to the Sabre. It was a simple lightweight fighter with no frills apart from a gyro gunsight. It outclimbed the Sabre with ease and its ceiling was considerably higher. Above 20,000 ft it was the faster of the two, the advantage becoming more marked as altitude increased. It could also out-turn its American opponent. It was heavily armed, with two 23 mm cannon each with 80 rounds, and a 37 mm cannon with 40 rounds. Its firing time was limited, just over seven seconds, but one or two hits were usually enough to destroy a Sabre.

By contrast, the American aircraft was heavier and more sophisticated. Its armament of six .50 Browning machine guns was light, even by World War 2 standards. This was to a degree compensated by 14 seconds of firing time. The gunsight had radar ranging and gave excellent results when it worked properly. Unfortunately it was somewhat unreliable.

Although generally outperformed by its Russian opponent, the Sabre possessed certain advantages. Its transient performance (the ability to change direction) was outstanding, particularly its rate of roll. At high Mach numbers it was a better gun platform as the MiG 15 tended to snake at speeds exceeding Mach 86. Below 20,000 ft it was as fast as the MiG and could generally turn with it.

Fighting at very high altitudes has special problems and as many encounters took place in the stratosphere, tactics had to be adapted accordingly. As altitude increases, the air gets thinner and gives less lift. It also contains less oxygen for the engine to burn and available power decreases. Hard turns at high altitude are therefore not possible. The stalling speed of an F-86F Sabre pulling 4 G at 40,000 ft was 580 mph. In anything other than gentle turns, the pilot risked 'dropping it', which could have proved embarrassing in combat. Even today in high altitude combat practice, the winner is often the pilot who can tease his opponent into tugging the pole a little too hard and stalling out.

A further effect of extreme height which applied to these early jet fighters was that large throttle movements caused the engine to 'flame out'. The throttle had to be handled very gently or preferably left alone. These two problems made keeping formation very difficult, even for just two aircraft. If the wingman lagged behind his leader, he was unable to catch up unless the leader pulled out to one side then back again, allowing the wingman to cut the corner.

The other problem of stratospheric fighting was, and is, visibility. The air is very clear and the harsh sun picks out the cockpit details in unnaturally sharp focus. These reflect strongly on the inside of the canopy. Also, the general lack of cloud gives the pilot's eyes nothing on which to focus and as the altitude approaches 50,000 ft the sky turns a darker blue, aggravating the problem. Thirty six years earlier, Oswald Boelke had been concerned at the way in which a hostile aeroplane could suddenly appear at quite close range. At 600 mph in the stratosphere the problem was much greater, a point illustrated by Lieutenant Colonel George Jones of the 335th Squadron, USAF, who was approaching the Yalu at 35,000 ft when: 'I spotted a glint in the sky, about 3 o'clock high. I wagged the stick, rocking my wings to get my wingman's attention. He looked across and I silently signalled "Drop tanks!" Again a silent signal for full military power, and we started a slow turn under that glint in the sky. Now there were many other flashes in the sun up ahead. All of a sudden I saw them. First there was nothing, then they jumped into focus. A flight of MiGs in loose trail, climbing as they crossed the river.'

Colonel Jones' words, 'they jumped into focus' are significant. The sun sparkling on either canopies or polished aluminium bodies, had told him where to look. Without this clue he might never have seen the MiGs until, aided by their radar and ground control, they appeared on his tail.

Any assessment of communist fighter tactics must be judged in the light of three factors. The pilots had a positional advantage with radar and ground control while the MiG 15 was definitely superior to the Sabre at high altitude. The communist nations including Russia, used Korea as a training ground to build up a nucleus of operationally experienced pilots. New units were posted into the Antung complex of airfields at intervals. Handled cautiously at first, their aggression grew as they gained experience and after a period a unit would 'graduate' and be replaced by a fresh one.

MiG tactics varied widely. Prior to February 1952 it was usual for them to form up north of the Yalu, crossing the border at high altitude well inland. Their basic flight was the 'finger four' and groups composed of seven or eight flights were common. Generally the 'finger fours' flew stepped down from the lead flight in line astern, although they were occasionally seen stepped up. For a really large effort, three groups in line astern were used, totalling almost a hundred aircraft. Two of these 'bandit trains' as they were known, would cross the Yalu about 40 miles apart. As Sabre patrols were spotted, flights were detached to engage. The remainder swept south at 40,000 ft or higher and met over Pyong Yang, where they turned and headed homewards, engaging Sabres en route. A third 'bandit train' would cross the border to cover their return. Potentially deadly, these huge sweeps achieved little. Such numbers of fighters were unwieldy particularly at high altitude and there were invariably stragglers.

Occasionally, the MiGs used a line abreast formation. This consisted of five flights in line astern. Each flight comprised eight elements of two aircraft in line abreast and could be even more unwieldy than the long drawn out 'bandit trains'. Turning a formation with an eight machine frontage at high altitude, through 90 degrees without losing cohesion, called for precision flying.

During February 1952, these large formations were replaced by flights of four, usually in 'finger four' but sometimes in line astern, or trail as it began to be called. Large numbers of MiGs were still put up, but they made no attempt to maintain a cohesive formation. They were content to patrol an area in company, giving each other mutual support. This was far more flexible than the massive formations and represented a major tactical advance.

Both piston and jet engine fuels contain water. This is converted into steam as the fuel is burnt and expelled into the atmosphere. At certain temperatures and atmospheric conditions the steam condenses into myriads of small water droplets, in effect an artificial cloud and this causes the vapour trails so often seen behind high flying aircraft, called contrails. Contrails can be seen from great distances and give away the presence of the aeroplane making them long before it would otherwise become visible. During February, the MiG leaders, aware that their contrails could be seen from well south of the Yalu, began to detach small formations before contrail height was reached. The intention was that the Sabres would be pre-occupied in watching the contrails and be surprised by the lower flights. A lucky accident aided the Sabres to discover this ploy. A section whose leader had pressurisation trouble, reduced altitude. This section ran across a flight of the low MiGs and shot down three of them. From this point on, the Sabres also kept some sections below contrail height to counter a new threat.

A further change of tactics came the following month. While retaining many MiG units in the contrail belt to distract the Sabre's attention, top cover was provided above the contrail layer where they were hard to see. At the same time the MiGs attempted to saturate the area between 18,000 and 25,000 ft with elements of two aircraft. These elements stayed in visual contact, ready to give mutual support. This was a hard phase for the Sabres. Each time they launched an attack other MiGs turned in on their tails. To counter this the Sabres also saturated the area with pairs. Finding the MiGs at an altitude where their performance advantages had all but vanished was just what the Sabre pilots wanted and they exploited the benefits.

With dozens of pairs of shiny swept-winged aeroplanes roaming the skies, recognition became a problem. Frequently Sabres were bounced by other Sabres, although little harm was done except to the adrenal glands. Some Sabre pilots took to using binoculars to aid recognition. The MiG pilots almost certainly had much the same problem.

Combat tactics for the MiGs were to a great extent conditioned by their superior altitude performance. Squadron Leader Harbison of the Royal Air Force was attached to the American 4th Fighter Wing. He later reported: 'Some MiG units make full use of their superior performance at height. Such units consistently stay at 35,000 ft and above, keep their speed well up, and use their altitude to dive down and attack the Sabres, pulling up again out of range after each attack. When flying in sections of two aircraft, they also use another quite effective manoeuvre, known as "Yoyo" tactics. If an element of MiGs is "bounced" by two Sabres, the MiGs will often split, the leader doing a climbing turn and his No 2 going level or diving slightly. Thus if the F-86s press home their attack on the low MiG, and they generally do (because it is a waste of time going for the high MiG, unless the attacking Sabres have enough speed), the high MiG eventually gets into a position from which he can dive down on the Sabres following his No 2. When this tactic is employed properly it is most effective.'

Squadron Leader Harbison's report is reinforced from the other side. The Russian Colonels, Babich and Dubovitskiy in articles published in the July and August 1977 issues of *Aviatsiya i Kosmonavtika* commented: 'The adversary should be drawn to a disadvantageous altitude by a combat formation in which one group engages, while the covering group continuously attacks the adversary vertically. It would be a gross error to change to horizontal manoeuvring immediately following the first pass. The initial altitude advantage should be maintained during the entire engagement and be expended very economically. In the war in Korea, the enemy's combat formation would be split by a dagger-thrust pass by the lead group, while the attack group would attack the enemy aircraft, which were deprived of support.'

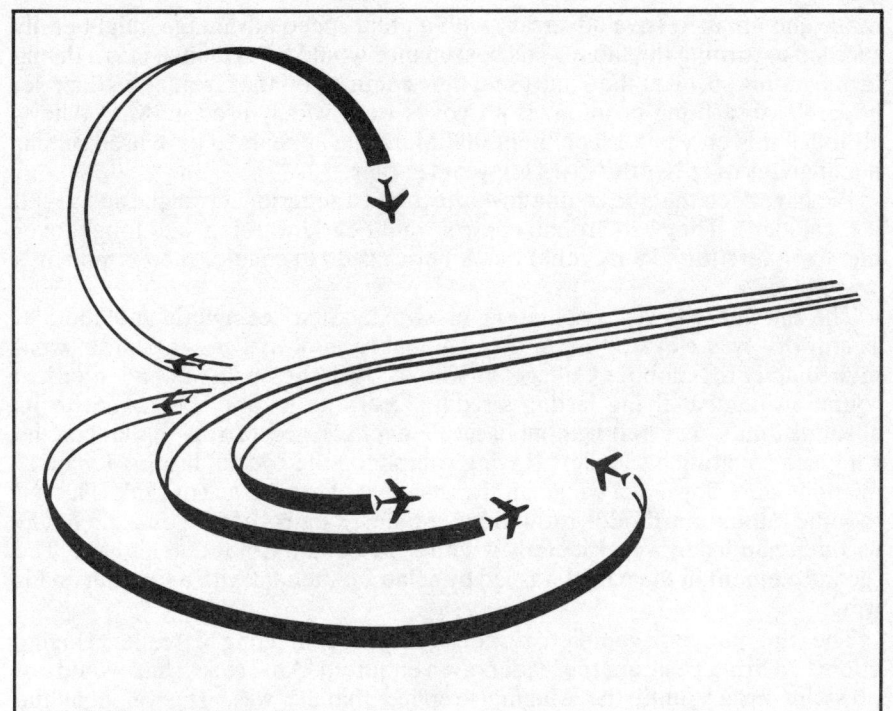

Fig 45 The defensive split.

The defensive split as described by Sqn Ldr Harbison. The lead MiG pulls high in a climb the Sabres cannot follow while his wingman turns hard into the attack. If the Sabres follow the wingman, the MiG leader gains an attacking position.

Harbison's reference to the 'Yoyo' is of particular interest and is reminiscent of the Godfrey/Gentile combat described earlier. The No 2 MiG holds the two Sabres in play while his leader positions for an attacking run. Thus the two aircraft manoeuvre independently, but in a co-ordinated manner. It emphasises the inability of the Sabre to stay with the MiG 15 in a climb. It is also the forerunner of three basic fighter manoeuvres which are today included in every fighter pilot's repertoire, but which were first formulated over 'MiG Alley'.

Basic manoeuvre No 1 was the defensive split. This instantly posed the problem for the attacking pair of which one to follow. Nowadays it is an established principle to take the high man. The climb performance of the MiG 15 left the Sabres no choice – it had to be the lower machine.

While the MiG No 2 led the Sabres around in a fast circle, his leader pulled high, aileron turning to keep the other machines in sight. As his speed fell, he pulled hard over the top, dropping down into a firing position as opportunity offered. This manoeuvre, soon to be called the High Speed Yoyo, came into general use against a horizontally turning target when the speed of the attacker precluded any chance of the attacking aircraft following its target in the turn.

A further derivative of this was soon developed; the Low Speed Yoyo. Faced with an opponent travelling very fast and executing a wide circle, the attacker could attempt to cut the corner. If this failed he would be left trailing far out of range and an aggressive adversary with a great speed advantage, might easily succeed in turning the tables. His best chance would be to launch into a diving turn, gaining speed at the same time, then zoom up on the far side of the circle, hopefully in a firing position. Both yoyos were widely used in 'MiG Alley', although it is only fair to comment that Marseille appears to have used similar manoeuvres over North Africa ten years earlier.

We have seen that the communist forces had a superior aeroplane and sound tactical ideas. They had ground control, radar early warning, and fought over their own territory. What could the Americans do to counter their opponent's advantages?

The answer was a combination of two factors, teamwork and morale. Teamwork was elevated to an art. The Sabre pilot arriving in Korea, went immediately to 'Clobber College' at Kimpo. Here he underwent an intensive course in combat flying lasting six days, learning to push his mount to its absolute limits. The pair was the basic element and great stress was laid on the wingman covering his leader. Having completed the course, his first ten or 15 missions were flown as a wingman, irrespective of experience or rank. This led to some rather unorthodox formations at times, a patrol of four on June 7 1953 was commanded by a 1st Lieutenant with a Lieutenant Colonel as his No 2. The second element in the patrol was led by a 2nd Lieutenant with a Captain on his wing.

The wingman took complete responsibility for protecting his leader. Having attained a firing position, the leader often enquired 'Am I clear', and would not press his attack until the wingman replied that he was. The value of the wingman is clearly demonstrated in the continuation of the combat account by Lieutenant Colonel Jones begun earlier: 'We were closing but slowly. I edged around in my seat and glanced behind. Bad news! A MiG was almost in position to swing in for an attack on me. I now realised that I had cut between the last two aircraft in the MiG formation. Where was my wingman? There he was, on my right wingtip and dropping his wing as if to start a pass on the MiG closing on my rear. Good Boy! I snapped my head around to the left. The MiG, which had tilted his wing down on the start of a firing pass, suddenly straightened up and levelled out. Now I got the picture – if the MiG pilot jumped me, my wingman would swing in behind him. The MiG driver backed off.'

It was not unusual for Sabres to turn in behind a MiG formation to find others on their tail. Poor high altitude visibility was one reason; the MiGs tendency to straggle was another. Colonel Jones' reference to his wingman on his wingtip is slightly misleading. It should be remembered that to see his wingtip he was looking backwards at about a 40 degree angle. The wingman would be 2–300 yds out and behind.

In the early days, the Sabres flew in squadron strength, particularly when great masses of MiGs were crossing the Yalu. This was later reduced to eight aircraft in two 'finger fours' but even this proved unwieldy when battle was joined. It then became standard to use four-aircraft flights sent off at three minute intervals. This ensured that there were plenty of Sabres about for mutual support and also that they did not all get low on fuel at the same time. For a maximum effort sweep, the 4th Fighter Interception Group, using three squadrons of 16 Sabres each, had a take-off spread of 33 minutes. They were often supported by the 51st Group, who timed the arrival of their first units in the patrol area to overlap with the last units of the 4th. The patrols operated at

The road to MiG Alley

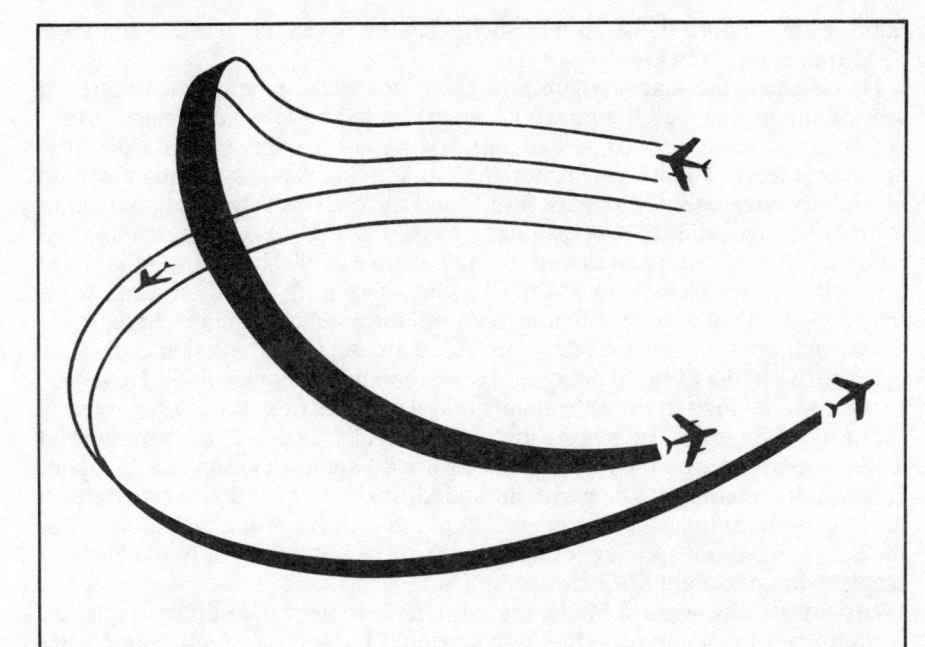

Fig 46 The high speed yoyo.

This manoeuvre is used to prevent overshooting a hard-turning target. It can also be used to prevent a more manoeuvreable opponent from scissoring. A simple looking manoeuvre, it requires precise timing and skilful flying to execute properly. If started too late, the attacker will have to pull his nose too high. This gives his opponent the chance to dive away and escape. If started too early, his opponent can pull up into a vertical ascending scissors.

varying altitudes up to 46,000 ft and the area was evenly saturated with Sabres for quite long periods.

The 'finger four' remained the standard Sabre formation for the duration of the war. Aircraft changed position during turns by crossing, but unlike the procedure adopted for the Second World War crossover, all aircraft crossed under the leader. Pulling up to cross over at high altitude cost distance.

In the combat area, the Sabres increased speed to Mach 0.9 or even faster. This made them less vulnerable to the high bounce. During combat every effort was made to keep the speed high. This frequently involved loss of altitude which had the advantage of pulling the MiGs down to a level where much of their performance edge was lost. Rather surprisingly, head-on attacks were possible despite closing speeds of nearly 600 yds per second. A few MiGs were shot down in this manner, but recognition in sufficient time was very difficult.

The general method of evasion for Sabre pilots was a hard diving turn. The MiG 15s found it difficult to pull enough 'lead' to score hits and generally broke off after one complete circle, although a few aggressive pilots followed Sabres right down to ground level on occasion. The slow-firing Russian cannon had a low muzzle velocity. The time of flight of the shells was correspondingly long and this made effective shooting at a wildly turning target, very difficult. Some

Sabre pilots reported the 23 mm shells passing above them while the large 37 mm shells went below.

By contrast, the machine-gun armament of the Sabre was much better at scoring hits but lacked the punch necessary to inflict decisive damage. Many American combat reports tell of hits sparkling all over a MiG with little apparent effect. The normal American gun loading was armour piercing and incendiary alternately, with each fifth round tracer. Tracer was optional but as in the First World War it occasionally caused a MiG to break, enabling the Sabre to cut the corner and close the range. Above 25,000 ft, the incendiary had little effect, presumably due to the lack of oxygen. MiGs often went down streaming fuel but without catching fire until lower levels were reached.

Instruction at 'Clobber College' included an escape and evasion course for pilots to use in the event of being shot down behind the enemy lines. However, Morale was so high in the Sabre units that few pilots took the possibility very seriously. The spirit of aggression was carefully fostered by experienced leaders, many of whom had years earlier fought against Germany and Japan. Headquarters pilots also flew with the squadrons. This kept them up to date on developments in the combat zone and kept *esprit de corps* at a high level. Thus the Sabres went out spoiling for a fight and it was not unusual for two F 86s to tangle with up to eight MiG 15s.

In contrast, the average MiG pilot seems to have been of indifferent quality, ready to run for home once the fight started. On the other hand, some MiG pilots and some units also, were exceptionally good. These were generally believed to be Russians.

The results of the air fighting over Korea are conflicting. Early figures released claimed a kill to loss ratio of 14:1 in favour of the Sabres. An official USAF document was issued in 1970 giving figures for the period July 1951 to July 1953, which covers the bulk of the fighting in 'MiG Alley'. The Sabres flew 76,500 sorties and shot down 757 MiG 15s for the loss of 103 Sabres. This gave a kill ratio of just under 7½:1 which was still very impressive. The average Sabre pilot flew 100 missions. Statistically his chances of shooting down one MiG during his tour were slim. This highlights the achievements of the aces who regularly beat the odds. However, the chances of an American pilot being shot down by a MiG were miniscule, nearly 7½:1 against. Nevertheless, a much higher proportion of the aces were shot down by MiGs, notably Major George Davis and Captain Joseph McConnell, the American top scorer with 16 victories. This would indicate that many aces took greater risks in order to achieve results. Major Davis was killed when he ignored MiGs on his tail as he pressed home an attack. Captain McConnell was rescued after bailing out over the sea in April 1953.

The primary lessons of MiG Alley are best summed up by Squadron Leader Harbison: 'Despite the advantages possessed by the enemy MiG leaders they have been outclassed and outfought by inferior numbers, due mainly to better American leadership, aggressiveness and a superior standard of pilot ability and training. The enemy is learning fast from his encounters with UN forces in Korea, his equipment is first class and the advantage might easily swing the other way. From the communist point of view, Korea can be classed, very broadly, as a second Spain. A testing and proving ground for their equipment and crews against the Western powers; invaluable in evolving their tactics.'

Fig 47 The low speed yoyo.

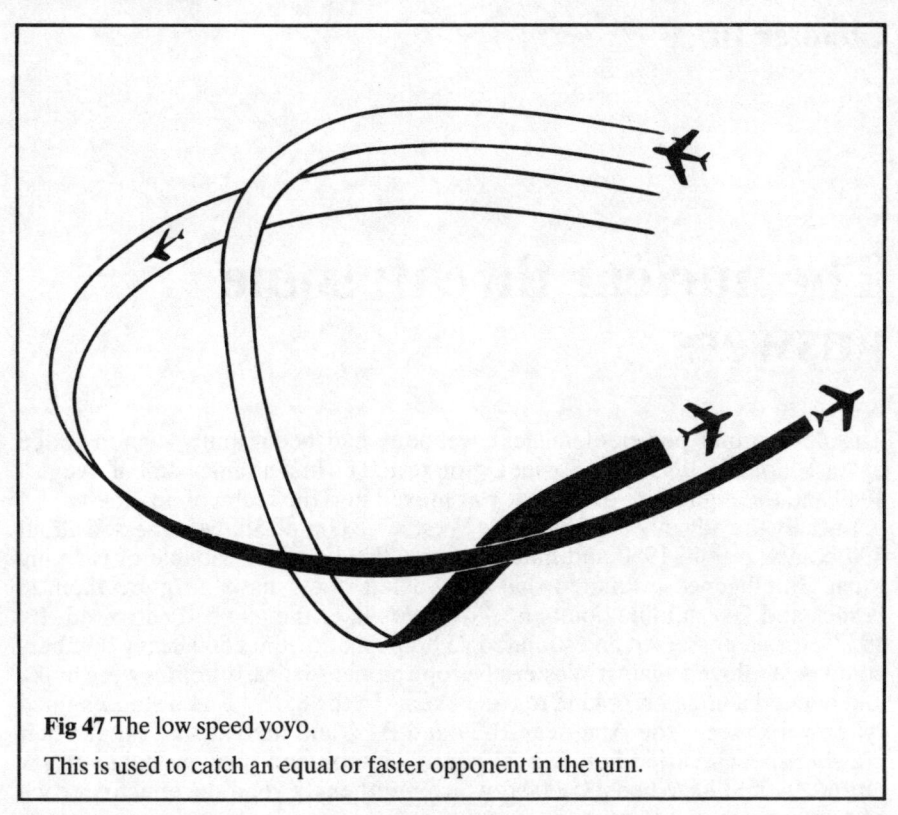

This is used to catch an equal or faster opponent in the turn.

The very high altitudes and high speeds of much of the fighting posed new problems. New techniques were evolved to solve them. When the fighting ended in the middle of 1953, the big fighter formation had gone forever. Other principles remained the same. The fighter with the height advantage held the initiative. Despite the improvements in gunsights, most kills were scored from astern. A high proportion of kills came from the surprise bounce, although the low proportion of losses indicates that surprise was more difficult to achieve than in the Second World War.

To sum up, the MiG 15 was in many ways superior to the Sabre. The major shortcomings in both aircraft lay in their armament. The six .50 machine-guns of the Sabre had insufficient hitting power, while the heavy Russian cannon suffered from a slow rate of fire, and the relatively long time of flight of their shells was unsatisfactory against a rapidly evading target. Regardless of whether there was any appreciable overclaiming or not, the Korean air war was decided by the superior ability of the American Sabre pilots. This lesson should not be forgotten.

Chapter 10

The nuclear threat: some answers

The devastating power of nuclear weapons had been amply demonstrated against Japan in 1945. The Soviet Union tested its first atomic bomb in August 1949 and the nightmare of nuclear war moved into the realm of possibility.

Initially the advantage lay with the West. The United States possessed about 300 bombs in mid-1950 and had in service 840 bombers capable of carrying them. Intelligence estimated that the Soviets could have no more than 25 bombs and 200 suitable bombers. Two years later the gap had narrowed. By 1952, Russia possessed an estimated 75 bombs, and about 500 heavy bombers could be deployed against Western Europe alone. The early bombs were bulky and needed a large aeroplane to carry them. In the early years piston-engined types were used – the American B-29 and B-36 and the Russian Tu 4. Their cruising speeds varied between 230 and 300 mph and their probable attack altitude would have been 35,000 ft which put them beyond the effective reach of piston-engined interceptors.

Modes of attack would have varied. The tremendous force unleashed by a nuclear explosion constituted a serious threat to the bomber. Immediately after releasing its weapons it would have been forced to carry out a steep diving turn through 180 degrees, leaving the target behind at full throttle. Therefore atomic bombs could only be dropped by single aircraft, not by formations.

The approach to the target could be carried out in a number of ways. A formation could fly in accompanied by escort fighters to the limit of their range, before splitting up to attack individual targets. This would have been particularly effective against targets in Western Europe and the British Isles as the distances involved are relatively short. It is reasonable to suppose that a considerable number of bombers would have carried electronic equipment to jam the opposing radar systems and ground to air communications. At a pre-determined point, the entire formation might have split up to confuse the defenders. Alternatively, the bulk of the aircraft in the formation might have carried old-fashioned iron bombs with only the nuclear-armed bombers breaking away to attack individually.

The large formation would almost certainly have attracted a good proportion of the defending fighters, leaving less to intercept the deadly nuclear-armed raiders. Or the entire raid would have come in well spaced-out over a wide front. Such an attack would also almost certainly have been carried out in weather conditions that hampered defence. This then was the threat. How could the fighters respond?

The nuclear threat: some answers

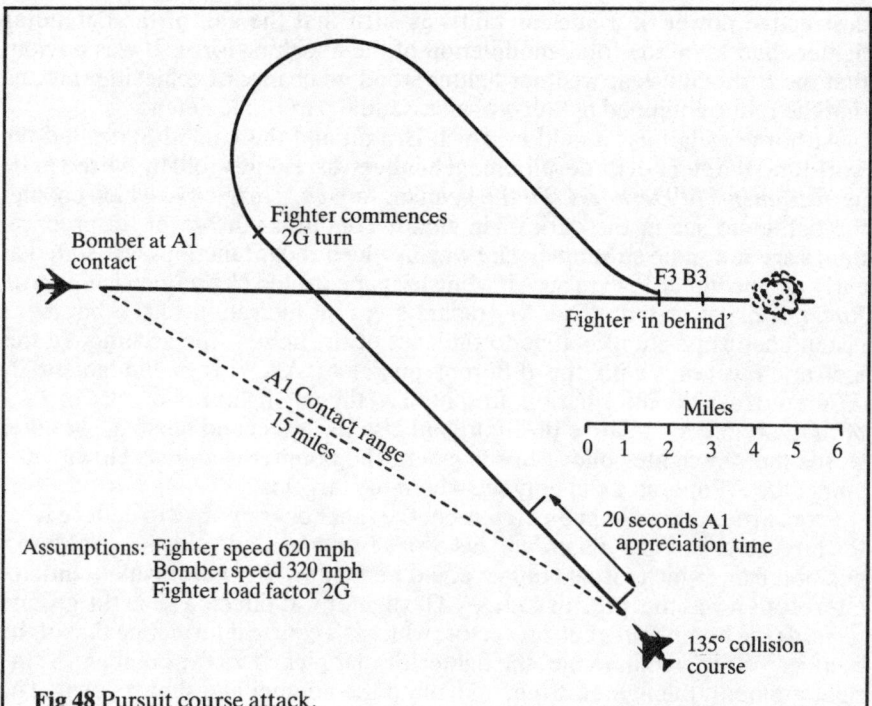

Fig 48 Pursuit course attack.

The difficulties of the pursuit course attack are clearly illustrated here. Radar contact is lost for a while until the fighter has turned around and a change of course by the bomber might well have enabled it to escape. The point at which the fighter begins its turn towards the bomber is determined by the course difference, the speed of the target, and the altitude at which the interception is made which restricts the fighter's turning ability. The threat was at this time the very high-flying fast bomber.

Up until this time fighter aircraft had fallen into two distinct categories. One was the single seat-fighter which depended entirely on directions from the ground and a pilot's eyesight to effect an interception. This gave excellent results in clear skies but was of limited use in cloudy weather. The Russian MiG 15, American Sabre, and British Meteor, all fell into this category. The heavy cannon armament of the MiG 15, coupled with its outstanding rate of climb, indicate that it was designed as a bomber destroyer although it was capable of holding its own against fighters.

The second category of aircraft had arisen from the World War 2 need to shoot down bombers at night. Traditionally, such a plane was a two-seater and carried airborne radar to hunt down targets invisible to the human eye. Generally it was larger and heavier than the single-seater and possessed inferior performance. However, its ability to find enemy aircraft in bad weather conditions was essential to counter a nuclear attack. It gradually became known as the 'all weather' fighter although this was a misnomer. It could not fly in *all* weather conditions; even today there is no aircraft that can, but it could operate in weather that rendered the day fighter impotent. The potential destructive power of a nuclear raid was such that the aim of the defending fighters had to be the total annihilation of the attacking force. It was obvious that the orthodox clear weather fighter stood no chance of achieving this and that the radar-equipped fighter was an essential part of the defence.

Airborne radar was a field in which Britain and the United States led the world and the story of its development has been excellently told by Alfred Price in *Instruments of Darkness*. To the layman, radar is a magic eye which enables the fighter to see in the dark or in cloudy conditions, however, in practice, things are not quite so simple. The way in which radar functions was stated as early as December 1943 in an Air Ministry paper called *Night Interception with Radar Aids*. It stated: 'The AI (radar) gives an indication of the bomber's instantaneous position relative to the axes of the fighter, the accuracy of this indication varying with the different marks of AI. This is fundamentally different from the information presented to the day fighter pilot who can see both the bomber's relative position, and also its aspect and heading. In other words the day fighter pilot can see where the bomber is and which way it is going; the AI operator can only see where the target is.'

From little spots of light on his screen, the radar operator had to deduce what the target was doing in relation to his own aeroplane, and guide his pilot into a position from which visual contact could be made. The traditional method of interception was the 'pursuit course'. The fighter was directed from the ground towards the bomber in a cut-off vector, which is a course intersecting that of the bomber. When within range, the fighter's radar picked up the bomber. At the right moment, the fighter turned in behind the bomber and shot it down. The problem was selecting the right moment to turn in. At high altitudes the turning ability of the fighter was very limited. Timing the moment to begin turning was absolutely critical if the bomber was not to escape. A further weakness of pursuit course interception was the attack from astern. The fighter would catch the full force of any radar counter-measures carried by the bomber: it would also become vulnerable to any radar controlled rear guns.

To overcome these problems, the United States developed the 'collision course' interception. The fighter received a cut-off vector from ground control which it followed until the target appeared on its own radar. A turn of a knob and a flick of a switch and the radar 'locked on' to the target blip. This meant that the radar scanner concentrated on the target blip to the exclusion of all else. The pilot had his own radar screen on which was shown a small circle. All he had to do was to keep the target blip inside the circle. If it wandered outside, a gentle manoeuvre would centre it again. An on-board computer did all the work, calculating the position the steering circle should be in. As the range closed, the pilot armed the system by pressing a switch. The armament was then automatically fired by the computer at the precise moment and range necessary to hit the target. The armament in this case consisted of a battery of unguided rockets, 104 of them in the case of the F-89D Scorpion. At 800 yds range they spread out and covered an area of sky the size of a football field, giving a fair chance of scoring a hit on a large bomber. The explosive power of the rockets was such that just one hit was likely to bring it down.

The advantages of the collision course interception were many. Even in clear conditions surprise was more likely to be achieved than with the pursuit course attack. The attack was delivered sooner, while time consuming manoeuvring into the tail position was eliminated. The fighter avoided the unhealthy tail

The nuclear threat: some answers

Fig 49 Collision course interception.

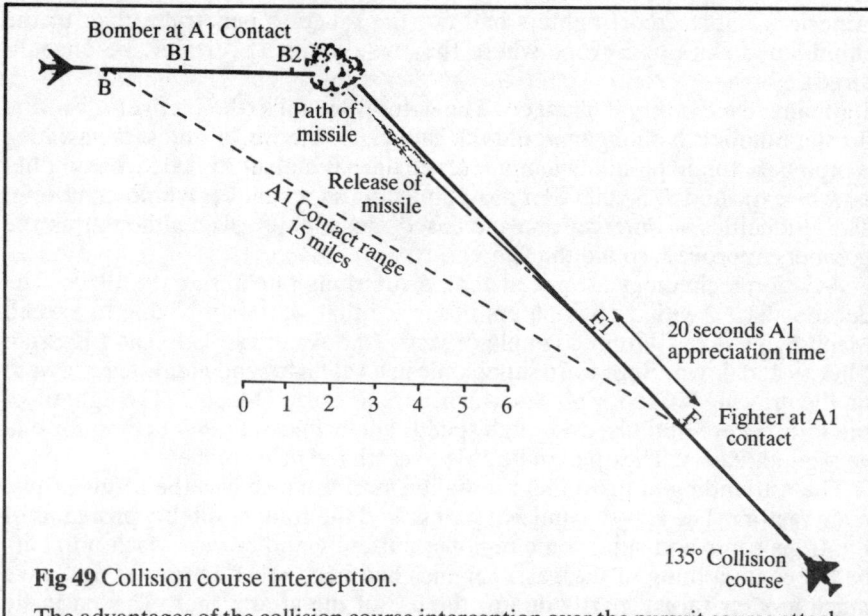

The advantages of the collision course interception over the pursuit course attack are demonstrated here. The fighter never loses radar contact. The attack is carried out much more quickly. The bomber has little chance of evading. No manoeuvring is needed by the fighter to reach a firing position. The weapons; either a battery of rockets or a guided missile are launched automatically by computer when the correct position is reached.

area. It was not essential for the fighter to have an appreciable speed advantage over the bomber, and attacks could be carried out while the fighter was still climbing to intercept. Finally, the bomber presented a bigger target from side-on than from astern.

There were, of course, certain disadvantages. The radar was vulnerable to countermeasures. If the bomber saw the fighter in time and took relatively minor evasive action, the computer was unable to cope and the rockets would miss. Should the bomber be flying through intermittent cloud with escort fighters in the vicinity, the interceptor might well be caught napping. The radar concentrated solely on the target, giving no warning of other aircraft. The pilot's head would be down 'in the office' as he concentrated on keeping the target blip within the steering circle. He would therefore have had no lookout. A two-seater fighter was preferable under these conditions, as the radar operator could take over the task of watching for enemy aircraft, however, the contemporary two-seater fighter was generally inferior in performance to a single-seater. Against single-seat escorts it would have been at a severe disadvantage.

The Americans built the first single-seater for collision course interception. This was a variant of the Sabre, the F-86D. It carried fewer rockets than the Scorpion and could look after itself in a dogfight. But while the pilot was peering intently at his radar screen, he was vulnerable to being bounced by enemy fighters. The F-86D was more suited to the air defence of continental

America, where escort fighters had not the range to penetrate, than to the cloud-laden skies of Europe where they would almost certainly be encountered.

Meanwhile the threat changed. The natural sequel to the jet fighter was the fast jet bomber. No longer would the carriers of the world's most devastating weapons be found plodding along at less than 300 mph at 35,000 ft. They could now be expected at 50,000 ft or more, hurtling along at over 8 miles a minute. The difficulties of interception increased many times over although as the bombers improved, so did the fighters.

Aviation technology advanced at an astonishing rate during the 1950s. The decade started with a few fighters in service that were barely able to exceed Mach 1 in a dive. Within a couple of years, the American F-100 and Russian MiG 19 had flown. Both were supersonic in level flight, and many designs were on the drawing board for planes which were to exceed Mach 2. The fighters of the future were optimised for high speeds and a colossal rate of climb for one very good reason. They had to be able to catch the new bombers.

The astounding improvement in fighter performance was the result of two main factors. The aerodynamicists had solved the compressibility problems of the trans-sonic and supersonic regions; buffeting and critical Mach numbers had become a thing of the past. Engines had been much improved and gave much greater thrust, partly due to the use of the afterburner. This basically consisted of a ring of nozzles which sprayed fuel into the hot tail pipe behind the engine. Once ignited, this fuel gave a tremendous increase in thrust, although fuel was used so quickly that it could only be used for short periods.

Weaponry had also made astounding advances. The batteries of unguided rockets described earlier were close range weapons. The tremendous closing speeds attainable by the new fighters, made the collision course interception hazardous for the interceptors. Something equally lethal, but with greater range was needed.

One early, rather crude answer, was the Genie. This was a large unguided rocket with a range of just over 6 miles, and a nuclear warhead. The pilot armed the warhead and the automatic fire control system tracked the target, fired the missile and automatically pulled the interceptor into a tight turn to escape the blast. The control system automatically triggered the warhead at the predicted moment. The explosion, equal to 1,500 tonnes of TNT had a lethal blast radius of several hundred yards. Unless the bomber made a radical change of course at the last moment, it stood little chance of survival.

More sophisticated were the new generation of guided or homing missiles under development. These fell into two main categories, infra-red and radar, depending on the guidance system used. They were designed to follow a manoeuvring target and destroy it.

With the advent of the guided missile, many pundits predicted the end of the manoeuvring dogfight. Future air combat was to be a contest of technology, missiles versus countermeasures, with the opposing fighters rarely, if ever, seeing each other.

However, what was the worth of these early missiles? The AIM (Air Interception Missile) 9B Sidewinder was built in greater numbers than any other. It homed in on infra-red emissions (heat) from an opponent and was a simple and cheap weapon. Weighing about as much as a man, and requiring little more than a switch and some wires and earphones for the pilot, it could be fitted to almost any aircraft with ease. To fire, the pilot activated the infra-red seeker. When the missile started to pick up heat emissions from its target, a growl was heard in the earphones. This increased in intensity as the emissions became stronger and at a suitable moment the pilot pulled a trigger on his control column to send the Sidewinder speeding on its way. The missile accelerated to a speed of Mach 2.5 in just over two seconds, and then coasted towards its target. Its range was about 2 miles (all missile ranges vary with altitude) and it remained under control for about 20 seconds. A direct hit was not necessary. The Sidewinder was fitted with a proximity fuse which detonated the warhead when it came within lethal range of the target. Its faults were its short range (although later models could reach out 11 miles with a flight time of one minute) and a tendency to home on to the sun, a convenient factory chimney or other heat source. Cloud or rain reduced its detection ability considerably, and the ground on a warm day would mask a low-flying target quite effectively. For many years it could only be used from the astern position from where the hot exhaust of the target aircraft formed an excellent heat source.

The AIM 7 Sparrow was typical of the other main type of missile, and was radar guided. The most common versions used semi-active radar homing, a system whereby the radar carried by the fighter bounces electronic signals off the target. The Sparrow then homes on the reflected signals. Nearly three times heavier than the Sidewinder, it was a much more complicated and costly weapon. With a speed of Mach 3.7 (about 2,500 mph at high altitude), its range was for most variants 25 to 28 miles. It was unaffected by cloud and could be used to attack targets beyond visible range. It could also be used for a collision course attack, a task for which the early infra-red missiles were not designed.

Many other missiles were developed during the 1950s and saw service later, but the Sidewinder and Sparrow were fairly representative. A fault common to both types of missile was that they could not be used at ranges of less than about ½ a mile, as they could not be guided during the acceleration phase.

By the early 1960s, the nuclear threat was changing yet again. The long range rocket was becoming the main delivery system for really large nuclear weapons. Against these the fighter was impotent. Bombers had, however, been retained to give a secondary strike capability and thus remained a threat. Although, as we have seen with the Genie, nuclear weapons had been successfully miniaturised. They could now be carried by small aeroplanes and delivered at high subsonic speeds at very low level. The high level nuclear bombing attack which gave plenty of radar warning to the defenders was now beginning to look a distinctly risky undertaking. Fighter and missile performance had improved to the point where the high altitude bomber stood an excellent chance of being intercepted. Large and sophisticated surface to air missiles (SAMs) compounded the dangers. Finally even the heavy bombers were switched to the low level role.

The tremendous improvement in fighter and weaponry performance had escalated costs out of all proportion. No longer could even the richest countries afford specialist aircraft for all roles. During the 1960s fighters tended to be designed as multi-purpose machines. The accent was on the fighter-bomber which could deliver ordnance and fight if it had to, or with a few minor changes perform a reconnaissance or an interception. Had anyone told the fighter designers of the early 1950s, that the most successful Western combat aero-

Fig 50 Fluid Four.

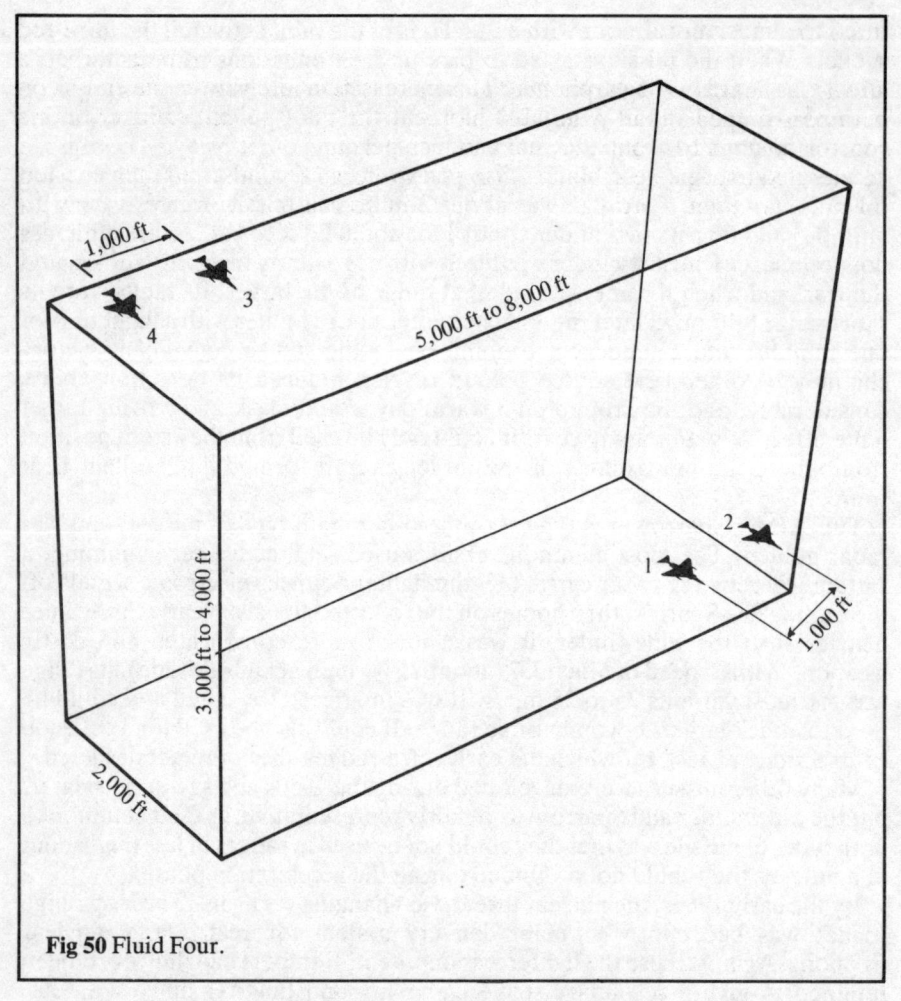

plane in 15 years time would be a two-seat, twin-engined, jagged looking, 25 ton monster designed as a jack of all trades, they would scarcely have credited it. Yet this is an accurate description of the Phantom II!

By the mid-1960s, the Mach 2 capable fighter was in widespread service among the technically advanced nations and once more the pundits forecast the end of the dogfight. Hard turns were impossible to perform at very high speeds without overstressing the airframe. The superior weapons systems would win the battle, not the better flying machine.

This argument would have been valid but for one thing. Few aircraft were even marginally supersonic without using an afterburner. And the afterburner was an expensive luxury. The F 4 Phantom II on maximum power (full afterburner, sometimes called wet thrust), guzzled fuel at an incredible five gallons per second. The result of this was that the afterburner could only be used when absolutely necessary, or the fighter would run out of fuel in a matter of minutes. Consequently, the Mach 2 fighters spend most of their time flying on military (dry) thrust at comparatively sedate subsonic speeds.

During the preceding 50 years, most air victories were the result of the surprise astern attack. In theory the Mach 2 fighters were so fast that they were almost immune although in practice, they were far more vulnerable. Right up to the end of the Korean War, there had been little difference between cruising speed in the combat zone and maximum speed attainable. Now the difference between combat cruise and maximum speeds became so great that the surprise bounce was even more likely. Given good controlling from the ground, a fighter could be positioned for its attacking run 20 or 30 miles away. It could then plug in 'burner', close rapidly to missile range, attack and break off with little chance of even being seen by its victim.

Another factor contributed to increased vulnerability from the astern attack. In their quest for greater performance, the designers had faired cockpits into the fuselage. This reduced drag but severely limited rearward visibility. The tear-drop shaped canopy of the Sabre had afforded an excellent all-round view. The Mach 2 generation of fighters had a very poor view astern.

One advantage of the new generation of fighters was their ability to light the 'burner' and gain large amounts of energy very quickly. This energy could be used for acceleration or a rapid climb. This increase in available energy, called specific excess power, led directly to a change in tactical fighter formations. Towards the end of the Korean War, a few Sabre units had begun to experiment with a formation called the Fluid Four. This was composed of two pairs, each of which retained the traditional shooter/cover relationship which at about this time came to be called Welded Wing or Fighting Wing. The pairs also maintained a shooter/cover relationship, the second pair flew in echelon formation a few hundred yards out and several hundred feet higher. The close spacing was dictated by the time taken for one pair to give support to the other. However, the vastly increased performance of the new jets changed the 'Fluid Four' radically. A formation of F 4 Phantoms typically consisted of a lead pair 300 yds apart with the second pair ½ mile astern, up to 1½ miles to one side and 3,000 to 4,000 ft higher. The name Fluid Four was retained although it bore little resemblance to the earlier formation.

Chapter 11

Limited wars

With the introduction of the new guided missiles, the gun lost favour as the primary air-to-air weapon. Many factors contributed to this. As fighter speeds increased, their effective gun range decreased. The early British 30 mm Aden cannon was a prime example. Its destructive power on hitting the target was excellent but the explosive was detonated by a fuse which only worked if the shell made its impact at 1,500 ft per second. This meant in practice that a fighter flying at 600 mph and firing at a target travelling at the same speed, had to close to within 240 yds for its shells to hit hard enough for the fuse to work. As aircraft speeds increased, so the effective range shortened due to the increased air resistance to the shell, and with designers thinking in terms of speeds of 2,000 mph or more in the next decade, the gun appeared very limited indeed. True, the fuse could be made more sensitive, but only at the risk of ground handling accidents. At very high speeds under certain flight conditions it was even possible that the fighter could overtake the shells it had just fired, with disastrous consequences.

Finally, the comparatively long ranges attainable with missiles suggested that the days of close combat were soon to be finished for ever. What good was a gun when it was totally outranged by missiles that could follow their target as it manoeuvred? This question was to be answered in a series of localised wars and clashes that erupted in the Middle and Far East between 1958 and 1973.

The first event of note occurred in September 1958. Sabres of the Nationalist Chinese Air Force from Taiwan, clashed with communist Chinese MiGs. Sidewinder missiles, homing on the infra-red emissions of their opponents were used operationally for the first time. Four MiGs were claimed by Nationalist pilots using Sidewinders, an event viewed as an encouraging start by the pro-missile, anti-gun faction.

A series of wars limited in duration and in scope began in 1965 and lasted to 1973. India and Pakistan clashed briefly in 1965 and again in 1971. Israel was engaged in frequent skirmishing with her Arab neighbours which erupted into short but vicious wars in 1967 and 1973. The United States began its protracted involvement in South-east Asia in 1965, and with the exception of an interim period lasting from the beginning of 1969 to the end of 1971, took part in much air fighting, albeit on a limited scale. As these periods overlap considerably, we shall look only at those sections of particular interest.

From Flanders to Korea aircraft had been fighting at ever increasing speeds

The F-104 Starfighter was designed to meet the requirements of pilots home from Korea who clamoured for more speed, greater climb rate and higher ceiling. The Starfighter gave all these but proved to be a turkey in a dogfight. Its true metier was as a low-level strike aircraft (*Minyon Prescott*).

The F-15 in action (*Minyon Prescott*).

Above F-5E Tiger IIs of an Aggressor Squadron at Nellis AFB. The Tiger II has a broadly comparable performance to the MiG 21 and the Aggressor Squadrons give valuable training in dissimilar air combat (*Northrop Corporation*).

Left Thomas C. Lesan, whose MiG kill was described in Chapter 11, pictured here as a Lieutenant-Colonel commanding the 527th TFT Aggressor Squadron at Alconbury (*Mike Spick*).

Above right Appalled by the mounting cost of sophisticated fighters General Dynamics developed the F-16 Fighting Falcon as an attempt to break away from the vicious spiral of rising costs. Probably the best dogfighter in the world, it has certain limitations in typical European weather (*General Dynamics*).

Right and overleaf The Tornado F-2 is designed primarily as a long range interceptor (*British Aerospace*).

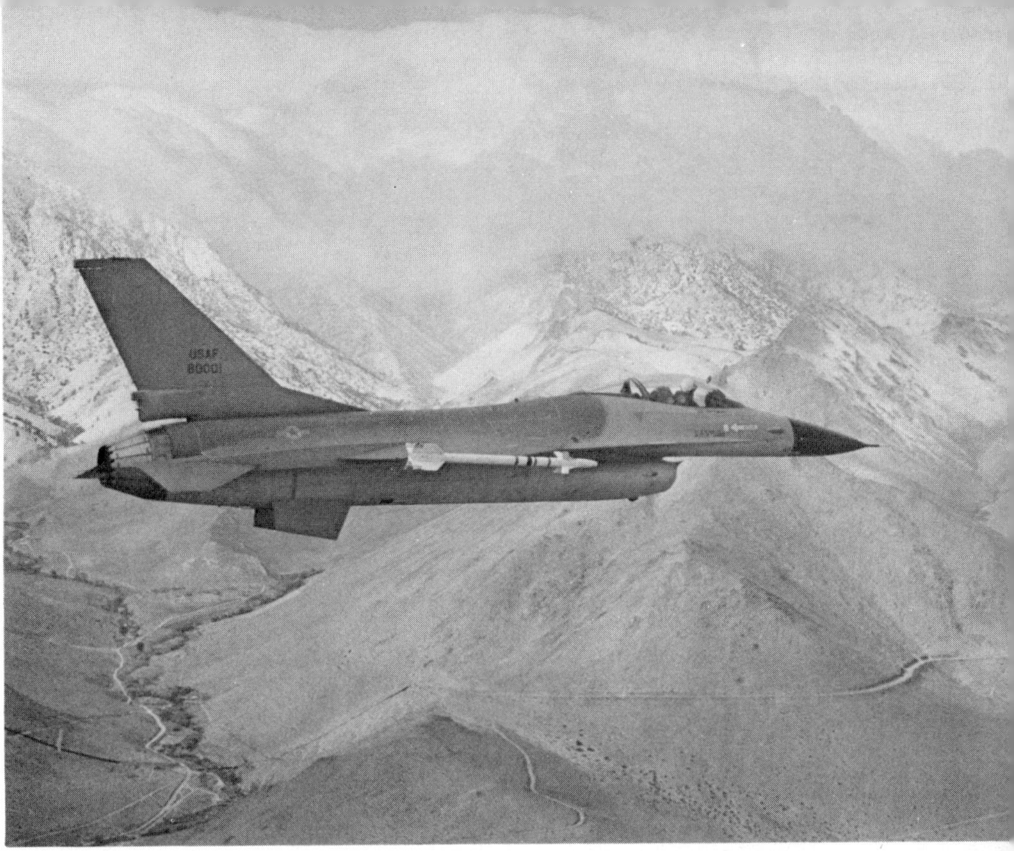
USAF
80001

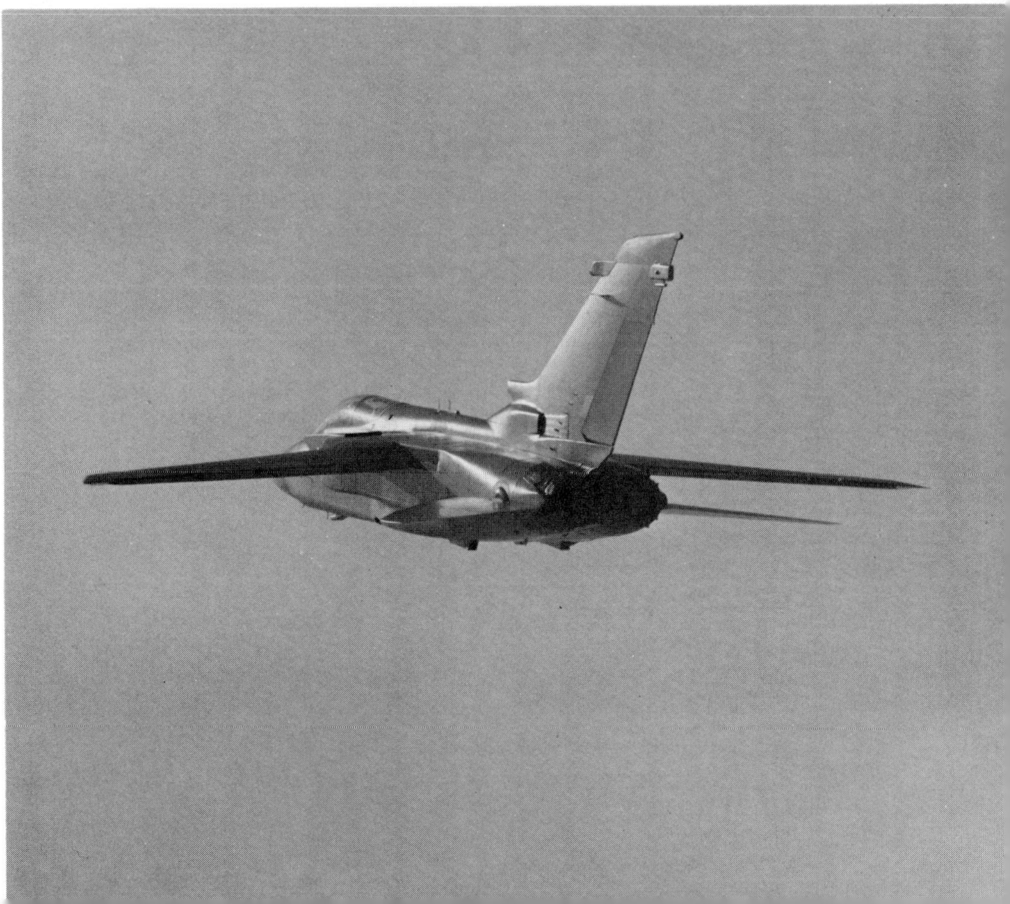

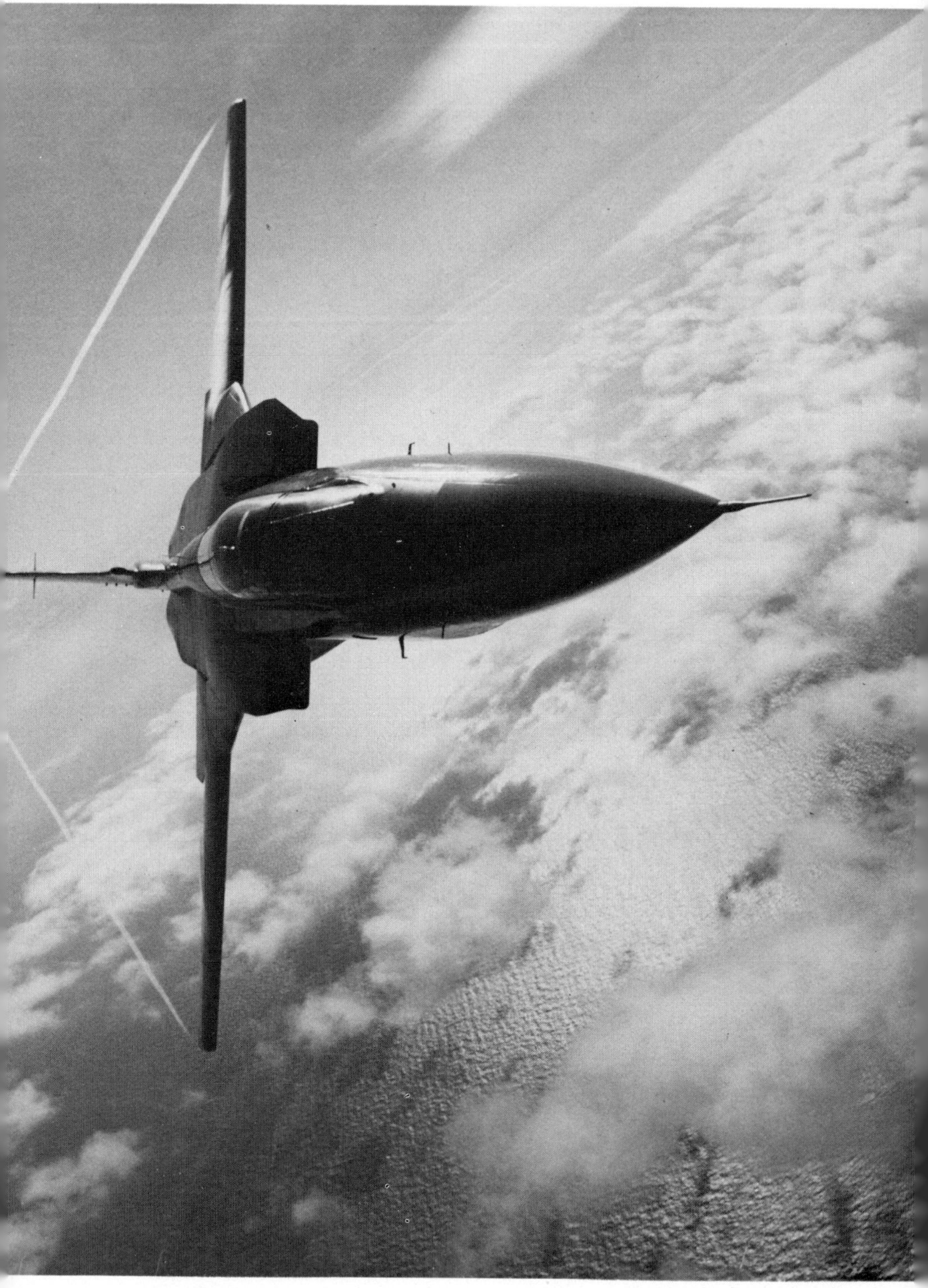

and heights. These trends were reversed by the Indo-Pakistan War of 1965. The majority of air combats took place at low level, often at less than 1,000 ft. The reasons for this are not hard to find. Both air forces were relatively small for the area they had to cover. Both sides possessed ground radar but the coverage was not comprehensive. Dust and haze frequently restricted visibility. The best method open to both sides to inflict a damaging blow on the enemy was to strike at their airfields, with fighter-bombers coming in low beneath the radar. The majority of combats occurred when these low-flying strikes were intercepted. At such low level the fighters had no altitude to trade for speed, which they quickly reduced in a series of hard turns.

The Pakistan Air Force was badly outnumbered and relatively ill-equipped. Their opponents possessed 118 Hawker Hunters and 80 Folland Gnats as their main fighting force, with 80 Dassault Mysteres. All these aircraft were subsonic, all possessed cannon armament. The supersonic component of the Indian Air Force was composed of ten MiG 21s. To oppose this powerful force, Pakistan could muster about 90 F-86F Sabres armed with machine guns, and a dozen Mach 2 Starfighters.

Against this numerical and qualitative imbalance, the Pakistanis had one trump card. About a quarter of the Sabres carried Sidewinders. In the heat of battle the Indians would have to assume that they faced missile-armed opponents. Their main fighter, the Hunter, was considerably faster and had much better acceleration than the Sabres. One method of evading a stern attack by a slower gun-armed fighter was simply to open the throttle and accelerate away out of range. The 2 mile reach of the Sidewinder made this manner of evasion distinctly unprofitable. The Hunters had to turn and fight, and in a high turn the Hunter lost speed faster than the Sabre.

Sabre pilot, Squadron Leader Alam, was credited with the destruction of five Hunters in one engagement during the morning of September 7. Two pairs of Sabres were patrolling the large Pakistani airfield at Sargodha at medium altitude with a Starfighter flying top cover at 15,000 ft. A low level strike by six Hunters was not detected until very late and the pair of Sabres led by Alam sighted them just short of the airfield. Alam fired his two Sidewinders, one of which accounted for a Hunter, then lost contact. Chasing back towards the Indian border he found them again, flying in loose line abreast at between 100 and 200 ft. As he closed, he was spotted and the Indian formation broke into a steep climbing turn to the left, ending in loose line astern. Alam turned across the inside of the circle, picking off four Hunters in quick succession. He later commented: 'I developed a technique of firing very short bursts – around half a second or less. The first burst was almost a sighter, but with a fairly large bullet pattern from six machine-guns, it almost invariably punctured the fuel tanks. . . . As we went round in the turn, I could just see, in the light of the rising sun, the plumes of fuel gushing from the tanks after my hits. Another half-second burst was then sufficient to set fire to the fuel, and as the Hunter became a ball of flame, I would shift my aim forward to the next aircraft.'

This brief encounter lasted barely 30 seconds. Alam pulled about 5G in the turn, about as much as his gunsight computer could handle. The turn lasted about 270 degrees, or three-quarters of a circle. During this turn, the Hunters lost speed at over 10 mph per second, from over 500 mph down to well under 300 mph. This enabled Alam to close the distance on the Hunters one after the other.

By all breaking in the same direction, the Indian pilots lined themselves up like ducks in a fairground. Had they all broken in different directions, Alam and his wingman could easily have been in trouble, outnumbered as they were.

The Indian Air Force did not have a monopoly on poor tactics. Minutes before the combat just described, Starfighter pilot Amjad Husain tangled with a Mystere. After a Sidewinder attack had failed, he closed the range and finished it with cannon fire. Another Mystere intervened and instead of using his tremendous climb or acceleration advantages, Husain tried to out-turn it. The Starfighter is arguably the world's worst fighter in a turning combat, and Husain ejected from his mortally stricken aircraft at low level. The Mach 2 wonder had been vanquished by a sub-sonic Mystere flown by a very determined Indian pilot. Bob Johnson's maxim of 'don't fight the way your opponent fights best' had once more been proved correct.

The two supersonic types in service appear to have seen little action. The small numbers available made effective action difficult. The Pakistan Air Force at first used single Starfighters as top cover for sections of Sabres. Later they tried keeping them low, beneath the radar, ready to zoom up and intervene if necessary. Neither ploy was very successful.

Little of value can be deduced from the three-week war between India and Pakistan. Most of the fighters of both sides were sub-sonic, missiles were little used and early warning and ground control seems to have been mainly ineffective.

India and Pakistan clashed again in December 1971. Both sides had increased their complement of supersonic fighters with India operating eight squadrons of MiG 21s and six squadrons of Su 7s. Against these, Pakistan could muster three squadrons of Shenyang F-6s (Chinese MiG 19s), one squadron of Mirage IIIs and a flight of Starfighters. Both sides were equipped with Sidewinder guided missiles.

Hostilities commenced on December 3. The Pakistani Air Force launched strikes at forward Indian airfields, with the intention of forcing the Indian Air Force fighters to operate at long range from airfields further back. The attacks, mounted with small numbers of aircraft, failed to achieve their purpose. As in the 1965 war, both sides concentrated on hitting ground targets and most of the little air fighting that took place was the result of low level interception. The only point of interest arising from this conflict was the ability of the supposedly obsolete sub-sonic types, the Sabre, Hunter and Gnat, to survive air combat consistently against the new supersonic fighters. We will return to this point later.

Further to the west air fighting had been a monthly, if not weekly occurrence for decades and mounting tension between the Arab world and Israel in the early months of 1967 made war inevitable.

The Israeli Air Force possessed about 70 Mach 2 capable Mirage IIIs, plus an assortment of inferior French designed aircraft. The main opposition was the Egyptian Air Force with between 100 and 120 Mach 2 capable MiG 21s its main force. The Syrian Air Force operated about 40 of these potent Russian-built fighters, and the Iraqi Air Force a further 60. Both in modern fighters and older types, the Israelis were outnumbered by three to one. To redress the numerical imbalance, the Israeli Air Force launched the now famous pre-emptive strike on June 6 1967. Air superiority was attained by the simple expedient of blowing large holes in Egyptian runways, rendering them unusable. The Egyptian Air

Limited wars

Force was quickly reduced to manageable proportions by this method, and nearly 300 aircraft were reported destroyed on the ground.

Despite this crushing blow, the Egyptians and their allies were not completely swept from the skies and a considerable number of air combats occurred. Unfortunately, first-hand accounts of clashes between Mirages and MiG 21s are few and lack sufficient detail for us to reconstruct. Rather surprisingly, a very high proportion of the Israeli victories were with the old-fashioned gun.

The popular view at the time was that missiles could do the job without the fighter ever closing to gun range and as a result many contemporary Western fighters carried no guns. The Six Day War disproved this contention, yet there were still doubters. Many viewed the stated Israeli preference for close gun combat, as part of a massive propaganda exercise. Of course there was a certain amount of propaganda. Israeli pilots were presented as supermen, the Mirage as a world-beating fighter, and the cannon as the primary fighter weapon. The Israeli stance was understandable. Even in victory they were still outnumbered and ringed by hostile Arab nations. One day they would have to fight again and before that day came they were determined to use every device to enhance the reputation and boost the morale of their airforce.

What were the facts? The Israeli fighter pilots were certainly better than their opponents. However, the Mirage was a very ordinary fighter. Its engine thrust in proportion to its weight was low; in fact the lowest of any Mach 2 fighter built. Its acceleration and rate of climb were inferior to those of the MiG 21 so what advantages did the Mirage possess? For a start its low wing loading gave exceptionally good turning performance and its handling qualities were excellent. It could perform descending manoeuvres at speeds of less than 100 mph without loss of control. By comparison, the MiG was limited to 130 mph and did not handle at all well at low speeds. The drag of the Mirage's large delta wing caused it to lose speed rapidly in a tight turn, but this could have been utilised to force an attacker to overshoot. As we have seen earlier, speed reduces in a turning fight. The slower the fight became, the more the Mirage came into its own.

The war of attrition between Egypt and Israel began in June 1969 and lasted until August 1970. The Israeli Air Force had been partially re-equipped with American-built Skyhawks and Phantoms. Egypt at this time abounded with Russian advisers and technicians. Much aerial skirmishing took place, with the Israelis as usual taking the honours. But in April 1970, events took a new and ominous turn. Five squadrons of MiG 21s arrived in Egypt complete with 150 volunteer Russian pilots to fly them. A confrontation could not be delayed for long and on July 30 it came.

Sixteen Russian-flown MiG 21s intercepted a Phantom strike force escorted by Mirages. The Phantoms broke into the attack and the Mirages plummeted down to the rescue. An Israeli pilot later recalled the action: 'They came at us in pairs and we let them pass in order not to be sandwiched between the pairs, as they had anticipated we would. They passed as couples in a procession. We waited and got in behind.'

From this it can be deduced that the Russian attack was most likely made by eight elements of two fighters, each element probably flying welded wing, with the elements in trail. 'The melee continued, planes turning and twisting around and firing guns and rockets at each other. More Israeli planes joined the battle.

Breaking hard, I succeeded in getting my sights on a MiG. He had guts and turned into the fight, but I quickly realised he was inexperienced. He made elementary mistakes. Diving down to 2,000 m I cut him off and soon locked on my radar – then we had time. It was clear that he could not get away. At a range of 1,000 m we fired a missile. The MiG exploded into a flaming ball. . . .'

This Israeli combat narrative is typical in that it gives virtually nothing away. We can however make one or two guesses. After the singular 'I' when referring to flying the aeroplane, the narrator reverts back to the plural 'we'. This means he was probably flying a two-seater Phantom and that the missile used was a radar homing Sparrow, as the Weapon System Officer in the back seat, would normally play a part in launching a missile of this type. Although from the astern position hinted at, a heat homing Sidewinder or Shafrir might have been used. At least one of the mistakes made by the MiG pilot appears to have been that he lost sight of his assailant, and failed to clear his six o'clock. But how much more this Israeli pilot could have told us! In the event, four more Russians were shot down during this engagement for no Israeli loss.

The next major clash in the Middle East came in October 1973. Claims and counter-claims were conflicting as usual. Once again the Israeli Air Force seems to have achieved a crushing victory. Pilot quality counts for much. Were any other major factors involved?

Four out of every five victims in air combat never see their attacker and there is no reason to suppose that the Yom Kippur War was any different. The obvious conclusion is that the Israelis were able to achieve surprise far more often than their opponents and this view is reinforced by the large number of missile kills claimed. The guided missiles of the day had little capability against a manoeuvring target which infers that a high proportion of shot-down Arab aircraft were unaware of impending attack. Why were the Arabs so much more vulnerable to surprise than the Israelis? Three possible reasons suggest themselves.

Firstly, many Arab aircraft were lost while engaged in low level strikes. Low flying makes it difficult to keep a good look-out astern since a pilot cannot concentrate on flying close to the ground at high speed and keep looking over his shoulder at the same time.

Secondly, the Israelis had refined their tactics to reduce the effectiveness of enemy radar surveillance. They sought not to evade detection altogether, but to disguise the composition of their force from which their intentions might be deduced at an early stage. Their aircraft flew very tightly spaced in the initial approach. This gave just one large blip on the Arab radar screens from which the minimum amount of information could be deduced. Three tactical devices were commonly used. Driving into their opponents at high speed and head-on to split their formation; drawing them towards an area where an attack force was lurking at low level beneath the Arab radar coverage, and splitting their own formation into pairs when action was joined to scatter the Arab formation still further. When the low level ambushing force climbed into the battle, mutual support between the aircraft of the Arab Air Forces was thus minimal. It was noted by Russian observers that single fighters rarely acted aggressively but sought to rejoin with friendly aircraft.

Thirdly, the Israelis possessed half a dozen aircraft equipped with electronic countermeasures. These, coupled with the jamming pods sometimes carried by Phantoms and backed up by jamming from ground stations, could conceivably have played havoc with their opponents detection and communications system, on which they were heavily reliant. The Egyptian and Syrian pilots may, at times, have been forced to fly electronically blind. If this was the case, the advantage of early detection and surprise would lie firmly with the fighters bearing the blue star of Israel.

During 1965 the United States became embroiled in a conflict in Vietnam. As in Korea it was the communist North versus the democratic South. There the resemblance ended. The Korean War had been fought out between conventional ground and air forces. The Vietnam War was in the main fought between the Viet Cong, a well organised and motivated guerilla army, and the conventional forces of South Vietnam and America. The Viet Cong proved an elusive opponent. It was rarely possible to strike at them direct and American air power was, therefore, mostly directed against the Communist supply lines and depots in an endeavour to reduce their fighting ability. It was the deep penetration raids into the North which led to air fighting, when the North Vietnamese Air Force rose in opposition.

The United States Air Force and Navy were extremely well equipped with modern aeroplanes and weapons. But their equipment was designed for fighting in support of conventional ground forces, against a numerous and well equipped opponent. The aeroplanes were mainly strike or multi-role types. Most widely used was the F 4 Phantom II, a massive 25 ton monster with a two man crew and exceptional all-round capability. It carried a powerful modern radar and as an escort fighter was normally equipped with four Sparrows and four Sidewinders. No guns were fitted in the early versions. The F-105 Thunderchief was also used in large numbers. The 'Thud' as it was affectionately known, was designed specifically for high speed, low level delivery of tactical nuclear weapons in a conventional battlefield scenerio. The largest and heaviest single-seat, single-engined aeroplane ever built, it carried only one Sidewinder for self-defence. A 20 mm cannon was also fitted, more for strafing than for air combat. The wing loading on both types was high, consequently neither was suited to a turning dogfight.

Many US Air Force units were based in Thailand. A deep penetration raid to the Hanoi or Haiphong areas involved a round trip of well over a 1,000 miles. They were thus dependent on in-flight refuelling which usually took place over the neighbouring country of Laos or well out over the Gulf of Tongking.

The North Vietnamese Air Force used mainly MiG 17s and 21s. The MiG 17 was a trans-sonic, cannon armed fighter. While lacking in speed and rate of climb, it out-turned its American opponents with ease. It was later equipped with Atoll heat-seeking missiles. The MiG 21 was later to be proven in the Six Day War. Possessing sparkling acceleration and armed with cannon and two Atoll missiles, it was a formidable opponent. Its only real weakness lay in its lack of structural strength that limited its speed at low altitudes. The American fighters were much stronger and at low level were generally over 100 mph faster than the MiG 21.

The Atoll was an infra-red homing missile similar to the Sidewinder although there was little to choose between them. They were ineffective if the firing aircraft was pulling more than 2½G. They were easily distracted by heat sources other than the target. They could not follow a hard-manoeuvring target and could thus be evaded by a tight turn. Their acceleration time was short and after the rocket motor burned out, the missiles coasted along losing speed

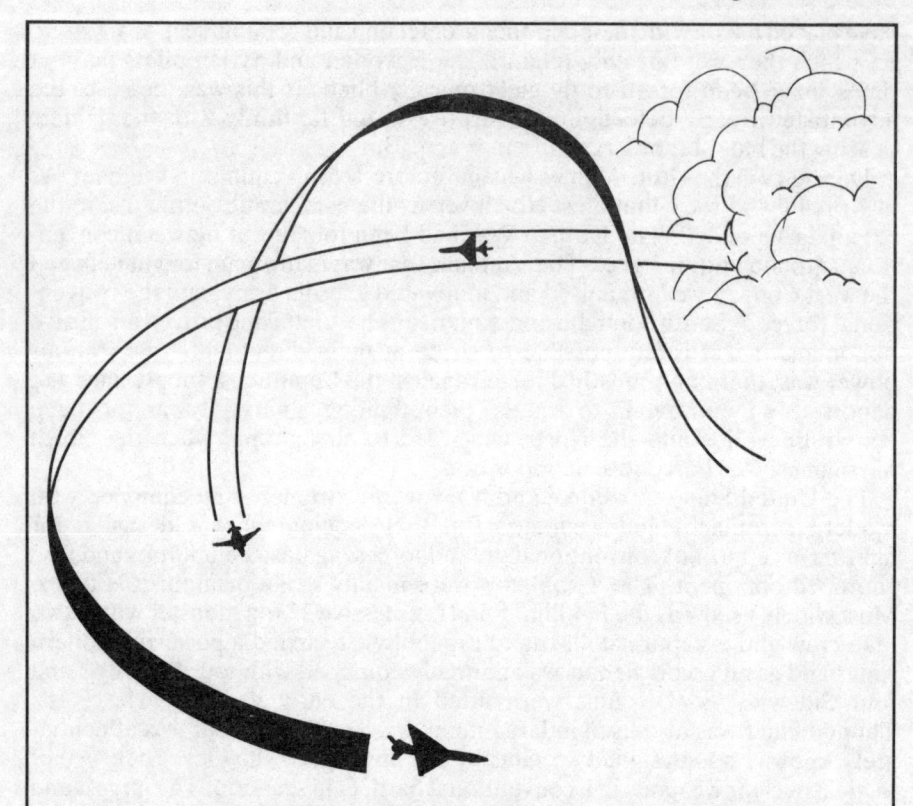

Fig 51 Barrel Roll Attack used by Colonel Robin Olds, Operation Bolo, January 1967.

MiG 21 emerges from cloud in a hard left turn. Colonel Olds pulls high and rolls away from the MiG, then down and below to achieve a successful Sidewinder shot. This is one more instance of a three-dimensional manoeuvre defeating a hard turn in the horizontal plane. This manoeuvre is sometimes called the Vector Roll.

rapidly. A fast-moving fighter could outrun them in the later stages of their flight.

The North Vietnamese had no equivalent of the Sparrow. This missile conferred the ability to shoot down an unseen target from very long range, when aimed by radar. The difficulty lay in positively identifying the target as hostile. After two friendly aircraft had been shot down by Sparrows, the Americans were forced to revert to positive visual identification.

Air combat effectively began during the morning of April 4 1965, when 48 F-105s attacked the Thanh Hoa bridge. Four MiG 17s, apparently directed from the ground, screamed out of the cloud and in a fast diving pass nailed two 'Thuds' before making their escape. The MiGs did not stay to fight – with so many Thunderchiefs in the area plus 20 escorting Super Sabres, there was little future in it. The surprising thing was that the North Vietnamese ground control had been efficient enough to get the small force of MiGs into position unobserved. The effective use of ground controlled interceptions was to remain the dominant feature of the North Vietnamese air defence.

The small North Vietnamese air force had to be used sparingly or risk destruction. Between September and December 1966, less than one in 20 American strike aircraft were intercepted. But of those that were, over half were forced to jettison their warloads before reaching the target. Thus the MiGs could achieve their objective of spoiling the American strikes without actually shooting down their opponents.

The American force's primary aim was to strangle the North Vietnamese supply lines. Shooting down MiGs was really a sideline. The purpose of a strike was to deliver bombs on target without losing aircraft. However, the spoiling tactics of the North Vietnamese Air Force were too successful, so in January 1967 a carefully prepared trap was laid. Codenamed Operation Bolo, the purpose of the mission was to bring the MiGs up to fight, and then destroy them.

Bolo was very thoroughly planned. The teeth of the operation consisted of 56 Phantoms in flights of four, timed to appear in the target area at five minute intervals, giving about an hour of intensive aerial coverage. They carried radar jamming transmitters in pods. This was an important part of the deception, as jamming pods had previously only been carried by Thunderchief strike aircraft. In their approach and communications they simulated a normal strike, even using the strike wing call-signs but they were backed by 24 Thunderchiefs, whose role it was, to suppress the ground defences, plus EB 66 C electronic countermeasures aircraft to jam the radars of the anti-aircraft guns.

The Phantoms were split into two forces. The 8th Tactical Fighter Wing was designated West Force. Their task was to bring up the MiGs and cover Phuc Yen and Giam La airfields. East force consisted of the 366th Tactical Fighter Wing. They were assigned to cover the airfields of Kep and Cat Bi. They were also responsible for blocking escape routes to the Chinese border. It was a formidable cast, and the stage was set for a battle to sweep the MiGs from the sky.

Battles rarely go according to plan. In this case two factors caused disruption. Heavy cloud made it impossible to cover the North Vietnamese airfields and provided a convenient bolthole for an aircraft pressed hard. In addition, the MiGs were slow in reacting to the strike threat. Only the first three flights of West Force made contact, but they made good use of their opportunities.

The MiG 21s operated in pairs. Apparently directed from the ground, they attacked simultaneously, one pair from ahead, the other pair from astern. Turning to meet the dangerous rear attack exposed the Phantom's tail to the pair from ahead.

World War 2 ace Colonel Robin Olds led West Force and commanded the leading flight. He saw plenty of MiGs that day. The first appeared directly astern and Olds broke left, turning just hard enough to spoil the MiGs aim, and waited for his Nos 3 and 4 to clear his tail. As he did so, another MiG appeared just off to the left at about 1½ miles range. Olds let fly with a brace of Sparrows but they failed to reach their targets. The Sparrow was notoriously unreliable unless fired under ideal conditions and battle conditions are rarely ideal. The initial range of about a mile and a half was probably reduced to less than a mile by the time the radar had been locked on and the missile fired. Against a manoeuvring target this distance was too short for the Sparrow's tracking capability to cope. The MiG 21 disappeared into the clouds, but another emerged off to Colonel Olds' left, in a hard left turn towards him. Olds pulled the nose of his Phantom up at about 45 degrees and rolled to the right. Half inverted, he waited as the MiG passed beneath, then rolled down astern to a position about 20 degrees angle off and just under a mile range. He launched two Sidewinders, one of which hit and blew the MiGs right wing off.

The Phantom pilots had been briefed beforehand not to engage in turning fights with their more manoeuvrable opponents. Colonel Olds pulled high when engaging his second MiG, using the vertical plane to offset his opponent's better horizontal turning performance. Colonel Olds fired his missiles in pairs probably because neither the Sparrow nor the Sidewinder was very reliable. As the war progressed, many American pilots set up excellent attacks only for their missiles to malfunction and although firing a pair was expensive, it greatly increased the chances of scoring a hit.

Colonel Olds was not the only successful pilot. Six other MiG 21s went down. No American aircraft were damaged. Operation Bolo did not cause the mass destruction planned, but it was a definite defeat for the North Vietnamese, who maintained a low profile for the next eight weeks.

Continued strikes by American fighter-bombers forced the North Vietnamese Air Force back into action and March and April saw no less than ten MiG 17s downed by gunfire from the unwieldy Thunderchiefs. During the same period, only two victories were claimed by their Phantom escorts; both were MiG 21s and both fell to Sparrows. This was a curious result during a time supposed to be the age of the missile. How it came about can be partly explained by a detailed look at one of the 'Thud' victories.

On the morning of April 30 1967, the 355th Tactical Fighter Wing attacked railway sidings northeast of Bac Giang. The run-in to the target was made at low level (1,500 to 3,000 ft) and 620 mph. Leading the third flight of Thunderchiefs was Captain Tom Lesan. He later described the action. 'One of the guys in the flight reported MiGs at 3 o'clock. They were in their standard Lufbery and had sighted us and were pulling off to attack. Since they were MiG 17s and pretty slow compared with us, I instructed my flight to hold formation. As I crossed the second element (pair of aircraft), to the left to position the flight in echelon for the push-up and pop, I observed the MiGs [three I think] on the attack from our right side.' Captain Lesan pointed out that the enemy opened fire while over a mile away and didn't pull any lead (deflection) at all but went on: 'Nevertheless the 37 mm rounds looked quite formidable coming across our tails. We had increased speed to nearly 700 mph at this time and left them in our wake. Our pop-up was a climbing turn to the right to between 7,500 and 8,000 feet in trail to allow a 35 to 45 degree dive eastward onto the target. I had briefed the flight to jink out of the target area individually and rejoin at a particular hill. At the top of the pop-up we encountered two more MiG 17s at about 11 o'clock. They came through from about 3,000 ft above firing at us, again without leading their shots and missed us all. Diving, I dropped my bombs on the rail yard from 6,000 ft and continued back eastwards, jinking hard left then right to confuse the ground gunners. I then headed for the re-join point. I was at about 3,000 ft and nearly 700 mph, when I sighted a two-ship flight of MiG 17s about 1,000 yds ahead, high, and going in the same direction. I estimate I was overtaking them at nearly 250 mph and I was closing fast. We always set our switches for missile air after the bomb run. This allowed either

Sidewinder or gun attacks. My Sidewinder was growling off the rail but I was closing so fast that I didn't think I had sufficient time for it to track so I elected to go for a gun attack. I selected the leader on the left and opened fire from about 500 yds. I had tracers about every eight rounds and saw that my aim was good. His wing root began to light up from the impacts, when I realised I was going to collide with the MiG if I didn't do something. I pulled up and rolled left to avoid collision and then rolled back right to re-position on the second MiG. He had broken hard right during my attack and was heading back inland, so I reformed my flight at the hill and we came home.'

The first point of interest in this account is the reference to the 'standard Lufbery'. The MiGs had adopted the defensive circle, which although considered dated in the jet era now fulfilled a new function. It enabled them to sit in one place ahead of the American strikes and wait, while giving all-round defensive cover should they be attacked. The 'wagon wheel' as the Americans now renamed it, had been re-invented, and was widely used by the North Vietnamese.

As we have seen earlier, a high proportion of fighter-bombers were forced to jettison their loads when attacked. Lesan was not easily deterred. Using the superior low-altitude performance of his aeroplane, he outran the first attack. The second attack was more dangerous as it could not be evaded without breaking off the bombing run. However, it caused no damage. At the debrief, the flight members discussed this attack and the general consensus of opinion was that the two MiG 17s pulled out after the attack and curved round to the left, trying to find the Americans. With the speed gained during their diving attack, they had got out in front of Lesan, with dire results for the leader who ejected as the Thunderchief overshot him.

The gun had proved its worth as a complement to missiles. While lacking the range of the missile, it was much more reliable, and the air battles over Vietnam proved conclusively that close range fighting was still possible. The Phantom, previously exclusively armed with missiles, now often carried a pod containing a 20 mm Vulcan cannon slung under the fuselage.

In August 1967 the North Vietnamese introduced a new ploy which was difficult to counter. The state of the art in airborne radar at that time was such that it was rarely possible to detect a low-flying target over land; the radar echoes from the hostile aeroplane were lost amid the reflections from the ground. The fast modern MiG 21s utilised this weakness. Taking off in pairs, they flew low, directed from the ground, until they were abreast of the incoming American strike. They then lit their afterburners and gained height astern of the Americans. Hurtling down from astern at supersonic speed in the classic bounce, they fired their Atoll missiles and either zoomed back high, or carried on down. Initial successes were achieved, but then when the nature of the attack was realised, flights of Phantoms were assigned to cover the rear of the American formations. A month later, air strikes were authorised for the first time against North Vietnamese airfields. Whilst damaging, these failed to counter the threat. In the seven months from August 1967, MiG 21s shot down 18 United States Air Force fighters for the loss of only five of their number.

The North Vietnamese fighters benefited from an efficient ground controlled interception service which greatly added to their defensive capability. The Americans initially had no such facility. Their EC 121 radar and control aircraft, orbiting at a distance, could give general warnings, but these were insufficiently precise to be of much help. This was in part remedied by 'Disco', the EC 121M which carried advanced radar detection and control facilities. Backed by 'Red Crown', a US Navy radar ship in the Gulf of Tongking, they were able to give much more specific information on the whereabouts of North Vietnamese aircraft.

Political considerations halted air fighting over North Vietnam from March 1968 and the hiatus lasted until 1972. The United States Air Force and Navy had time to consider their air fighting tactics. One thing was clear. The enormous kill-to-loss ratio achieved over Korea had not been repeated. There had been phases when the ratio was distinctly unfavourable to the Americans, despite their undeniable technical superiority.

During 1968, the United States Navy analysed the air combats that had taken place over Vietnam. Two main requirements emerged. The first was greater missile reliability. The second was that comprehensive training in air combat manoeuvres be given to pilots. The agile MiGs, with their low wing loadings, had consistently out-turned the heavy American fighters. The US Navy Post-Graduate Course in Fighter Weapons, Tactics and Doctrine was formed as a result, although this mouthful of a title was quickly shortened to 'Top Gun'. In essence it consisted of giving pilots the most realistic combat training possible by opposing them with aircraft of similar characteristics to those likely to be met in action. The T-38 Talon supersonic trainer and A 4 Skyhawk were first used as 'enemies'. Later they were supplanted by the F-5E Tiger II, chosen because its size, general appearance and performance were similar to those of the MiG 21.

Air fighting resumed in 1972 and Phantom pilot Bill Jenkins, flew a tour of operations at about this time. His comments make interesting reading. 'The MiG 21 is a very small airplane. From head-on it is difficult to see at more than 2 miles although a formation is easier. American aircraft were much larger and could be seen at greater distances, not least due to the smoky exhaust trail.'

Other things being equal, the North Vietnamese stood a better chance than the Americans of sighting the enemy first. Furthermore the exhaust smoke instantly betrayed the identity of the American machines. 'We flew a system called Double Attack. The first man to gain contact became the formation leader.'

Double Attack was one more example of re-invention of the wheel. The name was coined by Everest Riccioni, a Super Sabre pilot based in Germany in the early 1960s. A Canadian squadron based nearby flew F 86 Sabres, theoretically outclassed by the aircraft of Riccioni's unit. Mock dogfights often took place and the Canadians frequently beat their supersonic opponents. This set Riccioni looking for an alternative tactical system. His answer was Double Attack, in which an element of two machines split, and keeping their speed well above that of their opponents, carried out sequenced attacks in the manner of Godfrey and Gentile nearly 20 years earlier. It was fine for two against two in peacetime, but in a many versus many engagement it was risky, as both aircraft operated without cover. This was clearly unacceptable. Double Attack over North Vietnam consisted of sequenced high speed attacks made by elements of *two* aircraft, thus maintaining mutual cover at all times as Bill Jenkins explains: 'We flew in pairs although we often got split. Looking back, I think this was just as well. Flying in fighting wing (a close formation), the wingman's situation awareness is almost nil. He is just following the leader.'

Limited wars

This last comment highlights a tactical flaw. The purpose of the wingman is to cover his leader. With the long range of the weapons carried plus the tremendous acceleration available, the wingman would have been more effective a mile or more away than a mere 300 yds. 'Disco or Red Crown gave us warning of impending attacks. We used to generally turn towards them for a head-on shot with a Sparrow. Once we got within 5 miles range, our backseaters took their heads out of the office and became an extra pair of eyes checking our six o'clock. We figured they were more useful that way. I never got any kills in South East Asia, but I think it was possible to build up a score. What it needed was the determination to go in there and risk hanging your ass out. The guys who got results did just that!'

Turning into an attack had been standard procedure since the days of Boelke. Over Vietnam it carried the added advantage of turning the radar towards the attacker to assist in early detection. With the back-seaters responsible for keeping a look-out astern, the pilot was free to concentrate on attack once the range had closed to visual distance. But despite this advantage, Bill Jenkins also commented: 'A two-seat fighter is great in some ways. You've got a guy in the back seat to look after all the magic. In a fight you've got an extra pair of eyes looking out. But pilots do not always have complete faith in their backseaters. My personal preference in a shooting war would be a single-seater every time.'

Once again a reference, albeit indirect, to survival. Victories could wait until another day or even another war, but the first priority was to survive.

The Vietnam war produced few aces. So far as is known, the top scorer of the war was North Vietnamese, Colonel 'Tomb' with 13 victories. He is reputed to have flown both MiG 17s and 21s, and was shot down and killed by a US Navy Phantom flown by Lieutenants Cunningham and Driscoll on May 10 1972. Cunningham had benefited from the air combat training programme instituted by the Navy as described earlier. His attitude bears out Bill Jenkins' comment on determination. 'I never went into the air thinking I would lose. My own motto is borrowed from the Russians. It is: "Seek out your enemy. Don't ask how many, but only where he can be found." This attitude must prevail if you are going to win a war.'

Many top-scoring fighter pilots were much more cautious in their approach, often refusing battle if conditions were unfavourable. Was Cunningham's approach the right one? A look at the events of May 10 supplies the answer.

Phantom squadron VF 96, flying from the aircraft carrier *Constellation*, had just attacked the railyards at Haiphong. As Cunningham and his wingman pulled off the target, they were attacked by the MiG 17s. Cunningham broke to the left and the leading MiG, carried away by his speed, overshot. As he did so, Cunningham reversed his turn and lauched a Sidewinder, even though he was well within the minimum range for this weapon. The MiG was travelling so fast that it opened the range sufficiently for the Sidewinder to guide successfully.

Meanwhile, the second MiG had pulled up vertically and rolled right, where it was engaged by the second Phantom. Then three more MiG 17s appeared astern and the Phantoms nosed into a shallow dive and accelerated away out of range. At nearly 600 mph they pulled up in a half loop, rolling out level at 15,000 ft and headed back towards the fight. Below them they saw eight MiGs in a turning fight with three Phantoms. A Phantom broke away in a left turn, closely pursued by a MiG 17. Cunningham dropped in behind, but was unable to fire because his Sidewinder was just as likely to home in the on the Phantom as on the MiG. Four more MiG 17s were chasing him, then two MiG 19s attacked from 2 o'clock high. Cunningham evaded this attack by turning into it, then turned back after his original target; by now off to his left. Finally, the pursued Phantom broke right and cleared the danger area, enabling a Sidewinder to be launched. It struck the MiG in the tailpipe for the American flyer's second victory.

Evading an attack from above by four MiG 21s, Cunningham headed for the coast. On the way, he encountered yet another MiG 17, almost head-on. Its nose lit up with cannon fire. With no gun to reply, he pulled up vertically. The MiG, flown by Colonel 'Tomb', climbed vertically with him, canopy to canopy. The heavy Phantom had the better zoom climb, but all this did was to put it out in front of the MiG. As Cunningham pulled over, the top tracers flashed past. He went into a rolling scissors, disengaged, turned around and came back in again. Vertical rolling scissors, overshoot, tracers, disengage, come back. . . . On one of the vertical zooms, Cunningham throttled back, extended the air brakes and this time the MiG overshot. The North Vietnamese ace dived straight down, hoping his opponent's missiles would not guide. Although not very hopeful, Cunningham fired a Sidewinder anyway. In spite of the masking effect of ground heat, the missile guided and exploded close enough to the enemy fighter to inflict mortal damage. It dived straight into the ground.

Not satisfied with a hat-trick, Cunningham next turned towards yet another MiG 17 which appeared at his two o'clock. In doing so, he presented his tail to four more MiG 17s. He was saved by the intervention of another flight member, who in desperation, fired an unguided Sparrow. The big missile, trailing its customary plume of white smoke, passed just over Cunningham's tail. The MiGs, seeing it coming, broke in all directions to avoid it.

The conclusions to be drawn from this combat is that fortune favours the brave. The first kill was a combination of quick thinking and luck. The normal result of launching a Sidewinder at less than minimum range was the waste of a missile. The second kill highlighted the gravest deficiency of the heat-homing missile; its lack of target discrimination. Launched earlier, it could have as easily destroyed friend as foe. Two armament deficiencies stand out; the American fighter's lack of a gun and the Russian-built fighters lack of missiles. Had a few of the MiGs encountered by Cunningham during this action carried Atolls, he would have spent more time evading, and much less time in pursuit. The advantage of a two-seater fighter showed clearly. With Lieutenant Driscoll in the rear seat visually checking the vulnerable rear, Cunningham was able to concentrate on attacking. The air combat training programme also paid dividends. The heavy Phantom held its own against the manoeuvrable MiG 17 in the final combat, although perhaps Cunningham was a little lucky that his opponent's shooting was off target. However, as an example of determined action his fight would be hard to beat. The action was fought between seven F-4 J Phantoms and 14 MiG 17s, four MiG 19s and four MiG 21s. In all, six MiG 17s were destroyed for no American losses. Cunningham later commented: 'I personally feel that fighters in a multi-plane engagement cannot effectively remain in section with mutual support. Where several fighters are operating in one area, individual efforts can be made to help each other. . . . We should attempt to maintain section integrity, but when it breaks down be prepared to operate as a single fighter. . . . Speed is life. If you slow down to engage one bandit without mutual support, his wingman may get to you. Make slashing attacks. If he slows down or breaks, look for another tailpipe and clear your own six o'clock.'

He also remarked that Sparrow shots were impossible in this fight as the backseater was unable to use the radar in this environment. As we have seen, he was too busy keeping track of bandits astern. At least three missiles, probably Atolls, were fired at Phantoms during the fight. All missed.

The skies of the world remained relatively peaceful for a few years. Then in 1982 two more wars erupted, as different in character as the countries in which they occurred. The Israelis, provoked by the activities of guerrilla forces based in Lebanon, invaded. This brought them into a direct clash with the armed forces of neighbouring Syria. And in the southern hemisphere, Argentina made an ill-starred attempt to annexe the Falklands.

The Israeli/Syrian air battles were notable for the modern equipment used. The Syrian Air Force was equipped with MiG 21s, swing-wing MiG 23s together with the formidable MiG 25 and Su 22 fighter bombers. To counter this assortment of modern Russian-built aircraft, the Israeli Air Force possessed F-15 Eagles and F-16 Fighting Falcons, both designed for the air superiority role. In the course of a series of vicious dogfights, the Israelis claimed 84 Syrian MiG 21s and MiG 23s shot down *with no loss to themselves*. Israeli pilots had already proved to be of excellent quality. Now they had the equipment to match.

The F-15 is probably the world's best all-round fighter. It carries a mix of radar homing Sparrows and heat-seeking Sidewinders. With a Vulcan cannon for close range work, it is equally well equipped for medium range interception or the dogfight. A sophisticated range of electronics are incorporated for both detection and jamming. The F-16 is a more austere (and cheaper) clear weather dogfighter, armed with two Sidewinders and a cannon. Both fighters have outstanding acceleration, rate of climb, and manoeuvreability. Yet these qualities alone are not enough to account for the repeated aerial victories, and as previously noted, the Israelis do not give much away. Typical is this account by a young Israeli captain of a successful combat on June 8. 'During a sortie providing cover for our forces this morning I received a message about two Syrian planes getting too close to us. Almost immediately, I spotted them on my (radar) screen. Judging by the MiGs speed and direction they had taken off on an attack mission. I attacked the MiG closest to me while my No 1 (the element leader) attacked the second MiG. I acted according to our combat doctrine, aware of the specific performance of my plane. I hit the MiG and it went into a spin, dropped and crashed.'

Slightly more informative was the press conference held by Rafael Eitan, the Israeli Chief of Staff on June 15. While assessing the combat ability of the Syrian pilots as poor, he credited the Israeli integrated ground and airborne detection system with a large part in the success. In particular he singled out the Hawkeye airborne early warning aircraft which he described as 'marvellous'.

Reports have credited the Hawkeye with detecting taxying Syrian fighters on their airfields. This may well have happened once or twice when conditions were particularly favourable, but it should not be regarded as a normal operational capability. Nevertheless, we can reasonably conclude that very effective detection aided the Israeli flyers to a tremendous degree and that electronic countermeasures blinkered if not blinded the Syrians, who, with 350 modern jets at their disposal, could have been expected to have achieved more than they did.

From the clear skies and sunshine of the Middle East we now go to the clouds, fog and storms of the South Atlantic. The Falklands conflict was totally different in character to any war so far examined.

Argentina could muster about 120 jet aircraft, mainly Mirage IIIs and Skyhawks. The only runway on the islands with a hard surface was at Port Stanley. While it was too short to operate Mirages, it could be used by Skyhawks as a staging post for refueling after their attacks. This would have considerably extended their radius of action. In the event the Argentines were given no option. A Vulcan bomber carried out an epic long-distance raid which damaged the runway enough to prevent Skyhawks from using it. Argentina also possessed an elderly aircraft carrier from which Skyhawks could be operated. The Argentine jets were restricted to flying from mainland bases which severely limited their tactical options. Loaded with ordnance, the Falkland Islands were near the limit of their operational radius. Consequently, they could spend little time in the target area. The Mirages in particular were severely handicapped as they could not use afterburner for any appreciable time without depleting their fuel reserves to the danger level. Without afterburner, the Mirages were firmly subsonic, thus losing their greatest advantage over the British fighters.

Against the aging, but comparatively numerous Argentine jets, the British contingent appeared at first sight puny, consisting as it did of about 20 Sea Harrier fighters on two miniature aircraft carriers. It was clear that this tiny force would be stretched thin to cover an area the size of Wales.

Lacking airborne early warning aircraft, the Royal Navy was forced to resort to using ships as radar pickets well out from the task force, and operating combat air patrols. This was no substitute for an airborne detection system and the price the Royal Navy paid was high. Yet the small force of Sea Harriers, later reinforced by Royal Air Force Harriers, acquitted themselves well in combat, shooting down 38 Argentinian aircraft, mainly Mirages and Skyhawks, for no loss. As we have seen, supersonic performance had for years been considered essential in a fighter. But here we have the subsonic Sea Harrier successfully outfighting a proven, successful, Mach 2 fighter. We have seen that fuel limitations reduced the Mirage's performance, but we also know that the Mirage fights exceptionally well at low speeds. What was so special about the Sea Harrier?

The Harrier is unlike any other combat aircraft. Its unique vectored thrust engine, while designed to give it vertical take-off and landing capability, gives it certain unusual flying capabilities. Many air combat manoeuvres are designed to force an attacker to overshoot and fly through. Vectoring in forward flight (VIFF) can be used to assist this. Reversing the engine nozzles has a braking effect sufficient to cause the aircraft to lose 200 mph in a few seconds. In this situation no fighter in the world can stay behind the Harrier. An orthodox jet fighter can throttle back and extend the speed brakes to force an assailant to fly through. When the throttle is opened again, the engine takes a few seconds to wind up and accelerate the aircraft but not so the Harrier! When the nozzles are reversed to slow down, the engine continues to run at full throttle. Then when the nozzles are rotated aft, full thrust is instantly available and the Harrier, with a thrust/weight ratio exceeding unity, accelerates like a bat out of hell. Its subsonic acceleration is probably the equal of, if not better than the American super-fighters.

VIFF can be used in other ways. It can be employed to nibble off a few extra degrees of angle in a turning fight. It can be used to effect an Immelmann turn little bigger than that of the First World War ace. It can also be used to deflect the hot exhaust away from the aircraft to defeat a heat-seeking missile. For hovering flight, control is maintained by a reaction control system. This is high pressure air from the engine expelled from small nozzles at the nose, tail, and wingtips. Hovering would never be attempted in combat, but the control system allows the Harrier to be flown at speeds down to 70 mph.

The other advantages of the Sea Harrier were that it had a much better radar than the Mirage, the latest version of the Sidewinder, the AIM 9 L, and the fact that in normal flight its hot exhaust is emitted laterally. Its infra-red signature is therefore much larger than that of a conventional fighter but much more diffuse. To a heat seeking missile it presents an abnormally poor target. This was the machine in which British pilots tackled large numbers of Argentinian jets.

Flight Lieutenant David Morgan, an experienced Royal Air Force Harrier pilot, was attached to a Royal Navy Sea Harrier squadron when the Task Force sailed. At 10,000 ft above Bluff Cove in company with Lieutenant David Smith, he sighted a Mirage far below. 'I saw the Mirage attack a landing craft and we dived at full power. We were travelling at about 700 mph and closing fast. I fired off a Sidewinder from 1,000 yds and there was just a quick flash and a fireball. I pulled over and fired another 'winder at the next Mirage. The missile took the back of the Mirage off and as the aircraft came apart the pilot ejected . . . as his 'chute opened I just missed snagging him on my wing. There were two remaining aircraft and I fired a burst of 30 mm cannon as a Mirage drifted in front of me. . . . Dave Smith had seen my shells churning up the water and located a target flying about ten feet above the water. He fired and the Mirage went straight in. . . .'

This combat had all the ingredients of a classic if typical aerial victory. Detection was followed by rapid closing, the element of surprise was maintained and the attack was successful. The destruction of the enemy is always the best way to disengage.

Chapter 12

Summary

Changes in air fighting tactics are conditioned by two external influences. These are military necessity or threat, and the technical means available. Fighting effectiveness can be determined by four criteria. In priority order they are: (1) The attainment (and avoidance) of surprise; (2) Teamwork; (3) The ability to outmanoeuvre an opponent; (4) Weapon lethality.

As we have seen again and again in the preceding chapters, surprise is the dominant factor in air fighting as four out of every five victims are unaware of their attacker until it is too late. One exception to this rule exists. The massed daylight bomber raids of the Second World War were almost impossible to surprise, but the bombers were dependent on tight formations and massed cross-fire for defence and thus were unable to manoeuvre to evade attacks.

Teamwork enables the utmost advantage to be taken of the surprise attack; it also helps guard against being surprised. Fighters acting in concert are more effective than solo performers.

The ability to outmanoeuvre an opponent is the glamorous part of air fighting. Unfortunately, it is the area of fighting effectiveness which accounts for a mere fifth of all victims. This is why it has been placed a mere third in priority.

Finally, weapons lethality. Once the machine-gun had been accepted as the primary fighter weapon it ruled supreme until the advent of the guided missile. As technology developed, speeds increased and aeroplanes were made stronger. With greater speeds the average shooting range tended to increase. To compensate for longer ranges and tougher aircraft, more and heavier guns were introduced. But all in all, it is arguable that the AIM 9L Sidewinder of the 1980s is not significantly more lethal against modern jets than were the eight Colt Brownings of the Spitfire against the Me 109 in 1940, or the twin Spandaus of the Albatros D V, against the Camel in 1918. In air combat the weapons employed have generally been sufficiently effective.

Air fighting breaks down into five phases. In chronological order they are: (a) detection; (b) closing; (c) attack; (d) manoeuvre; (e) disengagement. In practice phases can be omitted. The detection of an enemy who has achieved a favourable attacking position, might well be followed by an attempt to disengage. We shall summarise the development of air fighting tactics by examining these five phases in turn. Of the four criteria for fighting effectiveness only teamwork affects all five phases of combat. This will be touched upon as necessary.

Detection

Early detection and identification of an opponent remains of the utmost importance, as it gives the pilot a vital few seconds to seize the initiative. During World War 1, detection was visual; there were no other means available. Inexperienced pilots saw little. They blundered round the sky creating a 'target-rich environment' for the aces. Accounts of the period (and of World War 2) abound with instances of a fierce fight going on around novices who remained completely unaware of their peril. If they lasted, they learned to see more and their chances of survival increased dramatically. The value of early detection is inversely demonstrated by the attention given by pilots to avoid being detected. McCudden in the 1914–1918 war was a classic example, and the papers by Malan and Tilley in the 1939–1945 war bear this out. The importance of achieving surprise (or not being surprised) cannot be overstated.

One man alone cannot see enough. Aircraft started to fly in company for mutual protection and this gave extra pairs of eyes to detect and guard against surprise. Conversely, a formation is easier to see at a distance than a single aeroplane, but the advantages of mutual protection offset this increased visibility. The most common formation used in the First World War was the Vic. This was not an ideal formation for pilots to search the sky and guard against surprise but with only the leader able to give visual signals, it was the best compromise possible.

The Spanish Civil War saw the development of the Schwarm or finger four formation. This was a major advance in avoiding the surprise bounce as each pilot was able to cover the vulnerable rear area of the other formation members. For this and other reasons, the 'finger four' was adopted by all the major combatant nations during World War 2.

The Second World War saw the introduction of radar and ground control. Enemy aircraft could now be detected at great distances and defending fighters directed to intercept. If time permitted, the fighter controller on the ground tried to place the defending fighters up-sun to increase their chances of making a surprise attack. The formation leader was directed where to look, which greatly increased his chances of seeing the enemy before they saw him. The system broke down when the situation became confused and fighter pilots were forced to fall back on visual detection.

Radar was first carried in aeroplanes in 1940. It needed a second crew member to operate it and a large fighter to carry it. The large fighter lacked performance compared with the single-seater and in a dogfight would have been severely disadvantaged. The range of the early airborne radars was short, and except in bad weather, there were no advantages in using the heavy radar-equipped fighter by day.

The air fighting over 'MiG Alley' should theoretically have produced ideal conditions for the MiG 15s to bounce the lower-flying Sabres. The MiGs had all the traditional advantages; height, position, and radar early warning coupled with ground control. How did they fail to capitalise on these advantages? The practice of the Sabre pilots was to fly at near their maximum speed in the combat area. This coupled with a high standard of training and alertness appears to have negated the ability of the MiG 15 pilots to achieve surprise.

The technological advances of the 1950s and 1960s, gave fighters a greatly increased detection capability. Single-seater fighters could carry quite sophisticated radars. The advances in engines and aerodynamics meant that a two-seater fighter with advanced radar and computers lacked nothing in performance when compared with a single-seater. However, the greatly increased detection capability raised as many problems as it solved. Positive identification was one, as the Americans discovered over Vietnam. After a couple of mishaps, they were forced to resort to visual identification. Another was how to remain undetected by enemy radar. Flying very low was one answer, jamming was another. A major problem was how to use radar for detection while remaining undetected. A radar set is a huge elecronic beacon in the sky which betrays its position and identity to ground monitoring stations. The only answer to this was for the radar to be used intermittently for search purposes and switched to 'standby' in between times.

Closing

This involves maintaining the element of surprise. In both First and Second World Wars it was customary to seek a position of advantage. The first priority was of course to avoid detection. This usually meant seeking a position up-sun. The second priority was to close from a direction which gave the best chance of a successful attack, ie, from astern. The third priority was to close the distance as rapidly as possible to reduce the detection times available to the enemy. This was generally achieved by attacking from a height advantage as the added speed of the dive reduced the closure time. It was rare that all three priorities could be met and the experienced fighter leader made the best of the options open to him. From the beginnings of air fighting to the jet fighter battles above MiG Alley, maximum speeds increased six-fold. This reduced the closure time considerably. The time taken to cover 3 miles was two minutes in 1916, 30 seconds in 1940 and less than 20 seconds in 1952.

The introduction into service of the Mach 2 capable fighter promised great advantages in surprise owing to its potentially huge rate of overtake. In fact, the maximum speeds seem never to have been used in combat. An analysis of more than 100,000 sorties over Vietnam by American Mach 2 capable aircraft was made. Time spent at speeds exceeding Mach 1.2 amounted to a few hours, while recorded time at Mach 1.6 or over amounted to a few seconds. The reason for this is not hard to find. By far the longest part of a mission is flown at cruising speed to conserve fuel. Cruising speed is firmly subsonic. Afterburner was only lit when combat was about to be joined and the closing time was too short for very high speeds to be attained.

However, the tremendous acceleration of the supersonic fighters allowed them to remain low where they were less likely to be detected by radar, then close in a fast shallow climb from astern, from which angle they were unlikely to be visually detected.

Even at the cruising speeds of today, an aircraft detected 50 miles away on an opposite heading is likely to be encountered within three minutes. Therefore, every unidentified aircraft within a vast area can very quickly become a threat. As Bill Jenkins noted over Vietnam, the standard procedure was to turn head-on towards them.

If an aircraft is positively identified as hostile, an attack can be made from beyond visual range. If long range identification is impossible, then closing must be done in a manner which ensures the earliest possible visual identification. If the bogey is on an opposite heading, the advantage will lie with the pilot of the smallest, ie least visible, fighter. A pilot flying a large fighter such as the F-15, can partially offset the size of his mount. The initial phase of closing is to turn away between 20 and 30 degrees, then turn back on an interception course after a few miles. The pilot will then be approaching the target from the front quarter, while presenting his smallest (head-on) aspect to the bogey. This increases his chances of spotting the bogey and diminishes his own chances of being seen.

Attack

Successful attacks are the logical outcome of early detection, swift closing and the maintenance of surprise. In fact, the attack flows on from the closing stage and it is difficult to define where one ends and the other begins. Perhaps we should consider the start of the attack as the moment when the attacker starts to align his weapons.

One aircraft attacking should be able to shoot down one enemy while a formation attack should be capable of destroying as many enemies as there are fighters in the attacking formation. With hindsight, the team attacks advocated by Sholto Douglas seem a little too rigid. The attacking flight leader was usually the only one who got a good shot, the other pilots being to a degree preoccupied with keeping station rather than aiming. The teamwork did, however, minimise No 84 Squadron's casualties while obtaining reasonable results. We should also remember the conditions at the time; a long-drawn out war which must have appeared to stretch ahead endlessly. In these circumstances Douglas was correct in minimising his own rate of attrition, while maintaining a favourable exchange ratio. The Vic formation, while best suited to the needs of the time, did not lend itself easily to the attack phase. The leader could get in close before opening fire, but the other pilots, staggered back from him, were forced to shoot from longer distances or risk breaking formation as the leader pulled up.

The finger four used so widely in the Second World War was much more adaptable, as there were two leaders in four aeroplanes. Each leader could take deliberate aim and fire, knowing that his wingman was guarding his tail. When opportunity offered, all four fighters could move into line abreast, thus all could attack effectively. The comparatively wide spacing between fighters made it easy to select individual targets without the formation losing cohesion.

The favoured position for attack was from astern. This gave a good chance of surprise, sufficient time to aim carefully, no return fire if the target was a single seater, and a good position if the attack failed. With no deflection to allow for, the target was relatively easy to hit. A determined fighter pilot in either World War adopted the 'stick your nose in the enemy cockpit' approach to ensure that his shots counted.

During the summer of 1940, some Royal Air Force fighter squadrons experimented with head-on attacks on the Luftwaffe bomber formations. This was only possible when the initial positions were right, but then it offered the quickest way of attacking the bombers before the escorting Messerschmitts could intervene.

The German fighters had a totally different problem to face when they tackled the American heavies later in the war. The traditional stern attack exposed them to a storm of crossfire for an unacceptably long period. They then reverted to attacking from head-on, but the short time available in which to aim

Fig 52

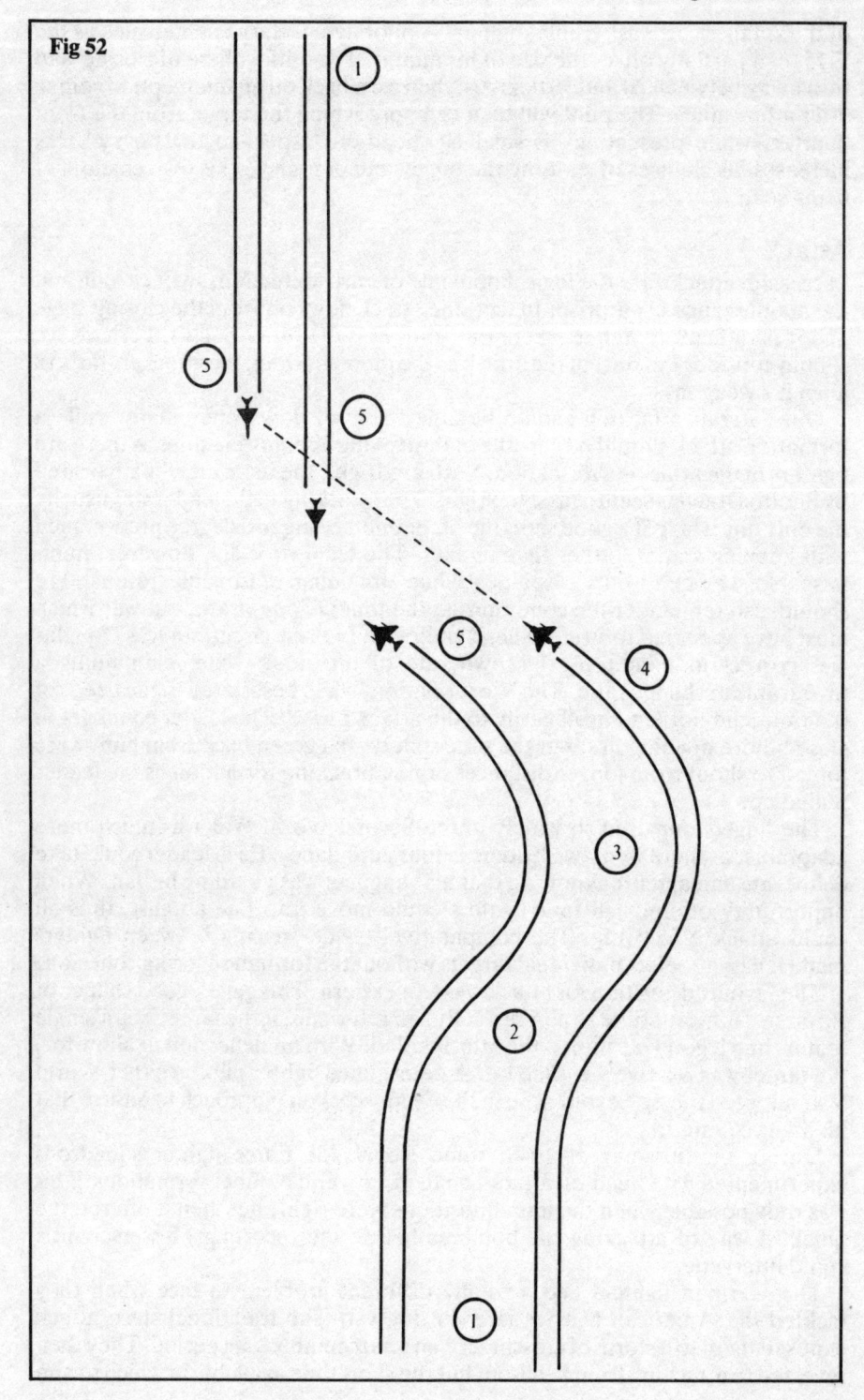

and fire did not secure the results they wanted. Finally, they introduced the Sturmgruppe; heavily armed and armoured fighters which attacked from astern, braving the return fire.

There were no new developments in the attack phase until the introduction of the guided missile. The radar homer promised the elimination of the closing phase with detection being immediately followed by attack. This fond hope was thwarted, as previously stated, by the difficulties of identification. The heat seeking missile has proved more effective in the traditional attack from astern. With its long range compared to the gun, it has enabled successful attacks to be made from distances of 2 miles or more, thus reducing the time taken in the closing phase.

However, the radar homing missile has its uses. In the closing stage we gave an example of an offset approach for visual identification. Let us take this one stage further and imagine opposing elements of two machines each. The first task of the attacking formation is to take up a very wide formation with the wingman 2 or 3 miles out and astern. The opposing formation is then established by radar; trail, fighting wing or whatever. The wingman in the attacking formation then puts his radar into the attack mode on the furthest enemy. As soon as his leader positively identifies the other formation as hostile, he is cleared to fire. If all works well, what started out as a two versus two combat, rapidly becomes a two versus one. If the attack fails, the two hostile fighters will have spotted only his leader. The wingman, if he remains undetected, is still a potential surprise factor in the ensuing fight.

Manoeuvre

This is the fourth phase of combat which, in encounters between small numbers of aircraft, only takes place if the first three phases haven't worked out. It is the most spectacular phase of combat and for this reason is often considered to be the most important. As we have seen, this is not the case. Manoeuvre is the phase in which only about one in five victims are brought down.

Manoeuvre started to become important with the introduction of a 'flying gun'. As the gun was aimed by aiming the whole aeroplane, the aim could be spoilt by target manoeuvring. The attacker could either break off at this point or follow the target, trying to achieve a new aiming position.

Air fighting, being three-dimensional, appears at first sight to be an open-

---

Opposite
Fig 52 Offset closing against unidentified radar contact.

1) Unidentified aircraft are detected at 50 miles range on a collision course.
2) The attackers turn away to offset the interception angle.
3) The attackers turn back onto an interception course.
4) The attacking wingman locks his radar onto the farthest bogey.
5) The attacking section leader, presenting his smallest aspect (head-on) to the bogeys, gains visual contact and identifies them as hostile. His wingman launches a radar homing missile (the leader is now too close to do so).
Should the missile attack fail, hopefully only the leader will have been spotted. His wingman will thus remain a surprise element in any fight that develops.
If the missile attack is successful, the ensuing fight is two versus one.

ended, manoeuvre/counter-manoeuvre sequence. However, this is not the case. In any given situation the options open to a pilot are limited. The limitations are imposed by the relative positions and speeds of attacker and attacked at the start of the engagement, and the performance abilities of the aircraft involved. Rarely will the manoeuvring phase start with the adversaries on level terms. Almost invariably one will have detected the other, sought an advantageous position, and have initiated closing or even attack before he in turn is detected. Manoeuvre is therefore born of a need to defend, or in extreme cases, survive.

The main evasive manoeuvre was the hard turn. In the First World War the attacker would usually attempt to follow. The two aircraft would then try to out-turn each other to achieve a firing position. In single combat a protracted circling match would then ensue, but in a multi-aircraft engagement, it was only a question of time before other aircraft joined in and the combat had to be broken off.

Max Immelmann seems to have been the first pilot to use the vertical plane. His fast diving attacks would rarely allow him to follow his opponent's turn, but pulling up into a steep climb and aileron turning as he did so left him well placed for a further dive. The Immelmann Turn was the direct ancestor of the high speed yoyo.

Few pilots of the era followed his example. A formation attack was usually followed by a free-for-all as fighters split up and engaged individual opponents. As we have seen, dogfighting was a very dangerous business as pilots, engrossed in outmanoeuvring one opponent were easily surprised by another. It was this that led Major Douglas to avoid dogfights whenever possible and break away after the attack had been delivered. One is reminded of Harold Balfour's comment 'We were too busy fighting to worry about the business of clever tactics.'

The outbreak of the Second World War brought few changes. The finger four formation gave much greater flexibility in the fight, coupled as it was with the cross-over turn. Horizontal manoeuvring combat still took place, but despite greatly increased speeds, turning was slower than it had been 20 years earlier. A Sopwith Camel at 100 mph pulling 3 Gs had a radius of turn of about 80 yds and an angular rate of turn of 36 degrees per second. By comparison, a Spitfire at 300 mph pulling 5 Gs turned on a radius of about 415 yds and its angular rate of turn was down to 20 degrees per second. This slower rate of turn, coupled with a much larger radius, made fighting in the vertical plane more advantageous and underlined the virtues of performance over manoeuvreability. Manoeuvreability remained important, but the accent shifted to transient rather than sustained manoeuvreability; the ability to change the direction of flight quickly rather than the ability to perform a very tight turn. The FW 190 A3 had a decided performance advantage over the tighter turning Spitfire V, and this made it a formidable opponent in the attack phase. In the manoeuvre phase, its exceptional rate of roll gave it the ability to change direction much faster than the British fighter. It is significant that some versions of the Spitfire had their wings clipped to increase their rate of roll, even though some turning ability was lost as a result.

Teamwork was the keynote of Second World War fighter operations. It enabled the American Navy Wildcat pilots to hold their own against the supremely agile Japanese Zeros during 1942. The leader/wingman element of two aircraft (welded wing) was almost universal during the final years of the war. Some experiments were made with a leader/leader, or 'loose deuce' style of fighting, but while effective it was rarely used, owing to the large number of aircraft in a fight.

The tendency in the early years of the war was for larger and larger formations to be used. That these were not very effective is shown by the results achieved by the huge British Circus operations. As speeds increased, it became more and more difficult to hold large formations together and by the final year the trend had begun to reverse among the Allied fighter forces. Not so the Luftwaffe, who were forced to use large numbers against the massive American daylight raids.

The jet fighter battles over Korea were fought at greater heights than ever before. The thin air near the stratosphere greatly reduced the ability of the aircraft to turn tightly. A Sabre pulling at 3 Gs at 600 mph has a radius of turn of nearly 1⅔ miles and its rate of turn is down to a pathetic six degrees per second. In practice combat today at high altitude, the winner is often the pilot who can tease his opponent into tugging the pole a little too hard and stalling out. To turn about would take half a minute! As a direct consquence, manoeuvres in the vertical plane became even more important than hitherto. The high speed and low speed yoyos, although not original, were first used extensively over MiG Alley. Teamwork retained its importance, but the difficulties of holding formation at extreme speeds and altitudes quickly reduced formations down to fours and pairs. Some MiG 15 pilots appear to have reverted to line astern or 'trail' during the conflict. This was an easier formation to hold than welded wing, but had the inherent disadvantage that the rearmost aircraft had no cover, and was therefore vulnerable.

The nature of the wars since Korea dictated that most fights took place at medium and low altitudes. Guided missiles had entered service and this vastly increased the range at which kills could be scored. Spacing between aircraft and elements for mutual cover widened dramatically, partly due to increased weapon ranges and partly due to increased speeds.

The spectacular success ratio achieved by American fighters over Korea was not repeated in Vietnam. The Russian-built fighters used by the North Vietnamese Air Force were better suited for close manoeuvre fighting than the heavy American Phantom. The dense air at low and medium altitudes is the domain of heavy manoeuvring, and horizontal manoeuvre assumes an increased importance. This was used to good effect by the North Vietnamese pilots and the Americans were forced to resort to three dimensional manoeuvring to counter them. The high and low speed yoyos were widely used, as were the barrel roll and vector roll. The American fighters were faster than the MiGs at low level and this was their great advantage. Provided they kept their speed high they could hold their own. Energy dissipating hard turns were avoided unless it became a question of sheer survival. As in all previous wars, teamwork was again vital. So was training in air combat manoeuvres; a field which had been sadly neglected.

Disengagement

The final phase of air combat is disengagement. As the Russian Colonel Dubrov has pointed out, it is necessary to consider the method of disengagement when the decision is made to attack. As the surprise bounce accounts for such a high proportion of total victories, it follows that the attack phase should, if possible, be followed by disengagement. This was the device adopted by Major Douglas in 1918. However, manoeuvring combat cannot entirely be avoided. The important point to remember about manoeuvring combat is that disengagement should take place when any initial advantage has been lost and that manoeuvring should be terminated if possible *before* the enemy has succeeded in gaining a positive advantage. Methods of disengagement vary according to the situation and the abilities of the opposing aircraft. Traditionally, a fast dive away out of the fight has been used, although the Russian training manual of the 1940s recommended a sharp pull up. Either method was usually sufficient to open a distance too far for effective gunnery. Cloud was also used to good effect.

When guided missiles entered service, disengagement became much more difficult. The accelerating shallow dive out of the fight became fraught with danger. Yet with afterburners gulping fuel at an incredible rate, an effective means of disengagement became more important than ever.

Two main methods emerged, both of which depended on manoeuvre. If the attacker was at close range, ie, 800 yds or less, the hardest possible turn into the direction of attack would cause the enemy fighter to overshoot it. In doing so he would probably lose contact, and disengagement could safely take place. At longer, ie, missile ranges, disengagement can be made by a series of turns hard enough to make it difficult for the attacker to achieve a good missile firing position, but not so hard that an undue amount of vital speed is lost.

Use of cloud may still be made to assist disengagement, but most pilots would only risk it in extreme circumstances. While destroying visual contact and acting as a shield against heat-seeking missiles, cloud is transparent to the radar of an opponent. Consequently, radar-guided missiles can be launched with every chance of success, or the attacker can pursue, waiting for his unseen victim to break out into the clear. Once visual contact has been broken, it is good policy to head for ground level to reduce the risk of radar detection.

The incident over the Gulf of Sidra involving American and Libyan aircraft, although starting as part of a peacetime training exercise, was in many ways a classic encounter. The US Navy Tomcats detected enemy planes at long range and closed on an offset interception course. When the leading Libyan aircraft launched a missile, the widely spaced American element enabled the wingman to swing in behind it leaving the leader to deal with the Libyan wingman. Both Tomcats were well placed when the manoeuvre phase began, and the Fitters attempted a defensive split. Each Tomcat fired one Sidewinder; they both scored. With both Fitters shot down, the disengagement phase was not needed.

The first fighter pilot to formulate rules for air combat was Oswald Boelcke back in 1916 and it is interesting to examine whether they have stood the test of time.

(1) Try to secure advantages before attacking. If possible keep the sun behind you. Advantages, in any shape or form, are always to be sought, usually advantages of position. The reference to the sun was in those days the best way of obtaining surprise through remaining unseen. Nowadays the sun is not so important, but remaining unseen, by whatever means, still plays a significant part.

(2) Always carry through an attack when you have started it. This still applies unless carrying through an attack is risking survival due to the appearance of a hostile fighter in a good attacking position. Modern technology has made this much more likely than in 1916.

(3) Fire only at close range and only when your opponent is properly in your sights. Close range is a relative term when launching guided missiles. It remains essential to attempt to achieve a 'heart of the envelope' shot. As speeds increased, gun firing ranges lengthened. While it is still possible to get in very close, it is no longer advisable. The modern jet engine at full throttle sucks in vast quantities of air. If lumps are being knocked off an opponent by cannon fire, some of them are liable to be ingested by the engine of a too-close attacker with serious consequences.

(4) Always keep your eye on your opponent and never let yourself be deceived by ruses. This rule is still very relevant. The ruses have changed over the years. A ruse involves presenting a picture of events as they are not. The decoy has been widely used, simulating a vulnerable single aeroplane, but all the while protected by others in a position of advantage. Ball's ruse of pretending not to have seen an enemy attacking him from astern was a classic of its day. Twenty five years later, the Japanese liking for staging mock dogfights to attract attention was remarkable. Todays ruses partly concern electronic wizardry, as in Operation Bolo, or are concerned with manoeuvres designed to 'wrong foot' an opponent. Typical of this type is a fighter attacking a more manoeuvrable type from astern. Let us say an F-5 E attacking an F-15. The F-15 pilot commences a hard turn towards the direction of attack. He knows the F-5 E cannot turn with him, and when he sees it roll its wings back level and lift its nose, he assumes that the F-5 E driver is attempting a high speed yoyo. The F-15 pilot immediately counters with a zoom climb only to find that his small opponent has snap-rolled back into a climbing turn and is on his tail!

(5) In any form of attack it is essential to assail your opponent from behind. While it is true that the easiest shot is from astern, records of successful attacks from head-on are commonplace in all eras. As missiles improve, this principle loses any value it may have had. Even with the gun as a weapon, head-on attacks at supersonic speeds are possible. Fire is opened at a range of 2 miles and the gunsight gently eased up through the target. This puts a spray of shells on a collision course with the target, although it is almost a case of the target hitting the shells than vice versa.

(6) If your opponent dives on you, do not try to evade his onslaught but fly to meet it. Increases in speed and vastly slower rates of turn have made it almost obligatory to evade an attack. Only in rare cases is it possible to fly to meet it. The lessons of history are clear; the attack phase is the most dangerous part of air fighting and it is therefore this phase which must be defeated. This is most easily done by evasion.

(7) When over the enemy's lines, never forget your own line of retreat. Disengagement is a difficult operation. When the opportunity offers it must be taken, regardless of direction. Never forget that the fuel state has become more important in modern times.

(8) Attack on principle in groups of four or six. When the fight breaks up into a series of single combats, take care that several do not go for one opponent. The performance of modern fighters is such that it is difficult for them to operate as more than a pair. It has been suggested in some quarters that it is

now a good idea to be outnumbered in the dogfight. The pair could take snapshots without having to worry overmuch about identification, while the more numerous enemy would have a very difficult time keeping track of who was who. In this context we must remember that a modern dogfight would take place in a vast area of sky, with fighters constantly getting beyond visual distance before pitching back in. However, this is a theory which remains to be proved. I leave the final word to ex-Aggressor, Major Joe Hodges. 'It sure as hell wouldn't do much for your morale.'

Air battles are lost rather than won. Well trained pilots rarely make mistakes. This being so, only ill-fortune can cause their downfall. The key to success in air fighting therefore, lies in pilot quality and teamwork. This is the lesson of history.

Acknowledgements

First and foremost I am deeply indebted to my good friend Alfred Price. His advice, encouragement and constructive criticisms have been invaluable, as has source material which he has generously made available. My thanks also to ex-Aggressor pilot Major Joe L. Hodges who cast the expert eye of a fighter pilot over the original draft and made many helpful suggestions. I also wish to acknowledge contributions made by Eric Coloney, Bill Jenkins, Mike Kempster, Tom Lesan, Julius Neumann, Christopher Shores, Darrol Stinton and Reade Tilley. Many thanks also to Pete West whose expertise translated the movements of my hands into informative illustrations.

Whilst I have used original material in the main, it was perhaps inevitable that some accounts of tactical innovations or relevant comments on them have previously appeared in print. One cannot ignore previously published material if it happens to be the most relevant, the best, or the earliest. I therefore wish to acknowledge the following sources from which I have drawn quotations.

Appendix

Approximate radius of turn in yards

Speed mph	2G	3G	4G	5G	6G	7G	8G	9G
100	130	80	60					
150	290	180	130	105				
200	515	315	230	185				
250	805	490	360	290	235			
300	1160	710	520	415	340			
350	1575	965	705	565	460	400		
400	2060	1260	920	740	600	525	450	
500	3215	1970	1440	1155	940	822	705	625
600	4630	2840	2075	1660	1355	1185	1010	900
700	6300	3865	2820	2260	1845	1610	1380	1225
800	8230	5050	3685	2950	2410	2105	1800	1600
900	10415	6390	4665	3735	3050	2665	2280	2025
1000	12855	7885	5760	4610	3765	3290	2815	2500

Radius of turn is essentially a function of speed. Generally speaking, the slower the speed, the smaller the radius of turn. But the slow aircraft is vulnerable to attack. Too many very tight turns, with the consequent loss of speed give rise to the situation best summed up as: 'out of altitude, airspeed and ideas'.

Approximate rate of turn in degrees per second

Speed mph	2G	3G	4G	5G	6G	7G	8G	9G
100	22	36	49					
150	15	24	32	40				
200	11	18	24	30				
250	8	14	19	24	30			
300	7	12	16	20	25			
350	6	10	14	17	21	24		
400	5	9	12	15	18	21	25	
500	4	7	10	12	15	17	20	22
600	4	6	8	10	12	14	17	19
700	3	5	7	9	11	12	14	16
800	3	4	6	8	9	11	12	14
900	2	4	5	7	8	9	11	12
1000	2	4	5	6	7	9	10	11

Rate of turn is more important than radius of turn. A defending pilot tries to generate enough 'angle-off' to spoil his opponents aim. An attacking pilot tries to haul his nose around the horizon to track his target. Very hard turns are only used when survival itself is threatened. At very high G loads accurate shooting, guns or missiles, is impossible and the pilot's visual acuity is impaired by 'greyout'.

Approximate Flight Envelope of an advanced fighter

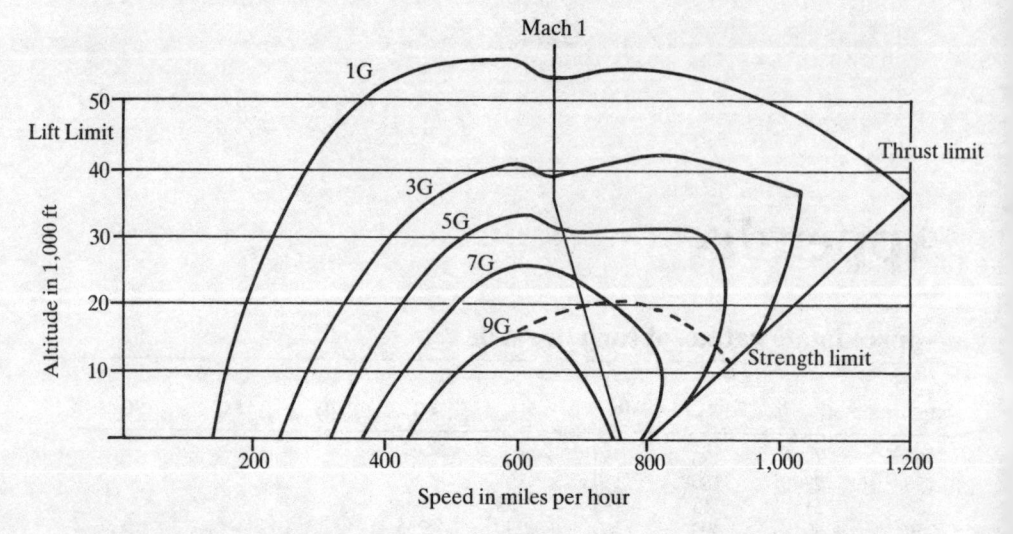

The lines on the diagram are limits set by three factors. These are lift, thrust, and structural strength. The left-hand part of the lines are the limits imposed by the lift available; the kink where the lines cross the speed of sound is caused by the drag increase in the trans-sonic zone and the downward taper is due to lack of thrust. Below the tropopause the maximum speed reduces sharply due to lack of structural strength (airframe and/or engine). The lines denote the limits of sustained manoeuvre. Instantaneous manoeuvre envelopes would be larger but would not exceed either the lift limitations or strength limitations. To clarify this point the 9G instantaneous manoeuvre envelope has been shown with a broken line. It must be emphasised that this data applies to a theoretical advanced fighter. The real thing would be classified.

Bibliography

Engineering, October 1914.
The Wind in the Wires, Duncan Grinnell-Milne.
Knight of Germany, Oswald Boelke.
The Red Baron . . . Manfred von Richthofen, Stanley M. Ulanoff.
Combat Report, Bill Lambert.
Saggitarius Rising, Cecil Lewis.
Wings of War, Rudolf Stark.
An Airman Marches, Harold Balfour.
Flying Fury, James McCudden.
The Command of the Air, Giulio Douhet.
Luftwaffe War Diaries, Cajus Becker.
Blitz on Britain, Alfred Price.
Nine Lives, Alan C. Deere.
The First and the Last, Adolf Galland.
The Soviet Air Force since 1918, Alexander Boyd.
Thunderbolt, Bob Johnson & Martin Caidin.
I Flew for the Führer, Heinz Knocke.
Look of Eagles, John T. Godfrey.
The Last Chance, Johannes Steinhoff.
Battle over Palembang, RAF Flying Review 1960.
MiG Alley, Larry Davies, Squadron/Signal.
Aviatsiya i Kosmonavtika, Colonels Babich & Dubovitskiy.
Battle for Pakistan, John Fricker.
And Kill MiGs, Lou Drendel, Squadron/Signal.
The Israeli Air Force – Mid East Wars, Eshel Dramit Ltd.
Royal Air Force News, 28.7.82 to 10.8.82.
Born in Battle No 27, Eshel Dramit Ltd.

Index

A 4 Skyhawk, 147, 154, 158
Afterburner, 136, 138, 139, 153, 162, 168
Air to air bombing, 11, 100, 119
Alam, Squadron Leader, 145
Albatros two-seater, 12
  D II, 17, 18, 19
  D V, 27, 160
Andrews, Captain, 18
Armée de l'Air, 46, 55, 56
Atmosphere, 19
Atoll, 9, 149, 153, 157
Avenger, 117
Aviatik, 10
B-17, 92, 99, 100, 110, 112
B-29, 119, 122
B-36, 133
Babich, Colonel, 126
Bader, Douglas, 71, 75
Balfour, Harold, 34, 36, 166
Ball, Albert, 23, 169
Bandit, 41
Basset, Ensign, 90
Blenheim, 50, 75, 76
Blunderbuss, 11
Boeing YB-40, 40, 94
Boelke, Oswald, 12, 13, 14, 17, 18, 124, 155, 168
Boelke's rules of air fighting, 14 et seq
Bogey, 41
Bowman, Captain, 35
Bristol Scout, 12
Brown, Russell, 122
Ceiling, 19
Cheek, Tom, 90
Chennault, Claire, 118
Circus, 73, 74, 75, 167
'Clobber College', 128, 130
Cloud, combat considerations, 22, 36, 71, 80, 81, 133, 137, 151, 168
Command of the air, the, 39, 40
Compressibility, 121, 122
Confusion factor, 39, 71, 79, 80

Contrails, 125, 126
Dahl, Walter, 114
Dassault Mirage III, 146, 147, 158, 159
  Mystère, 145, 146
Dauntless, 90
Davis, George, 130
Decoys, 14, 81, 151
Deere, Alan, 64, 69, 76, 77
Defiant, 50
Deflection shooting, 15, 16, 81, 86, 88, 120, 129, 152
Devastator, 90
DH2, 14, 17, 18
Dibb, Ensign, 90, 91
Disco, 154, 155
Dornier Do 17, 42
Douglas, W. Sholto, 25, 29, 30, 32, 45, 73, 163, 166, 168
Douhet, Guilio, 39, 53, 94
Dowding, Sir Hugh, 71, 73
Drag, 21
Driscoll, Willie, 155, 156
Dubovitskiy, Colonel, 126
Dubrov, Colonel, 110, 167
Duxford Wing, 71
Eaker, Ira C., 100
EB 66C, 151
EC 121, 153
Eitan, Rafael, 157
Electronic countermeasures, 9, 132, 134, 135, 148, 151, 157, 162
Escadrille Lafayette, 26
Escort considerations, 13, 40, 42, 61, 64, 74, 90, 94, 95, 100, 109, 110, 111
F-4 Phantom, 138, 139, 147, 148, 149, 151, 152, 153, 155, 156, 157, 167
F-4F Wildcat, 86, 88, 89, 90, 91, 166
F-5E Tiger II, 154, 169
F-6F Hellcat, 118
F-14 Tomcat, 7, 8, 9, 168
F-15 Eagle, 157, 163, 169
F-16 Fighting Falcon, 157
F-80 Shooting Star, 122
F-86 Sabre, 122, 124, 125, 126, 127, 128, 129, 130, 135, 139, 140, 145, 146, 154, 161, 167
F-89 Scorpion, 124
F-100 Super Sabre, 136, 150, 154
F-104 Starfighter, 145, 146
F-105 Thunderchief, 149, 150, 151, 152
Falklands dispute, 158, 159
FE-2, 14, 25
Fiat CR 32, 42
  CR 42, 77
  G 50, 77
Fighter sweeps, 60, 125
Flatley, James, 89
Flying Circus, Richtofen's, 26

Focke-Wulf FW 190, 76, 77, 96, 109, 111, 112, 166
Fokker D7, 32, 34
  Dr 1 Triplane, 34
  E 1 Eindecker, 12, 13, 14, 17
  G 1, 49
Fonck, Rene, 24
Formations
  Chutai, 86
  Echelon, 22, 43
  Fighting wing, 139, 154
  Finger four, 75, 109, 125, 128, 129, 161, 163
  Fluid four, 139
  Fours, 44, 62, 79, 81, 83, 89, 109, 115, 128
  Line abreast, 22, 43, 79, 125, 145
  Line astern (trail), 22, 62, 86, 125, 145, 147, 167
  Pairs, 13, 43, 44, 49, 62, 81, 83, 89, 91, 109, 116, 126, 128, 147, 151, 154, 169
  Shotai, 86
  Sweep formation, USAAF 14th AF, 119
  Vic, 22, 36, 43, 44, 59, 62, 79, 161, 163
  Welded wing, 7, 9, 139, 147, 167
Frantz, Joseph, 10
Galland, Adolph, 55, 56, 75, 99, 112
Garros, Roland, 12
Genie, 136, 137
German Air Service, Order of October 1916, 22
Gentile, Don, 110, 127, 154
Gintzen, Hannes, 52
Gnat, Folland, 145, 146
Godfrey, John T., 110, 127, 154
Goering, Hermann, 40, 61
Goering, Peter, 75
Grinnell-Milne, Duncan, 11, 12
Groupe de Chasse II/5, 52
Guided missiles, 136, 137, 165, 167, 168, 169
Guynemer, Georges, 23
Gyroscopic Computing Gunsight, 120
Halberstadt, 27
Hamersley, Lieutenant, 34
Harbison, Squadron Leader, 126, 127, 130
Hawker, Lanoe, 12, 17, 18, 19
Hayabusa, 115, 118
Height advantage, 10, 30, 35, 38, 131
Hein, 115
Heinkel He 51, 42
  He 111, 42, 54, 83
Herrman, Hans-Joachim, 114

Index

Hints on Hun Hunting, 79, 80, 81, 82, 83
Hodges, Joe L., 170
Hunter, Hawker, 145, 146
Hurricane, Hawker, 48, 54, 55, 61, 62, 63, 64, 77, 84
Husain, Amjad, 146
Immelmann, Max, 13, 166
Imperial Japanese Navy: ships
  Akagi, 90
  Chikuma, 90
  Hiryu, 90
  Kaga, 90
  Soryu, 90
Inayama, Hideyaki, 117
Infra-red homing, 136, 137, 149
Japanese air tactics up to May 1944 (Allied Report), 115, 116, 117
Japanese fighter pilots, instructions to, 117
Jenkins, Bill, 154, 155, 162
Johnson, Bob, 95, 96, 97, 146
Johnson, Johnny, 76
Jones, George, 124, 128
Junkers Ju 88, 83
Kawasaki Type 95, 44
Kleeman, Henry, 7, 8, 9
Knight, Lieutenant, 18
Knocke, Heinz, 100, 109
Knot (nautical mile per hour), 9
Kobzan, Boris, 83
Lacey, James H., 54, 55
Lambert, Bill, 31, 32
Lanchester, F. W., 10, 14
Lee, Kenneth, 64
Left hand bias, 69
Leigh-Mallory, Trafford, 71
Lesan, Thomas C., 152, 153
Lewis, Cecil, 34
Lift, 19
Lufbery, 26, 152
Luftstreitkrafte
  Jagdgeschwader 1, 26
  Jagdstaffel, 22
  Jasta 2, 17
  4, 26
  6, 26
  10, 26, 34
  11, 26
  35, 32
Luftwaffe
  Begleitgruppe, 111
  Gefechtsverband, 111
  Gruppe, 59
  Jagdgeschwader, 59
    JG 2, 75, 92
    JG 11, 100
    JG 26, 62, 75
    JG 27, 60, 84, 85
    JG 51, 64
    JG 77, 53
  Jagdgruppe 88, 43
  Jagdgruppe 102, 52

Jagdverband 44, 113
Kette, 92, 94, 113
Rotte, 44, 75
Schwarm, 44, 161
Sonderkommando Elbe, 114
Stabskompanie, 59
Staffel, 44, 59, 75
Sturmgruppe, 111
Zerstorergeschwader 76, 53
Lutzow, Gunther, 43
LVG two-seater, 13
Macchi MC 200, 77
Mach number, 120
Macomber, Lieutenant, 90, 91
Malan, Sailor, 61, 62, 64, 74, 161
Malta, 77, 79
Mannock, Edward, 24, 29, 30
Manoeuvres, attacks, and tactical moves
  Abschwung, half roll, or split-S, 94, 110
  Banking, 19
  Barrel roll, 27, 96, 97, 152, 167
  Beam defence manoeuvre (Thach Weave), 89, 90, 91
  Boxing, 82, 83
  Collision course interception, 134, 135
  Crossover turn, 36, 44, 75, 80, 129
  Curve of pursuit, 47, 48
  Cut-off vector, 134
  Defensive circle (Lufbery or wagon wheel), 25, 61, 85, 152, 153
  Defensive split, 9, 75, 110, 126
  Dive and zoom, 30, 44, 45, 53, 61, 85, 86, 126
  Double attack, 154
  Formation turn, 180 degrees, 36
  Head-on attack, 23, 43, 64, 69, 80, 88, 92, 94, 116, 129, 163, 169
  Immelmann turn, 13, 27, 36, 159, 166
  Loop, 18, 29, 116, 118
  Loose deuce, 110, 127, 167
  Overhead attack, 86, 88
  Pursuit course attack, 134
  Ramming attack, 83, 114, 116, 119
  Roller coaster, 112
  Scissors, 89, 156
  Side attack, 88
  Slashing attacks, 157
  Spin, 29
  Spiral climb, 17, 62, 63
  Spiral dive, 59, 88
  Stall turn, 27, 116

Turn comparison; Spitfire I vs Me 109E, 59, 60
Yoyo, high speed, 127, 166, 167, 169
Yoyo, low speed, 127, 167
Zoom, 21, 95, 96, 156, 169
Marseille, Hans-Joachim, 84, 85, 86, 128
Mayer, Egon, 92
McConnell, Joseph, 130
McCudden, James, 24, 25, 34, 161
Messerschmitt Me 109, 43, 52, 53, 54, 59, 60, 61, 64, 69, 71, 77, 80, 82, 84, 86, 100, 109, 110, 111, 114, 160
Me 110, 49, 53, 54, 61, 83, 96, 109
Me 163, 113
Me 262, 112, 113
Me 410, 109
Meteor, Gloster, 133
Meyer, John C., 109
Midway, Battle of, 90, 91
MiG alley, 124, 127, 128, 130, 161, 167
MiG 15, 122, 124, 125, 126, 127, 128, 129, 130, 133, 140, 161, 167
MiG 17, 149, 150, 152, 153, 155, 156
MiG 19, 136, 156
MiG 21, 145, 146, 147, 148, 149, 151, 152, 153, 154, 155, 156, 157
MiG 23, 157
MiG 25, 157
Mitsubishi Type 96, 45
Moelders, Werner, 44
Morale, 14, 16, 29, 37, 73, 92, 128, 130, 147, 170
Morane M, 83
Morane Saulnier Type L, 12
Morgan, David, 159
Muczynski, Lawrence, 7, 8, 9
Nakajima Type 97, 45, 115
Nesterov, Peter, 83
Nieuport 11, 14
Nieuport NiD 52, 42
No-allowance angle, 17, 50
Oesau, Walter, 75
Olds, Robin, 151, 152
Operation Bolo, 151, 152, 169
Operation Paula, 56
P-36 Hawk 75, 52, 53
P-38 Lightning, 49, 50, 94, 99, 118
P-40 Kittyhawk, 84, 118
P-40 Tomahawk, 84, 85, 86
P-47 Thunderbolt, 94, 95, 96, 97, 99, 109, 110, 111
P-51 Mustang, 109, 110, 111, 112, 113
Park, Keith, 69, 71
Patrouille, 46
Pearl Harbour, 86, 89

Penn-Gaskell, Lieutenant, 11
Pfalz D III, 27
Phoney War, 52
Pip-squeak, 56
Polikarpov I 15, 42, 44
    I 16, 42, 44, 45, 83
Potez 631, 49, 52
Price, Alfred, 134
Proximity fuze, 137
Quennault, Louis, 10
Raab, Wilhelm, 64
Radar, airborne, 133, 134, 135, 148, 153, 155, 157, 161, 162, 165
Radar, surface, 51, 56, 60, 61, 72, 90, 125, 128, 144, 145, 148, 155, 161, 162
Radio communications, 41, 80
Raleigh, Major, 11
Red Crown, 154, 155
Reinecke, Hauptman, 53
Rhys-Davids, Lieutenant, 34, 35
Riccioni, Everest, 154
Richthofen, Manfred von, 18, 19, 24, 35, 37
Rodeo, 73, 76
Roedel, Leutnant, 55
Royal Air Force
    Air Ministry paper, Night Interception with Radar Aids, 134
    Defence Plan, late 1940, 69
    Fighter Command Attack
        No 1, 48
        No 2, 48, 49
        No 3, 49
        A, 50
        B, 51
    Memorandum, November 1939, 53
    Tactical memorandum No 14, 73, 74
    November 1942, 79
    Tactical Bulletin, No 15, 79
    Squadrons No 32, 64
        No 54, 64
        No 65, 60
        No 74, 62
        No 92, 62
        No 111, 64
        No 403, 76, 77
        No 501, 62, 63, 64
    Training Manual 1922, 36, 37 1938, 46
Royal Flying Corps
    Manual, June 1914, 10
    Order, January 1916, 13
    Report, early 1915, 11
    Report, method of attack of hostile aeroplanes, 11

Squadrons No 16, 11
    No 20, 14
    No 24, 14, 17, 18, 31
    No 25, 25
    No 43, 25, 26, 34
    No 45, 26, 27
    No 56, 32, 34, 35
    No 60, 34
    No 84, 29, 163
Ruses, 14, 15, 23, 29, 61, 112, 116, 151, 156, 169
Saulnier, Raymond, 12
Saundby, Lieutenant, 18
Savoia-Marchetti Sm 79, 42
Schlichting, Joachim, 43
Schoepfel, Gerhard, 62, 63, 64
SE 5a, 24, 25, 27, 29, 32, 34, 35
Sea Harrier, 158, 159
Semi-active radar homing, 137
Sheedy, Daniel, 90
Shenyang F 6, 146
Shoki, 115, 116, 117
Sidewinder, 8, 9, 136, 137, 140, 145, 146, 149, 152, 153, 155, 156, 157, 160, 168
Signals, visual, 23, 125
Six Day War, 146, 147
Smith, David, 159
Sopwith 1½ Strutter, 25, 26, 27
    Camel, 27, 32, 34, 35, 160, 166
    Dolphin, 32
South African Air Force No 5 Squadron, 85
Sparrow, 137, 149, 150, 151, 152, 155, 156, 157
Spitfire, Vickers Supermarine, 48, 59, 60, 61, 62, 64, 69, 75, 76, 77, 79, 80, 84, 94, 95, 96, 100, 113, 160, 166
Stall, 19, 29
Standing patrols, 41, 42, 60, 72, 90
Stanford Tuck, Robert, 62
Stark, Rudolf, 32
Steinhoff, Johannes, 112, 113
Stratospheric combat, 124
Sukhoi Su 7, 146
Su 22 Fitter, 7, 8, 9, 157, 168
Supersonic flight, 120, 121
Surprise, element of, 10, 14, 22, 23, 24, 35, 37, 56, 62, 63, 64, 75, 80, 113, 131, 139, 148, 159, 160, 161, 168

Survival, 30, 32, 34, 36, 83, 109, 167, 169
Synchronisation gear, 12
T-38 Talon, 154
Taitari Units, 119
Talalikhin, Lieutenant, 83
Tempest, Hawker, 113
Teranishi, Major, 44
Thach, John S., 89, 90, 91
Thach Weave, 89, 91
Tilley, Reade, 79, 80, 81, 82, 83, 99, 161
Todd, Captain, 11
Tomb, Colonel, 155, 156
Top gun, 154
Transient performance, 124, 166
Trautloft, Hannes, 112
Trenchard, Lord, 11, 40
Tupolev Tu 4, 132
United States Air Force
    4th Fighter Interception Group, 128
    51st Fighter Interception Group, 128
    8th Tactical Fighter Wing, 151
    355th Tactical Fighter Wing, 152
    366th Tactical Fighter Wing, 151
United States Army Air Force
    4th Fighter Group, 95
    401st Bomb Squadron, 99
United States Navy
    Fighter squadrons VF 3, 89, 90
    VF 41, 7
    VF 42, 89
    VF 96, 155
    Aircraft carriers
        USS *Constellation*, 155
        Forrestal, 7
        Hornet, 90
        Nimitz, 7
        Yorktown, 90
Vickers FB 5 (Gunbus), 10
VIFF, 158, 159
Voisin Type 3, 10
Voss, Werner, 34, 35
Vulcan, Avro, 158
Warning systems, 39, 42, 51, 56, 57, 60, 61, 69, 70, 72, 125, 128, 145, 148, 150, 151, 155, 161
Weavers, 59, 62
Wellington, Vickers Armstrong, 53, 54
Yom Kippur War, 148
Zero, 86, 88, 89, 90, 91, 115, 118, 166